Early Intervention Every Day!

Early Intervention Every Day!
Embedding Activities in Daily Routines for Young Children and Their Families

by

Merle J. Crawford, M.S., OTR/L, BCBA, CIMI

and

Barbara Weber, M.S., CCC-SLP, BCBA

·P A U L · H ·
BROOKES
PUBLISHING Cº ®

Baltimore • London • Sydney

Paul H. Brookes Publishing Co.
Post Office Box 10624
Baltimore, Maryland 21285-0624
USA

www.brookespublishing.com

Typeset by Cenveo Publisher Services, Columbia, Maryland.
Manufactured in the United States by
Bradford & Bigelow, Inc., Newburyport, Massachusetts.

The individuals described in this book are composites or real people whose situations are masked and are based on
the authors' experiences. In all instances, names and identifying details have been changed to protect confidentiality.

Library of Congress Cataloging-in-Publication Data

Crawford, Merle J.
  Early Intervention Every Day! : embedding activities in daily routines for young children and their families / by
Merle J. Crawford, M.S., OTR/L, BCBA, and Barbara Weber, M.S., CCC-SLP, BCBA.
    pages   cm
  Includes bibliographical references and index.
  ISBN-13: 978-1-59857-276-6 (alk. paper)—978-1-59857-574-3 (electronic)
  ISBN-10: 1-59857-276-8 (alk. paper)—1-59857-574-0 (electronic)
  1. Children with disabilities—Services for—United States.   2. Children with disabilities—Education—United States.
3. Early childhood education—United States.   I. Weber, Barbara, 1956– II. Title.

HV888.5.C73 2013
362.4'04808320973—dc23   2013018059

British Library Cataloguing in Publication data are available from the British Library.

2017   2016   2015   2014   2013

10   9   8   7   6   5   4   3   2   1

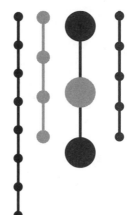

Contents

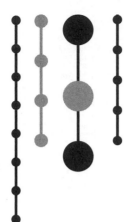

About the Authors

Merle J. Crawford, M.S., OTR/L, BCBA, CIMI, is an occupational therapist who has a private practice in central Pennsylvania. She has a bachelor of science degree in special education and elementary education and a master's degree in occupational therapy. In addition, Ms. Crawford has graduate certificates in applied behavior analysis and autism. She has extensive training in relationship-based interventions and is a Board Certified Behavior Analyst and a Certified Infant Massage Instructor. Ms. Crawford works primarily with infants and toddlers in early intervention, integrating strategies from her varied training when coaching families and working with young children.

Barbara Weber, M.S., CCC-SLP, BCBA, is a speech-language pathologist who has a private practice in central Pennsylvania. She received her bachelor of science degree and master's degree in communication disorders. Ms. Weber has a graduate certificate in applied behavior analysis. She holds the Certificate of Clinical Competence from the American Speech-Language-Hearing Association and is a Board Certified Behavior Analyst. She has worked with children and adults with a variety of disabilities for more than 30 years in school, clinic, and home settings. Ms. Weber works with infants and toddlers as her primary clinical focus and concentrates on collaborative processes to help families integrate routines-based intervention.

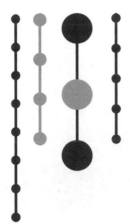

Acknowledgments

MERLE CRAWFORD

Thanks are not enough to those who have inspired me, helped me, and taught me so much. Thanks to Paul H. Brookes Publishing Co. for the opportunity to publish this book and for all of the help along the way. Linda King-Thomas, who imparted the philosophy that there is always more to learn about typical development, started the process of this book many, many years ago when I thought I knew about children. Professionally, many have had an immense impact on me. Ed Feinberg, Juliann Woods, Pip Campbell, and Jeannie Goryl shaped me through their work in early intervention. Interacting with co-workers throughout the years, especially Jenny Fornberg, Kim Beard, Lynn Cummings, and Liz Kelly, taught me so many tips and expanded my knowledge base. I am grateful to Madison and Phin and their families for their help and to Jeannie Goryl for her edits and ideas. Thanks so much to Barb Weber, who persevered and graciously gave so much in collaboration to make this book possible, and to Christopher, Alyssa, and the rest of my wonderful family for their love and support. There are no words to express the extent of gratitude for my husband Greg's technical and emotional support, his help with editing and typing, and the happiness and love he has given me.

BARBARA WEBER

I wish to acknowledge first and foremost my husband, Howard, who is my greatest cheerleader and who always supports me. Thanks to my children, Andrea, David, Rachel, Sarah, and Michelle, who inspire and delight me in so many ways. I wish to thank my college professor, Larry Shriberg, Ph.D., who has inspired and encouraged me from miles away and over many years. Whenever I send him an e-mail, he answers quickly, and it never ceases to amaze me. Countless colleagues and teachers, far too many to name, have contributed to my professional growth and development, and I am deeply grateful to them on a daily basis. I am honored to have completed this book with my friend and colleague, Merle Crawford, and am grateful for her dedication, patience, and brilliance in guiding our book in so many ways. Thanks to Jeannie Goryl, for her sensitive edits based on her professional and personal experiences. Special thanks to our in-house editor, Greg Crawford, for his tireless efforts and countless hours of editing, revising, and providing suggestions. Thanks too to everyone at Paul H. Brookes Publishing Co. for your dedication in disseminating knowledge to countless professionals and for the guidance and support you gave us in making this process easy to understand and navigate.

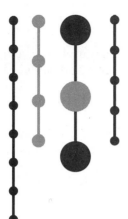

Introduction

This book was written to give early intervention providers a comprehensive resource for working with children from birth to 3. In 2008, the Workgroup on Principles and Practices in Natural Environments of the National Early Childhood Technical Assistance Center delineated principles for early intervention services. They included the statement that "infants and toddlers learn best through everyday experiences and interactions with familiar people in familiar contexts" (p. 2). Such experiences are said to take place in the child's *natural environment*, a term that implies not only a setting but also a context in which everyday routines offer many opportunities for skill learning and practice (Campbell, Sawyer, & Muhlenhaupt, 2009). After following more than 100 families for more than 15 years, Bernheimer and Weisner (2007) concluded, "If there is one message for practitioners from our parents and from our longitudinal studies, it is that no intervention, no matter how well designed or implemented, will have an impact if it cannot find a slot in the daily routines of an organization, family, or individual" (p. 199). According to McWilliam (2010), "Children learn throughout the day, not in 'lessons,' 'sessions,' 'work times,' 'exercise times,' or 'goal times' that concentrate the learning into just one time a day" (p. 148).

Another principle delineated by the Workgroup on Principles and Practices in Natural Environments (2008), one that lies at the heart of this book, emphasizes that "the primary role of a service provider in early intervention is to work with and support family members and caregivers in children's lives." Parents and caregivers are the true facilitators of learning for young children, not the early intervention provider. McWilliam (2010) describes this truth aptly:

> When the regular caregiver's role is framed as "following through" with some supportive activities, rather like it might be for parents of school-age children who are given homework, caregivers could be forgiven for thinking that their role is incidental rather than central to the child's learning. In fact, all the adult–child interactions that occur between specialists' visits are where learning occurs, with some learning occurring in child–object interactions—also *between* specialists' visits. (p. 120)

Another goal of this book is to improve the quality of family life and help children with delays and disabilities participate fully in family routines. Early in the 21st century, the World Health Organization (2002) endorsed the *International Classification of Functioning, Disability and Health* as a model for disability and functioning. In essence, this model looks at social and ecological contexts to define disability. To the extent that one is unable to participate in daily routines, the disability is accordingly increased or decreased. The more one is able to participate within daily activities, the less one seems to be "disabled"; the less one is able to participate, the greater the disability (Wilcox & Woods, 2011). Early intervention's focus on family-centered strategies and participation in routines and activities is consistent with this classification system. Thus, the book focuses not only on skill development but also on ways parents and caregivers can scaffold learning within daily routines and activities. It is intended to be a guide but is not comprehensive, as each child and each family is unique and deserves coordinated strategies that go beyond a sourcebook

The book is composed of three main sections and two appendixes. Section I provides an overview of early intervention, recommended practices related to teams that include parents and other caregivers, and recommended practices related to facilitating skill acquisition.

Section II of the book details the developmental progression of functional skills across six domains of learning (behavior regulation and social skills; cognitive and receptive language; expressive language; gross motor skills; fine motor skills; and self-care/adaptive skills) and provides ideas for ways early intervention providers can help parents and caregivers facilitate skill development and achieve many individualized family service plan (IFSP) outcomes in typical routines and activities. Developmental domains are often considered to include physical development, social-emotional development, cognitive development, adaptive development, and communication development. A strong relationship exists between cognition and receptive language skills (Fagan & Montgomery, 2009), and the authors synthesize these two domains that overlap in many activities and routines in which infants and toddlers participate.

Section III provides charts for daily routines across domains, which give early intervention providers a framework with examples to help parents and caregivers facilitate early development and achieve IFSP outcomes when children participate in activities such as grocery shopping, riding in the car, or looking at books. Helpful resources regarding skill acquisition and behavior management appear in Appendix A. Appendix B includes progress monitoring examples. (See Chapter 1 for more information.)

Children interact with parents, extended family, child care providers, neighbors, and many others during typical days, weeks, and months. Many of the suggestions offered in this book are relevant to all of these people who may have opportunities to facilitate skill acquisition. In this book, the term *caregivers* is used broadly to encompass these people.

The authors hope readers will find this book so useful that it resides, ready to provide ideas, dog-eared in the early intervention provider's car.

REFERENCES

Bernheimer, L.B., & Weisner, T.S. (2007). "Let me just tell you what I do all day...:" The family story at the center of intervention research and practice. *Infants & Young Children, 20*(3), 192–201.

Campbell, P.H., Sawyer, L.B., & Muhlenhaupt, M. (2009). The meaning of natural environments for parents and professionals. *Infants and Young Children, 22*, 264–278.

Fagan, M.K., & Montgomery, T.R. (2009). Managing referrals for children with receptive language delay. *Clinical Pediatrics, 48*(1), 72–80.

McWilliam, R.A. (2010). *Routines-based early intervention: Supporting young children and their families.* Baltimore, MD: Paul H. Brookes Publishing Co.

Wilcox, M,J., & Woods, J. (2011). Participation as a basis for developing early intervention outcomes. *Language, Speech, & Hearing Services in Schools, 42*(3), 365–378.

Workgroup on Principles and Practices in Natural Environments. (2008). *Agreed upon mission and key principles for providing early intervention services in natural environments.* Retrieved from http://www.nectac.org/pdfs/topics/families/Finalmissionandprinciples3_11_08.pdf

World Health Organization. (2002). *Towards a common language for functioning, disability and health: ICF, the International Classification of Functioning, Disability, and Health.* Retrieved from http://www.who.int/classifications/icf/training/icfbeginnersguide.pdf

To all the children and their families
who have taught us so much and to those who will continue to do so

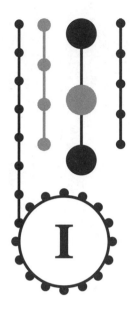

Early Intervention Basics and Recommended Practices

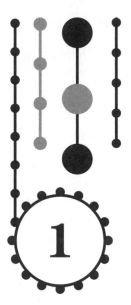

Overview of Early Intervention

This chapter provides an overview of early intervention (EI), including regulations, evaluations, individualized family service plans (IFSPs), and models of service delivery. Considerations regarding the first and ongoing sessions, as well as progress monitoring, are also discussed.

REGULATIONS

In 1986 Congress passed an amendment to the Individuals with Disabilities Education Act (IDEA; PL 99-457) that mandated preschool services for children with disabilities. Part C of IDEA delineates services to children from birth to 3. EI regulations specify guidelines for referrals, evaluations, IFSPs, and service provision. In the early years of implementation of EI, many programs were housed in clinics, centers, or hospitals, but later the services were mandated to be provided in natural environments, "settings that are natural or typical for a same-aged infant or toddler without a disability" (34 CFR § 303.26). Such settings include homes, child care facilities, fast food restaurants, community playgroups, swimming pools, and libraries. According to Bruder (2010), because most infants and toddlers have "short attention spans and active learning styles" their "tolerance of isolated, episodic, and structured time-intensive interventions" is limited (p. 40). In addition, infants and toddlers learn in the context of their families, and thus, EI must target not only the children but also their families and caregivers whose priorities become the focus of intervention. The supports and services provided by EI, such as speech and language therapy, physical therapy, special instruction, and occupational therapy, make up a small percentage of infants' and toddlers' waking hours, and thus there is much more potential for families and other caregivers to have an impact on the child's development. Educating and empowering families and caregivers are key components of EI.

Federal regulation mandates IDEA eligibility of all children who are experiencing a developmental delay. Each state, however, determines the criteria for what constitutes a developmental delay, and hence eligibility for services differs greatly across the United States. Some states such as Alabama (Alabama Department of Rehabilitation Services, 2012) and Pennsylvania (55 Pa. Code § 4226) currently have eligibility requirements of a 25% delay in one or more areas of development (physical, adaptive, communication, cognitive, and social) or a physical or medical condition that will likely result in a developmental delay. In Alaska (Alaska Department of Health and Social Services, 2011), the current eligibility requirement is a 15% delay in at least one area of development or a diagnosed condition that will likely result in a developmental delay. Arizona's (Arizona Department of Economic Security, 2012) eligibility criterion as of 2013 was a 50% delay

3

in one or more area of development or a diagnosed condition that has a high probability of causing a delay. In New Jersey (New Jersey Early Intervention System, 2012a), current eligibility is a 25% delay in two or more areas of development or a 33% delay in one. It is at each state's discretion to include children who have a "diagnosed physical or mental condition that has a high probability of resulting in developmental delay" (20 U.S.C. 1432[5]).

Just as states vary in eligibility requirements, there are differences in lead agencies and funding. In Vermont, EI is administered by the Vermont Department for Children and Families with funding coming from "a variety of sources, including insurance, Medicaid, participating agencies, local schools, family cost share, etc." (Vermont Department for Children and Families, 2012). Some families in New Jersey, where the lead agency is the Department of Health and Senior Services, also pay out of pocket for services (New Jersey Early Intervention System, 2012b), whereas Early Intervention services in Pennsylvania, under the Department of Public Welfare, at this time do not cost any families directly (Pennsylvania Department of Public Welfare, 2012). In Maryland, the Department of Education oversees the infant-toddler program, which also does not cost participants (Maryland State Department of Education, 2011). In North Carolina, where administration is from the Department of Health and Human Services, service coordination and evaluations are at no cost to families; however, other services are based upon a sliding scale (North Carolina Department of Health and Human Services, 2012).

EVALUATIONS

When a referral is made a timeline begins, and services must be in place for an eligible child within 45 days. Before services can commence, there must first be an evaluation of the child, an assessment of the child and the family, and the creation of an IFSP. The evaluation of the child must include the use of an evaluation tool; an interview of the parent; the identification of the child's functioning in the areas of cognitive development, physical development, including vision and hearing, communication development, social or emotional development, and adaptive development; the gathering of information from other sources who have information regarding the child's strengths and needs, such as other caregivers and medical providers; and the review of relevant records. The assessment of the child includes observation of the child and identification of the child's strengths and needs in each developmental area. A voluntary family assessment is also part of the process and includes the family's concerns, priorities, resources, and supports related to the child's development.

Initial evaluations as well as some annual evaluations can be very stressful for families. In many cases, at the initial evaluation parents' fears are confirmed: their child is not developing as expected. It is critical that evaluators be sensitive to the families' feelings and needs at this time. It can be quite challenging for providers to ask questions in a sensitive manner, to ask questions in a way that reveals the information they wish to glean, and to set the stage for what may be a long-term relationship with service providers. Often during evaluations, new information that was not discussed at the intake is revealed. For example, on occasion a child may have been asleep during the intake, and when the evaluators begin to interact with the child they may see red flags for autism that were not observed at the intake. Learning how to tactfully discuss concerns discovered during the evaluation as well as throughout the EI process, whether they are medical issues that need to be ruled out such as seizures or signs of possible autism, is a skill that often evolves over time. Strategies such as asking open-ended questions and using reflective listening are beneficial during conversations throughout EI processes, and providers should consider supplementing their skills in these techniques, as well as in observation skill building, through training opportunities.

INDIVIDUALIZED FAMILY SERVICE PLANS

After a child is found eligible for services, the next step is the creation of the IFSP. The IFSP team must be composed of the parent and two or more individuals from separate professions, one of which must be the service coordinator. The IFSP must contain information regarding the child's developmental status based on the evaluation; the family's resources, priorities, and concerns; measurable results or outcomes that are expected to be achieved through service provision; and the types of services to be provided, with a delineation of their length, duration, frequency, and intensity.

The IFSP is the framework for a child's EI services, yet its critical importance is often not understood by caregivers and EI providers. Unlike in the medical model, where goals are determined by the providers treating the child, in EI the services are determined by the outcomes developed by the family with input from other team members. These outcomes should be both functional and measurable. Parents can benefit from learning about the importance of their input in developing the IFSP; many resources exist to assist both families and EI providers. Some parents are easily able to express their thoughts about their child's plan, while others need guidance through this process. The phrasing of the questions posed to parents can make a great deal of difference in helping parents and caregivers formulate outcomes. In the authors' experience, when asked, "What are your concerns and priorities?" families often are not sure what to say. However, when asked "Thinking of the next 6 months; what would you like to see your child doing that he is not doing now that would be helpful for you or for him?" families are much more able to generate an answer. This type of question often reveals information regarding priorities, challenges, and the parents' understanding of next steps in development, all of which the IFSP team can use to assist in the development of the IFSP.

In the authors' experiences, many times families begin the initial IFSP meeting being very involved in this process, but by the end of the meeting they are less engaged, because the providers are struggling to complete the document according to local and federal guidelines. As a result, the parents' input is lost in the shuffle of papers. Often at the end of the meeting the families are trying to console children who need attention and providers are looking at their watches to ensure they won't be late to their next appointment. To help alleviate this breakdown at the initial IFSP, it would be helpful for the service coordinator or other EI personnel to prepare the family before the IFSP meeting, explaining the process, which entails first reviewing parent priorities and identifying outcomes and then delineating strategies the team will use to help achieve the outcomes. The next steps would be identifying whose expertise and how much is needed in achieving those outcomes and how progress will be monitored. For IFSP reviews or annual IFSPs, it would be helpful for providers to review the outcomes and brainstorm with families about ideas for revising current outcomes or formulating new ones, as well as reviewing the IFSP process so the team meeting can be as productive as possible.

Regardless if the IFSP meeting is an initial (I), a review (R), or an annual (A) meeting, the team must contemplate many factors to determine the frequency of services. Questions such as the following should be considered:

- How many service providers and weekly or monthly appointments does the family feel they can handle with their schedules? Many families are very busy and cannot accommodate multiple providers due to work schedules, health concerns, or needs of family members. (I, A, R)

- In how many settings does the child spend time where support is needed? For example, a child who is in a child care setting may need support there as well as at home. In addition, a child who spends time in homes of multiple caregivers may need services in these different settings in order to support the child and/or the caregivers with various activities in which the child is involved. (I, A, R)

- Are the service providers showing the parents and caregivers something new at each visit? (I, A, R)

- Are the parents and caregivers feeling the need for more support between visits? (A, R)

- Do the parents and caregivers implement the recommendations of the service provider? If not, is a change in service or service provider needed? (A, R)

- Are the skills of the service providers necessary on an ongoing basis or can parents and caregivers implement the strategies, for example, range of motion? (I, A, R)

- Is the child making progress at the current frequency? (A, R)

- Would an increase or a decrease in frequency likely cause a benefit or risk for the child? For the parents and caregivers? (A, R)

- Is there duplication of services due to the expertise and experience of the team members? (A, R)

- Would consultative services to the team be appropriate rather than having direct service provision? If so, which team members should provide and receive the consultative services? (I, A, R)

- Is the decision in the best interest of the child, the family, and the rest of the team, and is it financially responsible? (I, A, R)

MODELS OF SERVICE DELIVERY

Three main models of team intervention can be found in the literature: multidisciplinary, interdisciplinary, and transdisciplinary (Woodruff & McGonigel, 1988). Members of multidisciplinary teams function independently and interact minimally, much as young children parallel play (Peterson, 1987). Interdisciplinary teams collaborate more, and team members incorporate portions of the plan that are outside their discipline into their services as they are able. Members of transdisciplinary teams use one service provider as the main interventionist and use consultants as needed. McWilliam (2003, 2010) writes extensively of transdisciplinary service delivery, calling it a primary service provider (PSP) model. Some EI programs have moved from a multidisciplinary to a transdisciplinary model to decrease costs, but McWilliam identifies other reasons that the PSP model is preferable. The model implies that intervention 1) occurs between visits instead of during them, 2) helps to ensure routines-based rather than domain-specific intervention, and 3) decreases the amount of time the family must be "hosting the professional" (McWilliam, 2010, p. 119).

Leaders in the field examining the issues of best practice and service delivery models have discussed the impact on society not only from a financial perspective but also from the perspective of the impact on the family. Dunst, Hamby, and Brookfield (2007) reported that the intensity of EI services was negatively related to family well-being. Stress can be caused by conflicting information given by service providers and struggles to fit appointments into families' busy schedules.

In addition, professional associations such as the American Physical Therapy Association, the American Occupational Therapy Association, and the American Speech-Language-Hearing Association have developed position statements and scopes of practice that refer to issues regarding direct service and crossing boundaries into other disciplines. Though leaders in the field discuss transdisciplinary and PSP models, many therapists question providing services outside of what they feel their profession allows. To help providers with this situation, some EI programs use consultations. For example, in the area in which the authors work, if providers feel they need the expertise of a therapist from another discipline to contribute ideas or to determine if the child might benefit from the addition of another team member on an ongoing basis, the EI provider initiates a consultation by speaking with the service coordinator and the family. Ideally, the consultation occurs with the EI provider(s), the family, and the service coordinator so the team can then amend the IFSP if needed. Depending on the needs of the child, the family, and the team, in some cases the consultation leads to recommendations for the current team, while at other times the team decides to add a team member or to substitute one team member for another.

Just as there are no hard and fast rules regarding frequency and duration of services, the team's decision regarding when a specific service is needed is also individual and somewhat subjective. A consideration that may help a team decide if another service should be added is whether the child has a delay in learning or a difference in learning. For example, if a child has been receiving special instruction to facilitate overall play skills and has motor delays but no significant difference in muscle tone, gait, or symmetry of movement, a physical therapist may not be needed to provide direct therapy or consultative services. However, if the child has atypical muscle tone, gait, or range of motion, the expertise of a physical therapist may be needed to provide direct therapy or consultation to the team. This expertise may be needed frequently or infrequently, depending on the child's and the family's needs, as well as the expertise of the service providers who are already working with the child. Similarly, if a child is delayed in speech and language skills but is following the typical developmental trajectory and acquiring skills as expected but at a slower pace, service providers who have training and knowledge in communication development may be able to meet the needs. For a child who is only labeling and not requesting or for a child who has excellent receptive skills but very few expressive skills, the expertise of a speech-language pathologist may be needed as the child's developmental progression is atypical and the child may need the specialized expertise.

Another way to look at models of service delivery is from the perspective of family routines and participation. According to Sawyer and Campbell (2009, p. 326), the various models, including "'routines-based intervention' (e.g., McWilliam & Scott, 2001), 'family guided routines-based intervention' (e.g., Cripe & Venn, 1997; Woods, Kashinath, & Goldstein, 2004), 'activity-based intervention' (e.g., Pretti-Frontczak & Bricker, 2004; Valvano, 2004), 'learning opportunities' (e.g., Dunst, 2001; Dunst, Bruder, Trivette, Raab, & McLean, 2001; Dunst, Hamby, Trivette, Raab, & Bruder, 2000), and 'participation-based services' (e.g., Campbell, 2004; Campbell & Sawyer, 2007)" have different components and emphasis, but they all stress the role of the family and the use of typical routines and activities as learning opportunities.

Providers in EI are charged with embedding intervention into family and child care routines to help increase learning opportunities in order to achieve outcomes. Embedding skills and strategies within routines is an effective way to help caregivers provide the child with the support that the child needs to facilitate development and increase participation. Any activity a family is engaged in offers opportunities for their child to learn. Some families have more predictable routines than other families; however, all exchanges between adult and child offer the potential for learning. Embedding strategies into family routines offers multiple opportunities to practice throughout the day and is far more effective in helping the child master skills and reaching outcomes than is confining practice to only an hour or two of therapy.

In discussing where to embed strategies to help a child participate and develop, a discussion with the parent and caregiver as to where strategies can be embedded or when the strategy may be most successful needs to be a collaborative effort between the parent and caregiver and the EI provider. Suggestions for how to embed skill development can be demonstrated and practiced with the parent and caregiver. A sensitive conversation about how easy or difficult it is for the them to incorporate the strategies developed and how well the intervention strategy is working is imperative.

A vignette illustrates successful collaboration between an EI provider and a parent. Ava's outcome was to use words and word combinations so that she could make her wants and needs known to her family. The provider usually arrived in the morning, when Ava was engaged in play with her family. Ava brought out a ball, wanting to play catch, and the provider helped Ava's mother, Sandra, embed strategies for helping Ava imitate words or use words spontaneously during the play. Sandra modeled simple words like *ball*, *catch*, and *throw*. Watching for imitation, the provider and Sandra noticed that Ava approximated the word *ball* when Sandra said "ball" and paused before throwing the ball. The provider then started to help Ava "call" for "ball" prior to each time her mother threw the ball by modeling calling for the ball. Ava imitated the model, which helped Sandra embed word use into an everyday play routine, and this helped Ava practice words and learn that words get things she wants (the ball). The provider then asked Sandra where else, in the family's day, she thought this strategy could help Ava use words. Sandra identified how motivated Ava was by helping to water the family garden and was going to try to have Ava call for "hose" and "water" to see if Ava would begin to use different words to request things she wanted. Another idea that Sandra proposed was to see if Ava would begin to ask for "eat" when it was snack time if Sandra began to model "eat," playfully say "eat," and pause for Ava to imitate. The session concluded with Sandra's plan to use the effective strategy seen with the ball play in other places. When the provider returned the next week, she began the session by asking if the strategy was successful throughout the week. Sandra reported that it was successful for "hose" and "water" while watering the garden. She said that Ava seemed reluctant to say "eat," thinking that maybe when Ava was very hungry was not the best time to practice because it was more difficult for her to talk when she was excited or upset. The EI provider and Sandra continued to use ball play and watering the garden to expand Ava's communication skills and over time found many other family activities to use.

In the prior example, the provider helped the caregiver identify functional and important routines specific to the family, which empowered them to facilitate their child's development and help to make progress toward the outcome. When providers can help caregivers embed strategies within the family's daily activities, the result is more functional, efficient practice and leads to more opportunities for achievement of outcomes.

Terminology used in EI has changed throughout its history and one can find references to family-centered, routines-based, and participation-based services. This evolution reflects the emphasis on EI's goal of promoting young children's participation in the same activities as peers who do not have a disability or developmental delay. Though routines-based and participation-based services are considered best practice, Campbell and Sawyer (2009) identify discrepancies between the belief of the providers and the delivery of participation-based services.

In the experience of the authors, there are factors related to families and factors related to providers that account for this discrepancy. Some families embrace the opportunity to explore various routines with providers while others do not. The family's knowledge about the scope and purpose of EI is a major factor. How families are introduced to the purpose of EI during their first contacts with the service coordinator appears to make a significant difference. In addition, during the first contact, when EI providers come into the home or other child care location to discuss the collaborative process with caregivers about how they will work on outcomes during various routines, the stage is set for this philosophy to be implemented. In contrast, it is very difficult for EI providers to implement a routines-based, participation-based model when the stage has not been set. This happens many times when EI providers change or a new provider is added and there is a mismatch in service delivery model implementation. When a provider who uses a routines-based, collaborative approach begins with a family who has had experience with a provider who always brings a bag of toys, which are used only during the session, or works with the child independent of the caregiver's active participation, the family may initially think the new EI provider is doing something wrong and is not teaching skills correctly. Unless told otherwise, families and some providers may think that EI services are traditional hospital, clinic, or rehabilitation models of therapy used for older children but in a home setting. In 2000, Hanft and Pilkington discussed how "therapy without ramps, swings, gyms, adapted tables and chairs and specific objects to cue targeted responses may not be perceived by some therapists and families as good therapy" (p. 3). Teaching families about the purpose of EI sets the stage for successful collaborative partnerships that benefit families and those working with them.

Learning about family concerns and family routines is a process that often takes time as providers and families establish rapport and trust and as families gradually learn more about what EI entails. One of the authors was working with a family whose child had a significant speech and language delay. The child's outcome was related to communication and participation in play activities. Though the family appeared most comfortable watching, over time the author was able to increasingly engage the family and coach them to interact more directly with the child. During a session, the author modeled an activity with the child and asked the mother to then try. As soon as the mother began to do the activity with the child, he began to hit her, a behavior not seen with the author. The author asked some probing questions and the mother, after several months of being in EI services, felt comfortable enough to admit that her son hit her daily during the diaper changing routine. As the discussion went on, the mother admitted many more routines that were challenging. She was afraid to take her son into the community alone because she didn't know what to do. She feared someone might report her to child protective services if she tried to discipline him in public. The author offered to help with these behaviors and they planned a community outing for the next session to practice communication and to help the mother gain the skills and the confidence so she and her son would have a successful experience. Many times when help outside of the home setting is offered, families remark, "I didn't know you could do that" or "Are we allowed to do that?" Families may be unaware of the scope of support EI providers can give and it is important for all team members to teach families about the various settings in which EI can provide support. These collaborative, problem-solving activities within functional daily routines provide opportunities for providers to coach parents in helping children develop skills and empower parents to be able to help the child independently within and between sessions.

THE FIRST SESSION AND BEYOND: SETTING THE STAGE AND CONTINUING THE MESSAGE

EI professionals need to be aware of the importance of providing clear information about EI supports right from the start. Many families are unsure about what EI entails. Some families are familiar with EI from friends and relatives or from experiences with older children, but many have never heard of the program until they receive a referral from a doctor. Depending on their own experiences or what they have heard from others, some families may confuse EI with child protective services and are hesitant to get involved. Some families have reported they thought EI is only for families who cannot pay for private therapy. Getting involved with EI can be difficult for some families. Regardless of whether the parents bring up a concern to a doctor or if a doctor brings up a concern to the parents, the thought that something might be "wrong" with their child evokes stress and anxiety in most parents. Though some report relief that the doctor validated their concerns, the process of intake, evaluation, and the beginning of services can be quite stressful.

The first contact with the family has the potential to set the stage for a successful partnership with families. During the intake, when a family is introduced to EI, important groundwork is laid. Some parents, particularly parents of children who are premature, have reported that the purpose of EI is to help babies catch up. In some cases, EI does enable children to catch up, but this does not always happen, and parents can be left feeling betrayed and disappointed. For children who have significant developmental delays, in order to catch up the children have to learn at a greater than typical pace and, in some cases, this challenge is too large to overcome. EI providers should never take away hope, but at the same time they must not mislead families. EI does make an impact on the child's development and the family's competence and confidence in helping facilitate development (Hebbeler et al., 2007), and this is the message that should be shared.

The first contacts are also important times to establish the role of the parents and caregivers and the EI providers within the EI process. The message is quite different when a parent or caregiver is told they need to attend and observe the EI sessions than when told the purpose of EI is to support them in helping them facilitate their child's development with an emphasis on collaboration and partnership. Emphasizing the collaborative process during the first contacts puts the provider in the position to assume the role of a coach so he or she will be able to demonstrate with the child and then transfer skills to the caregivers. Discussing this partnership between the provider and the caregivers sets the stage for working together. When practices are family centered, they are characterized as individualized, strength based, and capacity building and are reflective of the culture of the family. The family is involved in decision making, problem solving, and self-efficacy (Dunst, Trivette, & Deal, 1994). A great deal of information is provided to parents at the intake, evaluation, and IFSP, and it is not uncommon for parents to report feelings of confusion and being overwhelmed. There are paperwork requirements at each process that are important, but at times the completion of forms and discussion about processes can interrupt the flow and understanding of meaningful conversation. To assist with helping parents and caregivers understand the collaborative role, it is essential for EI providers on their first visit not only to complete required paperwork such as authorizations and privacy forms but also to review the parents' priorities and concerns and the IFSP outcomes. It is extremely helpful for providers to discuss their roles and responsibilities and those of the caregivers for such things as procedures for illness and cancellations and issues related to mandated reporting for protective services, and it is important to emphasize the parents' rights to services to meet their and their child's needs. Parents should know that if services are not meeting their needs they need to communicate this as soon as possible to the provider and/or the service coordinator. Another important discussion to have at the initial session is one pertaining to household rules and discipline. In some households, shoes must be taken off and left outside or just inside the door, children may not be allowed on certain furniture, or children may not be allowed to eat in certain rooms. In some homes, bubbles are only for outside. Often caregivers may be embarrassed by a child's behavior and not know what to do or may have a method of disciplining the child that the provider may not know or condone.

For families who have multiple service providers, another important topic to discuss early in the relationship between caregivers and providers is the approach each provider uses during sessions. Families may be confused when each provider uses a different type of intervention practice. Some providers may tend to coach, others may tend to provide hands-on therapy, and others may tend to model. An example of this occurred when one of the authors began working with a child who had been receiving physical therapy and special instruction for several months. After the first visit, when the EI provider explained that her style typically was to coach families, the mother reported she was grateful to know this as she did not know what she was supposed to do during the other therapies. In another personal experience, the therapist took over for another EI provider who was on maternity leave. The previous therapist's style was to bring in a toy bag and provide hands-on intervention with the child, whereas the new therapist tended to coach parents and use toys, objects, and activities in the home. Soon the new therapist discovered that the parents found her style of intervention to be very different than what they were used to and that they were not at all interested in her methods. This helped her realize that discussions about expectations, roles, preferences, and philosophies need to occur very early in the relationship between caregivers and EI providers.

PROGRESS MONITORING

The purpose of EI is to improve skills, competencies, and participation in family routines. Change and progress are fundamental components of intervention (McConnell, 2000). Progress monitoring is not meant to be comprehensive, but rather it serves as a measurement of the progress on a current outcome. Progress monitoring measures help determine whether or not a child is making adequate short-term progress (Walker, Carta, Greenwood, & Buzhardt, 2008). Unlike "critical skill mastery" or "developmental skill mastery," progress monitoring reflects progress toward the long-term outcome (McConnell, McEvoy, & Priest, 2002). The way progress monitoring is implemented varies by state. Some states such as Pennsylvania, Washington, Virginia, Maine, and West Virginia have a specific place on the IFSP to note how progress toward the outcome will be measured, whereas other states such as North Carolina have the measurability criteria in the outcome statement itself. According to the 2011 Part C regulations, each IFSP must have documentation of the criteria for measuring progress, the procedures by which progress will be measured, and the timelines at which progress will be measured (Early Intervention Programs for Infants and Toddlers with Disabilities, 2011).

In some states such as Pennsylvania, early interventionists are required to submit a quarterly report to document progress toward the outcomes. Typically the team creating the IFSP will determine a variable or set of variables that will be measured to determine whether or not a child is making satisfactory progress toward the outcome(s). The IFSP team delineates how progress on each outcome will be monitored. For example, for the outcome "Billy's family would like him to talk so he can ask for what he wants rather than screaming," the provider might make a list of gestures, sounds, and words that Billy uses during the session and that his parents report he used between sessions, and these would be documented in session notes and summarized in quarterly reports given to the service coordinator and to the family. For the outcome "Mary's family would like her to walk so they don't have to carry her," progress could be monitored by charting the number of steps she takes pushing her toy, the number of steps she takes independently, the places she walks to rather than crawls, and/or the types of surfaces she walks on. These also could be documented by the provider during the session and/or reported by the caregivers and summarized quarterly. See Appendix B for samples of completed charts that illustrate progress monitoring.

Another aspect of progress monitoring in EI is known as Early Childhood Outcomes. In 2005, the U.S. Department of Education's Office of Special Education Programs began requiring states to report data on child outcomes, specifically, the percentage of children who have IFSPs who "demonstrated improvements in positive social-emotional skills, acquisition and use of knowledge and skills, and use of appropriate behaviors to meet their needs." States are also required to submit data regarding the percentage of families who "know their rights, effectively communicate their children's needs, and help their children develop and learn" (Early Childhood Outcomes Center, n.d.). It is crucial for EI providers to understand EI regulations and EI philosophy in order to optimally serve and positively affect families and children. The interaction that occurs between providers and families during the families' introduction to EI sets the stage for helping children make progress and helping families learn to advocate for themselves and their child.

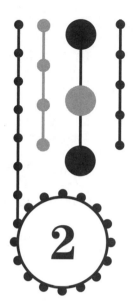

Recommended Practices
Caregivers

This chapter focuses on important factors that EI providers must consider to best help caregivers achieve their goals for their children: cultural considerations, learning styles, the grieving process, family priorities, and the dynamics of working with multiple caregivers, siblings, and peers. According to McWilliam (2010), "early interventionists provide three types of support: emotional, material, and informational" (p. 155). To make the greatest impact, EI providers must consider not only the children but also the caregivers or adult learners to be their clients. According to Hanft, Rush, and Shelden (2004),

> Adult learners are influenced by their level of motivation to engage in new experiences, their desire for self-direction, the presence of a supportive environment that uses their unique learning styles, their ability to build on prior experiences, and ongoing support to put new knowledge into practice. (p. 21)

EI providers must tailor their intervention to the caregivers, for it is the parents, the grandparents, aunts, uncles, and child care staff who are in the best position to affect development and facilitate a trajectory of growth and change.

CULTURAL CONSIDERATIONS

It is important that providers consider a family's cultural background. The American Speech-Language-Hearing Association's Issues in Ethics Statement: Cultural Competence (Speech-Language-Hearing, 2005) pertains to all disciplines, not only to speech-language pathologists or audiologists. The association recommends that therapists ensure that materials are not offensive, accommodate families who choose alternative treatments, understand that differences are not deficiencies, use interpreters when needed, understand that bilingual skills do not equal cultural competence, and avoid making assumptions based on culture. In addition, this statement notes that providers must be aware of their own cultural biases, must be open and flexible so treatment strategies are aligned with family choices, and must refer to others with the needed experience or knowledge when cultural or linguistic differences affect service delivery.

Some cultures do not recognize disability or developmental delay, an important consideration for early interventionists whose own attitudes regarding disability have shaped their practice. It is important that providers make the effort to understand cultural beliefs and attitudes that determine behaviors, guide decisions, and have an impact on the way the family members interact with each other and with their community. In some cultures, chronic illness and disability are seen as forms of punishment. An inherited disorder may be envisioned as a family curse. In cultures where belief in reincarnation is strong, a disability may be seen as evidence of a transgression in a previous life. Some cultures have a strong gender bias in favor of male children. The family may go to great lengths to obtain care and services for a male child, whereas daughters may be considered a poor financial risk.

Some caregivers may believe that they were singled out to parent a child with disabilities. Providers must keep in mind, however, that just because a person is part of a certain culture, it does not mean he or she holds the same beliefs that are commonly associated with that culture. For example, if a child's delay is viewed as a sign that the parent had done something wrong, another family from the same culture may not share that belief. It is important to consider a multicultural focus whenever working with a family and to be aware that cultural influences may influence belief systems about the child (Groce & Zola, 1993).

EI providers must have an awareness of the impact of culture on their collaboration with families. One of the variables that may affect the relationship between the provider and the caregivers is dress. For example, a family may have a strong preferences for shoes on or off in the home or might wear clothing that may or may not lend itself to taking certain positions or movements. Attire of the provider may be of importance to the caregiver. Modest attire may be more comfortable for some families who have conservative dress mores, and providers need to be respectful of this. Considerations regarding eating may be a factor in some homes. Parents may offer the provider food or tea, which may be used to establish rapport or respect. The authors have been offered tea, specialty dishes, pieces of birthday cake, and tastes of new recipes the family is excited about. The family may have dietary preferences or limitations that are culturally based that must be understood and respected. Developmental milestones such as the age of self-feeding, toilet training, and independent dressing vary by cultures and often influence family priorities. The role of extended family may be part of the provider's consideration in making recommendations. Some of the caregivers, when multiple caregivers within the family are involved with the child, may vary in language fluency. One author worked with a family in which the father was present every other week, and communication was challenging because his ability to understand English necessitated repetition, slow rate, and visual cues. The mother of the child was fluent in English. The author had to adapt her speaking style depending upon who was present at the session. Age and gender differences may influence the relationship between the provider and the caregiver as well as the relationship between the child and the caregiver. In some matriarchal or patriarchal role definitions, the caregiver may feel more comfortable directing or teaching than playing. Some families may have staff to help with children in their homeland, and they may be unaccustomed to playing with their child.

A family's immigration status can affect attitudes or even access to benefits. If a family has residence in one country on a provisional basis, consideration of impending transition may be part of service delivery. At times, extended trips to the country of birth may be part of what providers need to incorporate into the course of treatment: absences of 3 weeks to 3 months at a time. Providers need to respect privacy in the home, and may need to be sensitive as to whether or not the family welcomes questions about the religious icons, use of incense or candles, religious texts, food restrictions, and other practices or items specific to a family's culture. One of the authors had the following experience at an IFSP review with a Hindu family. Not thinking about how cows are considered sacred in the Hindu culture, one provider continually responded to the child's wonderful progress with the exclamation "holy cow!" While the family did not seem to react, providers need to be sensitive to the origin of exclamations and potential offense a family may take from their use. Early interventionists are likely to provide services to families who are affected by influences such as ethnicity, gender, religion, sexual orientation, family composition, race, and immigration status. These influences, as well as anger management style, discourse style, and child discipline choices, to name a few, may differ from the provider's belief system or cultural values, but differences need to be put aside in order to treat all families with respect.

One of the more common questions that providers have is whether or not the use of more than one language at home results in confusion or whether a child knows one language better than the other. According to the U.S. Census Bureau (2009), approximately 1 in 5 school-age children (20%) spoke a language other than English at home in 2009. From 1980 to 2007, the number of speakers of non-English languages at home increased by 140 percent (U.S. Census Bureau, 2010). If a child has a speech or language problem, it will show up in both languages. However, these problems are not caused by learning two languages (American Speech-Language-Hearing Association, 2005).

Cultural competency is much more than knowing about practices within an ethnic group, or speaking the language; it is ongoing, social and multidimensional. It requires open dialogue to meet cultural needs and individual family needs as well.

LEARNING STYLES OF CAREGIVERS

Just as children have varied learning styles, so do their parents and caregivers. It is important for EI providers to discuss the parents' and caregivers' preferences for exchanging information regarding recommendations and child progress. Along with the typical modeling and coaching that occur during sessions, many caregivers appreciate and benefit from multiple opportunities and methods to practice a technique including the use of photos, videos, and/or written instructions. Personality factors also influence the relationship. Some caregivers prefer to jump in and implement a new strategy while others prefer to watch a few times and then try, just as some children warm up quickly while others need more time. Lindeman and Woods (1999), project directors of FACETS (Family-guided Approaches to Collaborative Early Intervention Training and Services), provide a useful online resource, *Implementing Information about Adult Learners in Family-guided Activity Based Intervention: A Checklist*, which assists providers in collaborating and communicating effectively. Each family has unique needs, and in some cases the caregivers have challenges that can affect the EI process. These challenges may include a learning disability, an intellectual impairment, or a mental health condition. EI providers can learn more about parents who have disabilities from resources, including Through the Looking Glass (http://www.lookingglass.org/home), a center dedicated to research, training, and services for families in which a child, parent, or grandparent has a disability, and the U.S. Department of Health and Human Services Office on Women's Health (http://womenshealth.gov/illnesses-disabilities/parenting/parents-with-disabilities.html).

COPING AND ACCEPTANCE

Children come into EI services through a variety of referral paths, and many different outcomes may occur. At times, a child is referred for a delay in one area and more than one area of delay is discovered. For example, a child may be referred initially for not talking, and as time goes on, that initial referral may lead to the discovery of a complex need profile, such as in the diagnosis of an autism spectrum disorder. Some parents come into EI with an idea about a child's delay or disability because it was identified at birth, such as when a child has Down syndrome, but others may be very surprised that their child qualifies for EI.

As families adjust to learning that their child has special needs, they may experience a wide range of emotions. Many researchers suggest that the families cope in diverse ways and do not go through specific stages of grief, as was once popularly believed (Featherstone, 1980; Howard, Williams, Port, & Lepper, 1997; Miller, 1994). Ulrich and Bauer (2003) identify four stages of adjustment that parents go through: in stage one, parents don't realize the impact of the disability; in stage two, parents seek help; in stage three they try to make differences in their children less apparent and may decrease services; and in stage four they don't see their situation as better or worse but merely different. According to Gallagher, Fialka, Rhodes, and Arceneaux (2002), parents and early interventionists may view the same processes quite differently:

> Parents and professionals often enter into a working relationship with different expectations and perspectives. Such differences affect how each partner perceives the next step in intervention. For many professionals, a label, diagnosis, and/or prognosis can give direction and insight to their work with a child. They can consider which intervention techniques work best with children with that particular diagnosis. They know what they expect to happen with the child. During the initial diagnosis and during transition periods, parents may not appreciate the importance of a diagnosis or label. To parents, labels may be like foreign words creating chaos and a sense of inadequacy. Parents may question the meaning of the diagnosis, unsure about how it might affect the future of their child and family. They may feel unprepared for this new twist in life, and wonder how to assimilate so much information at once. Professionals should be cautious not to expect all parents to integrate new information about their child in the same manner or within the same time frame as the professional (p. 13).

Though having a child who has developmental challenges can be stressful to parents, Turnbull and Turnbull (2001) found that having a child with a disability can also have many positive effects and can strengthen a family. EI providers will find families with varying attitudes and also will find that a given family's attitude may change over time. Some families are eager to join support groups or look for families who have children with similar challenges, whereas others do not want to "join the club," as one family termed it.

The Florida Department of Education Technical Assistance and Training Center (2009) suggests several ways in which early interventionists can support families, including providing open and regular communication, listening to concerns with acceptance and understanding, building a relationship based on trust and mutual respect, avoiding excess criticism or praise, being encouraging and realistic, providing documentation that supports statements, providing appropriate resources, being honest, and building confidence in parenting skills.

Many of these suggestions resonated in the responses given when one of the authors e-mailed parents of children with autism with whom she had worked in order to gather information for a presentation. The EI provider e-mailed the following:

> I am doing a training for service coordinators and evaluators in early intervention about autism. One of the topics is how to best talk to parents about 'red flags' if the evaluators suspect autism and the parents have not mentioned it. Thinking about your experiences, do you have any advice or anything you would like to share about your experience when someone first mentioned autism to you—what they did well and what would have been better?

In the following responses, one can see the parents' wishes for honesty and resources. One parent replied,

> For me, I sort of knew in my heart early on that autism was a possibility, but as a parent you want to try and deny it for as long as you can. What many therapists might not be aware of is that the parents might be getting a ton of outside influential opinions. What I mean is that, for me at least, since I have been blessed with a very "hands-on" family, many will give their opinions even if they aren't solicited. Therefore, during the initial evaluation and for the first few months, I kept hearing, "Oh give him time." I would tell everyone to try and be very sensitive to the parents and always think, "What if this was me? How would I want to be told that this therapist believes my child has autism?" Everyone is different, and if you can try and first get to know the family and, more importantly the mom and dad, figure out what's the best way to tell them. In my opinion, honesty is the only way to go, because time is such a critical component in treatment here. Try and be sensitive on the presentation, of course. As much as it hurt, looking back and knowing what I know now, I'm grateful my son's therapist was so honest and up front in her way of dropping hints. I think if I were a therapist who knew in my heart early on that a child I was working with was definitely on the spectrum, no matter how severe, I would first discuss all of the red flags in depth with the parents. I just know, the earlier the parents accept the diagnosis and move on to getting the label, since that is what opens up so many more doors, the more intensive the services can become, and the better off the child will be overall.

Another parent said,

> With both of my children, I had to mention autism first. I also had to request a developmental evaluation. Especially with my older child, I felt I was going it alone, so to speak. His developmental therapist obviously saw red flags, but I had a really hard time getting her to talk about it, so I

actually contacted [my son's] service coordinator and asked for an evaluation from the developmental pediatrician. Even at the time it bothered me, because I wondered how long his diagnosis would have been put off if I had not been working on educating myself.

A parent commented,

I do not know why the special instructor did not tell me. Fear of hurting my feelings? Fear of causing an emotional breakdown? I do not know. I just wish more practitioners would lose the fear and look at the best interest of the child. And hope that the parents are adults who would cope and rise to the occasion. The special instructor did not have to come out and say to me that my daughter has autism. But when I gave her an opening like questions about my child's behavior, she should have seized it as an opportunity to tell me to check it out. Even recommend a doctor or two. I had little experience with children before my own child, so I had no benchmark for normal. But, I could sense that something was wrong. I could also sense when people were holding back and not saying that something was up with my daughter. I would have been grateful for anyone to point me in the right direction.

Finally, another parent said,

I would advise the evaluators to be sympathetic, which they are, but honest. The parents need all the facts. They may not understand everything right away, but they have it and can ask questions later. It is a lot to absorb if the words *autism* or *special needs* come in to play in relation to their child. The Internet is a scary place for parents wanting information. It always gives you the most grim facts, not the wonderful things a child can become.

Whereas some families may openly discuss feelings about coping and adjusting to their child's needs, others may not. Parents' attitudes and perceptions about having a child with a developmental delay are very individualized, and EI providers must support all families without passing judgment or making assumptions about their experience. Empathy and knowledge aid in the understanding of others, but one can never fully be in the shoes of another person. One of the authors had an experience that greatly affected her when two mothers of children with disabilities met each other at a focus group for parents of children in EI. One of the children has cerebral palsy, an intellectual disability, a visual impairment, and seizures. The other child is intellectually advanced and has a progressive neuromuscular disease with a prognosis for limited life expectancy. At each of their EI sessions after they met, both mothers said to the therapist, "I don't know how she does it. I wouldn't be able to cope with a child like that."

In summary, coping and adjustment are parts of a process that is unique to each family. EI providers need to be aware of this process and support families by providing strategies to help them with their priorities and concerns, by providing resources, and by listening.

FAMILY PRIORITIES

Given the context of teaching within family routines and the active involvement of the caregiver, it is imperative that the provider work with the family's priorities rather than focusing on the provider's ideas of what needs to be targeted. When skills are learned within an activity or routine, providers help caregivers identify a context for learning particular skills. For some children, the opportunity to practice a skill within the routine will provide enough opportunity for learning. For other children, the opportunity to practice may not be enough, and intervention strategies beyond practice may be needed.

In building a reciprocal process of sharing information between providers and families, the focus should be on the individual family's interests, beliefs, and unique characteristics. What is identified as an excellent activity by the provider may not be preferred by the family when discussing when and where skills might be embedded. For example, some families might want to leave mealtimes as relaxed times rather than a time to work on skills (Woods & Lindeman, 2008). Conversations about where and when families are most comfortable focusing on skills, which skills caregivers would like to focus on, and how they would like to embed skills into their daily routines should be approached with respect and flexibility. Caregivers have important knowledge about what motivates their child, what works best for their family, and what they value as important to them.

The following example illustrates the importance of an early interventionist asking families their priorities rather than coming in as the expert and assuming priorities. Priorities may change week to week, especially as participation in family routines increases.

Kamir was a 27-month-old boy who was eating soft textures such as yogurt and pureed foods. He expressed little interest in the spoon. When given solid food such as crackers or bread, he moved the food around in his mouth until it was moist and then opened his mouth, letting the food drop out. When the provider asked Kamir's mother if she had concerns about his eating, the mother said "No," believing Kamir would start to eat different kinds of foods and use a spoon when he was ready to do so. The EI provider felt conflicted, as she wanted to honor Kamir's mother's wishes but felt that the mother might not be aware that Kamir's difficulties chewing textured foods and disinterest in the spoon could have an impact on his diet and nutrition in the future. She felt professional responsibility to educate the family in a sensitive manner without making them question their beliefs or the provider's motives. She decided to bring up the subject a few weeks later, when Kamir's mother was talking about sending him to a preschool program. The provider discussed how snack time was part of the preschool program and that Kamir would be expected to feed himself. The mother then asked the EI provider to help Kamir learn to eat a variety of foods and feed himself with a spoon.

In addressing the outcomes on the IFSP, which are based on parent priorities, providers may want to ask what the caregiver's priority is for a particular session. Very often, providers may have one idea and the caregiver another. To assist in focusing on the needs of the caregiver, the interventionist might ask sensitive questions, such as "Is there anything you would like to practice today?" or "Were there any challenges this week that you would like to address?" Providers can also review notes from the previous session and ask, "How did this go?" or "Did you get a chance to try _____?"

WORKING WITH MULTIPLE CAREGIVERS

In many situations, EI providers have opportunities to interact with multiple caregivers for a particular child. Many children have multiple caregivers, which may include two parents, extended family, child care providers, and teachers. A child's living situation may necessitate intervention with caregivers in different locations, as a child may spend time with parents who do not live together. Many children act differently in different settings or have difficulty generalizing a skill from one environment to another. Observing children in various settings and with different caregivers gives the provider a wealth of knowledge about the child's strengths and needs as well as supports that may be beneficial for all of the caregivers.

Brianna was seen at home for occupational therapy due to difficulties related to eating as well as self-regulation and behavior. At home, she had frequent tantrums and her behavior was very difficult for her parents to manage. When her parents told the therapist that Brianna was going to attend child care, the EI provider feared that the adjustment to the structured setting would be quite difficult. Brianna and the child care center benefited from the interventionist's suggested strategies to facilitate peer interaction and direction following, and Brianna's behavior was much less of a problem at child care than at home. Seeing her in both settings allowed the therapist to learn more about her behavior in order to help develop strategies to assist all of her caregivers.

Though being in multiple settings with multiple caregivers has many advantages, the EI provider must be cognizant of the dynamics of the relationships and remain neutral and professional when there are conflicting opinions and philosophies among the various caregivers. While working with Brianna's family, the EI provider often found herself in the middle of the parents' disagreements and in a role that she felt was outside her area of expertise. With the help of the service coordinator, resources for family counseling were given to the parents.

EI providers frequently serve children in child care settings and preschools. As Hanft et al. (2004) note, "A family's agreement to participate in an early intervention program does not ensure that care providers from group settings will automatically be interested as well" (p. 138). The authors identify challenges that EI providers frequently face, including respecting the group setting's philosophy, developing partnerships with staff, supporting other children in the group, finding time to have conversations, maintaining confidentiality, and sustaining support with staff retention challenges. EI providers must determine the needs of the child in the group setting as related to the IFSP, explore the needs of the staff related to the child, define the provider's roles in the context of the routines of the group when services begin, and adjust strategies as time goes on so everyone's needs are being met.

Early interventionists are in a position to coach child care providers; however, this must be done skillfully and tactfully. Though the child care facility has given permission for the EI provider to be present, the teacher may or may not actively be looking for suggestions about how to increase a child's skill. One provider was giving a teacher tips on how to use visual supports to benefit all the children in the group, and though she thought she was being sensitive to the teacher, the teacher looked at her after a suggestion and said sarcastically, "Fine, you run circle time." It is imperative that EI providers discuss their role not only with the director of the child care setting but also with the direct care providers. Asking questions such as "What can I do to help with Jessica's behavior?" or "Are there any parts of the day difficult for you because of anything Jessica is doing or not doing?" can help child care providers see the EI provider as an ally and a collaborator. In addition, child care providers should be asked how they prefer to obtain information, just as families should be asked at the beginning of EI services. Many child care providers are always busy and in demand, and they may find taking time to talk before, during, or after a session to be very stressful. Asking "When is a good time for me to talk with you?" and "How would you prefer I provide information?" as well as offering to demonstrate, leave session notes, and/or follow up with emails or phone calls will provide a forum in which the child care providers can share ideas on how they can best interact with EI personnel. Some child care providers may prefer that the director have a discussion with the EI provider and then relay information to them later, perhaps during the children's nap time.

In addition to discussing their role, EI providers should have conversations about how the family or child care provider would like the early interventionist to handle discipline—not only of the child in services but also of other children who are present. Examples of common occurrences include when a child shows unwanted behavior toward another child or toward the EI provider. Just as families have different styles of discipline, different child care and early childhood settings have different rules and philosophies that must be considered.

Working with children who are seen in child care settings, the early interventionist often faces a challenge to find time to collaborate with primary caregivers at home. Email, phone calls, or sessions during drop-off or pick-up times, during holidays, evenings, or weekends can help to ensure coordination of services. The authors have been in child care and preschool settings where administrators, teachers, and aides have been very welcoming and where great partnerships were formed, but they have also been in others where the collaborative process was difficult due to many of the same reasons that working with certain families can be challenging: a lack of understanding about EI, stressors staff are dealing with, differences in personality or styles of interaction, or the EI provider's lack of understanding about issues facing the group setting. Just as the first session is so important for families to lay the foundation for EI processes, relationship building during the first session in a group setting is also critical.

SIBLINGS AND PEERS

Many homes where children receive EI have other children present, including siblings, cousins, and friends, and as noted, many children receive services in child care settings with peers. Because EI services focus on natural environments, daily routines, and participation, other children are often present during sessions and naturally become part of the interaction, which has many benefits. When EI providers suggest ways to embed strategies into daily routines, they need to be cognizant of the caregivers' responsibilities to other children present. For example, in a home environment, many parents feel stressed about being able to meet the needs of the child receiving EI services while also fulfilling household responsibilities and meeting the needs of other children. Similarly, in child care settings, teachers must meet the needs of the entire class as well as try to implement strategies suggested by the EI provider.

Some families identify IFSP outcomes that target interactions with other children, which can make it very easy to incorporate other children into the sessions. In other instances, however, families may find it difficult to focus on the child who is receiving EI services in the presence of other children. Some families have been known to feel the need to have siblings go to a neighbor's home or to a relative's home during the therapy session. Although the EI provider may have told the families the benefits of having siblings present, some parents find it difficult to multitask and prefer to concentrate on one child at a time. In this situation, it works well to start where the parents and caregivers are comfortable and over time suggest and find ways for siblings to be present, at least for a portion of the session on a trial basis.

The presence of siblings and other children during EI services has many advantages. When siblings are incorporated into the sessions, the EI provider can coach the family using real-life situations rather than leaving the family to figure these out after the provider leaves. Sometimes parents are uncomfortable when siblings interrupt a session to get their own needs met, but these kinds of interruptions are also likely to occur when the parent is on his or her own without the provider present, and the provider can coach the caregiver in managing such situations. This situation occurred for a provider who frequently had sessions during which an older sister often interrupted with many demands. The mother's comment "This is your brother's time" not only increased the sister's demands but also resulted in the caregiver feeling stressed, inefficient, and frustrated. Although the sister's behavior was more pronounced during the session, the mother said, "She is like this all the time. I don't know what to do. This is what my entire day is like." Together, the provider and the mother problem solved ways to help the sibling share the mother's attention, and after several sessions the interactions between the girl and the mother were much more peaceful.

Other children present during sessions can serve as models or even directly teach specific skills. In some cases, other children are more successful than adults in eliciting specific behaviors (Kresak, Gallagher, & Rhodes, 2009). Children can be used as models in a variety of situations. For example, children who have hearing impairments or difficulty following directions can be cued to look at peers to help them follow the class routine. Caregivers can be coached to use peer influence to change behaviors. For example, when a peer or sibling demonstrates a targeted behavior such as using gestures with songs, turning to the child and complimenting him or her on how well he or she listened and used hand movements may result in other children using gestures for the next song. To help caregivers identify ways to involve peers or siblings, providers can ask questions such as "How do you think the other children could help with this skill?" For example, when asked this question, a father realized his older son could play catch with the younger son, giving the exact same prompts the father would.

In child care settings, when an EI provider arrives in the room, he or she is often swarmed by many children eager to interact with an adult who sits on the floor and is not busy changing diapers or involved in getting ready for the next activity. This affords many opportunities to use peers as partners in dyads to develop specific competencies: using words or gestures to make requests or using peers as role models to teach specific skills, like how to play with a certain toy in the room.

BUILDING EFFECTIVE TEAMS

Much of the literature on building an effective team comes from business models; however, basic tenets can be extrapolated as a framework for EI teams. Effective teamwork involves trusting, collaborating, sharing ideas, working toward a common goal, being open to feedback, avoiding self-interest, sharing responsibility for conflicts that occur, having appropriate knowledge, and working toward a common goal (Lencioni, 2002). In EI, the common goal of a team is to help the family achieve the outcomes they have identified for their child. This goal is accomplished by team members whose knowledge includes information about the family, the child, development, learning, and their area or areas of expertise. EI providers may find themselves in the position of needing to balance their personal values and skills with those of others with whom they interact throughout service delivery, but each team member brings unique information and insight to the collaborative process in order to facilitate the common goal.

EI providers often become very involved in families' lives. In many instances, the providers come into the home weekly, participate in daily routines with the family, and are privy to personal information and conversations. Sometimes close relationships develop between EI providers and families. A provider may be in a home for three years or even longer if another child in the home begins EI services. According to a study by Blue-Banning, Summers, Frankland, Nelson, and Beegle (2004), parents expressed the desire for professionals to "go the extra mile" and "be like family," and EI providers had similar feelings but also were aware of the need to balance empowerment and codependency. It is important for many EI providers to find the balance between providing resources and teaching the family to find its own resources. It is tempting for some EI providers to bring toys, food, clothing, or other necessities to a family that may be struggling financially; however, when the relationship ends, the family may not have the needed supports and resources. Objectivity may be lost because an EI provider may be unable to separate professional and personal feelings. For example, one of the authors overheard an EI provider who was a close friend of a family reassure the mother that the child would walk and talk, a hope that was not fulfilled. Furthermore, EI providers are mandated reporters when abuse or neglect is suspected, and this situation is very stressful for all involved under any circumstances but perhaps particularly so if the provider has a close relationship with the family.

EI providers are often seen as "the experts," which, at times, can put the family in a position of being hesitant to give honest opinions. In addition, parents and caregivers may be hesitant to reveal true opinions for fear of hurting the provider's feelings. In addition, EI providers need to be cognizant of how they ask questions to ensure they are not leading families to answer a certain way. This often occurs when EI providers are scheduling make-up sessions. EI providers have been overheard asking questions such as "I need to make up the sessions I missed so is it ok if I come on Tuesday?" or "Would you like me to come next week?" Though both of these questions were asked with good intentions, to an observer it seemed that the parents did not feel the make-up sessions were necessary but were hesitant to say so. Phrasing questions carefully can help facilitate honesty. For example, after discussing a missed session, asking the questions "How are you feeling about your use of strategies and how your child is doing? Do you feel as if it would be helpful to schedule make-up time for the missed session or are you feeling comfortable with where we are at right now and with your resources and tools?" may facilitate an answer reflecting true feelings. In general, asking open-ended questions reveals more information than yes or no questions and should be considered when communicating with parents and other team members.

EI providers need to be cautious that they do not put families in positions in which they feel badly for not implementing recommendations; instead the providers need to find out what precluded the recommendations from being implemented. Perhaps the family was very busy, decided the recommendation was not practical, felt the recommendation did not fit into their routines, felt a lack of competence, or felt uncomfortable for some other reason. Instead of considering the family "noncompliant," the EI providers should see such situations as opportunities to explore with the family what would be helpful. There are many reasons a family may continually struggle to implement suggestions or may not seem invested in EI services. These could include stressors that are priority issues for the family, such as illness, housing, financial difficulties, or responsibilities to care for other family members. Some families may truly not be interested in EI services but are afraid to admit this for fear of being perceived negatively. Nonjudgmental conversations need to occur in these situations.

EI providers also need to make sure they bring clarity rather than confusion to interactions with the family. For example, when a child has multiple service providers, it is necessary to ensure that conflicting information is presented as infrequently as possible. When conflicting opinions do arise, care must be taken to help the family consider all the information. Families should be coached to weigh conflicting information so they can make the best decision for their child and themselves. Parents, as well as other team members, may interpret comments in ways that were not intended. In cases when a family has multiple providers but one team member has a closer relationship with the family, other team members may feel less valued. The parent may confide in one team member, providing information that would be beneficial for all team members to know, but the confidante may feel that telling the other team members would betray the parent's confidence. On occasion a caregiver may make comments about other team members, and it is imperative that the caregiver be encouraged to discuss any concerns with that provider and with the service coordinator. If a parent or caregiver is dissatisfied with a provider, the situation must be rectified so the needs of both the caregiver and the child can be met.

To successfully collaborate, team members must be honest, open minded, nonjudgmental, empathic, and tactful. Team members may have differences in their philosophies, practices, ethical or professional guidelines, personalities, commitment, styles, communication, and expertise, but EI providers are in a position to learn continually from each other, from child care providers, from families, from children, and from the myriad of others who work together with the common goal of positively affecting the lives of families with young children.

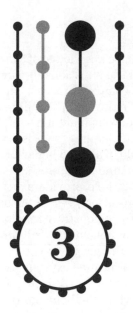

Recommended Practices
Facilitating Skill Acquisition

This chapter discusses important considerations for facilitating skill development with infants and toddlers. Factors in skill acquisition as well as electronic and other therapeutic and educational materials are highlighted.

Developmental progress and mastery of outcomes are related to many factors, some pertaining to the child and others pertaining to service providers. Factors pertaining to the child include the extent of developmental delay. For example, a child who has minimal delays or a delay in just one area has the potential to make faster developmental gains than a child who has more extensive or global developmental delays. Further, because of the complexity of development and the interrelatedness of the developmental domains, the type and extent of developmental delay affects progress in different ways. A child who has challenging behaviors and difficulty communicating may not make progress as quickly as a child who is very interactive. The child's temperament and personality also affect the ability to make progress, as children who are dysregulated and irritable, although interactive and communicative, may not make a lot of progress until they are better able to interact with others and their environment.

Numerous factors related to skill acquisition pertain to activities or qualities of the EI providers. For example, the way an outcome is written is very significant in terms of measuring a child's rate of progress. Some outcomes are very specific, such as "Johnny will walk from the living room to his high chair without falling," while others are more general, such as "Johnny will walk inside and outside without falling." Achieving the first example will take less time than achieving the second example. The expertise of the EI providers also has an impact on progress. Providers' knowledge base, interpersonal skills, and depth and breadth of experience greatly affect provision of service. Extensive knowledge of typical development in all developmental domains, including those outside their discipline, is essential for all EI providers. In addition, providers must keep in mind the developmental appropriateness of not only the skill but also the materials used to develop it. For example, a step toward fine motor development might be learning to pick up small objects, but if the child puts nonedible items in his mouth, it would not be appropriate to use a sensory bin of raw rice and beans or small pom-poms to facilitate a pincer grasp. Similarly, to work on imitation of actions and sounds, using plastic containers, a large ball, or pudding finger paint would be better choices than modeling dough for children who continue to mouth objects. Providers must understand that most skills include reliance on previous skills in the developmental trajectory and that interrelatedness of skills greatly affects skill targets.

When a parent or caregiver tells the EI provider that the child is having difficulty playing with a certain toy, asking for a drink, walking without falling, assisting with dressing, or feeding him- or herself with a spoon, to be of optimal help the provider must have knowledge of the child's strengths, needs, and preferences, the components of the skill, and the situations in which the difficulty occurs. Assisting an individual in gaining a new skill is a complex process. One must understand not only the child's strengths and needs but also what motivates the child so that those preferences, interests, and strengths can be used to enhance developmental needs. Young children will quickly lose interest and avoid activities that are too challenging, so it is essential that activities and interactions be filled with success and fun. The field of applied behavior analysis (ABA) provides a helpful framework for understanding motivation and learning.

ABA examines human behavior and provides strategies that can help providers and caregivers change behaviors, facilitate acquisition of new skills, and monitor progress. It focuses on objectively defining behaviors of social significance and intervening to demonstrate relationships between the interventions and improvements in behavior, whether that behavior is drinking from a cup, communicating with gestures or words, walking outside on the grass, or completing a puzzle. ABA is based on the scientific principles of behavior and learning and is systematic, both in procedures and documentation of change. A critical focus of ABA is *operant behavior*: voluntary behavior that evolves from the history of "what happened" when the behavior occurred in the past, in contrast to involuntary respondent or reflexive behavior. This concept comprises what are often referred to as the ABCs of behavior analysis: the behavior's *antecedents* (what happened before), the *behavior* itself, and the *consequence* (what happened after) (Cooper, Heron, & Heward, 2007).

The ABCs are exemplified in the following scenario. Ricardo sits under a toy bar and bats at a suspended rattle. When he hits the toy, he feels the rattle, sees it move, and hears it make a sound. The antecedent is a rattle suspended in front of Ricardo, the behavior is Ricardo batting at the rattle, and the consequence is tactile stimulation from the rattle, visual stimulation from the movement of the rattle, and auditory stimulation from the sound of the rattle.

MOTIVATION, REINFORCEMENT, AND PUNISHMENT

In the preceding scenario, Ricardo finds the sensations he receives when hitting the rattle to be pleasant and interesting, so he continues to bat at the toy for several minutes. The feel, sight, and/or sound of the rattle reinforce Ricardo's behavior of hitting the toy, and such *reinforcers* are defined as "a stimulus change that increases the future frequency of a behavior that immediately precedes it" (Cooper et al., 2007, p. 702). Jodi, in contrast, dislikes unexpected sound and touch, and the three times she accidentally hit a suspended rattle she became startled and started crying. Jodi then stopped moving her arms. The presentation of the rattle and the sensory feedback she received when hitting it serves as *punisher* for Jodi. A punisher is "a stimulus change that decreases the future frequency of behavior that immediately precedes it" (Cooper et al., 2007, p. 702). Reinforcers increase a behavior and punishers decrease a behavior. Since reinforcers are anything that increases a behavior, praise, a toy, food, a smile, a high five, or being picked up can be reinforcers, but only if the behavior increases. A reinforcer for one person may be a punisher for another person, as illustrated by Ricardo and Jodi. An item or an activity may be a reinforcer at one particular time but not at another, depending on satiation and competing reinforcers. For example, Mary has been happily playing with a cause-and-effect toy for 5 minutes. Mary's button pushing is reinforced by lights and music. Her brother walks into the room eating cereal. She drops the toy and runs to get some of his cereal. If Mary had just eaten lunch, she may have continued playing with the toy rather than running to get some food. Likewise, if her brother had walked in when Mary was just starting to play with the toy, she may have continued to play with the toy as the toy may have been more reinforcing than food at that particular time.

What motivates an infant or toddler can be gleaned by asking caregivers questions about what makes the child become calm, smile, or laugh and by observing the child's responses in various routines and activities. Knowing what motivates a child in a given situation is paramount to facilitating learning skills and encouraging appropriate behaviors. Ongoing assessment of reinforcers and motivation is necessary, as is making adjustment to the environment to facilitate learning opportunities. EI providers need to be aware of how to help parents and caregivers set up the environment to facilitate learning so competing reinforcers are minimized. For example, if a caregiver is trying to interest a child in a book but the television is on, the child may be more likely to attend to the television. If a child is working on using gestures or words to communicate, putting items out of reach, using clear containers the child cannot open, filling the child's cup with only a small amount of his or her favorite beverage, and using other communication temptations facilitate skill development as opposed to an environment where the child can play, explore, and get his or her needs met without interacting.

For many children, skill development happens in fairly predictable sequences. Sometimes, however, children develop splinter skills, skills generally found in older children and without some of the other skills that are usually seen as prerequisites. Though splinter skills are often not functional, they frequently are very motivating. For example, fascination with the alphabet or numbers is often seen in children who are on the autism spectrum. It is not unusual for young children with autism to say the names of numbers and letters but be unable to use words to request. Though it is important for the earlier developing functional skills to be addressed, it is sometimes beneficial to use the splinter skills for motivation. For example, for the child who names numbers and letters but does not make requests by using words, having the child request the numbers and letters may help bridge the gap by asking "Do you want the *b* or the *f*?" when holding up two alphabet blocks. This may help the child experience the power of communication, which will then generalize, often with intervention, to asking for more functional items such as a drink.

TASK/ACTIVITY ANALYSIS

In addition to creating learning opportunities by using motivation, EI providers must be able to analyze a skill or an activity into its components and be aware of any prerequisites needed. A common clinical issue facing providers occurs when families are focused on obtaining one skill in the outcome that is dependent upon skills that precede it developmentally. A good example is when parents want their child to talk. Talking is reliant upon communicative intention, motivation, oral-motor sequencing skills, cognition, and receptive skills, to name just a few. Teaching the child to reach for or point to what he wants may seem unrelated to talking to a parent or caregiver; however, strong and persistent communicative intent represented by gesture will precede talking for most children (Iverson & Goldin-Meadow, 2005). The sequential nature of skills can be difficult for parents and caregivers to understand. As providers systematically address precursor skills, it is important to explain why these skills are important, how best to facilitate the skills, what routines the caregiver can use to teach the skills, and how these earlier skills will lead to acquisition of the desired outcomes.

Observing parents and caregivers engaged in their routines with their children provides EI providers with a great deal of information about what is working well to facilitate a skill and what may need targeting for modification. For example, Mario's mother wanted him to help more with undressing. The EI provider watched Mario's mother get him ready for the day. She dressed him standing and, although she asked him to put his legs into his pants and to give her his foot for his socks and shoes, Mario did not follow any of the directions. The EI provider knew Mario could identify clothing and body parts and follow directions well. The provider suggested Mario sit down so he would not have to work on balancing and standing on one foot while working on the new skill of helping with dressing. With that change in the requirements of the activity, Mario was easily able to put his feet in the opening of his pants and help to put on his shoes and socks.

By coaching the caregiver in how to facilitate specific responses or by personally attempting to facilitate responses hands on, EI providers must constantly analyze strengths and needs relevant to skills necessary to achieve the child's outcomes. For example, if a child does not roll over, the provider must informally assess the reason, determining if strength, motor coordination, and/or responses to the sensation of moving and/or being on the stomach are barriers. If a child does not follow the direction to go get his or her shoes, the provider must figure out if the child knows what a shoe is (to assess receptive language) and if he or she can find a shoe when it is nearby as opposed to across the room or in another room (to assess memory, attention, and problem solving). If a child struggles to complete a three-piece puzzle, the provider must assess if the difficulty arises from the inability to match the pieces to the openings and/or from the inability to turn the pieces to orient them correctly. Once the barriers to successfully completing the skill are discerned, the appropriate strategies can be implemented to facilitate skill development.

SHAPING AND PROMPTING

Once the specific reason or reasons for the child's difficulty is determined, the EI provider and the parents and caregivers collaborate, and the provider coaches them on how to support the child for success. There is both an art and a science to knowing when, how, and how much to help a child master a new skill. When adults provide too much help, children become reliant on adults' cues; when adults provide too little help, it can cause frustration and avoidance in children. Every child's sensory system and pattern of learning is different, and each opportunity to practice may result in progress, necessitating that caregivers and EI providers be able to make adjustments. *Shaping* and *prompting* are two techniques that are used in this process.

Shaping involves starting a learning process where the child is successful and working toward the target behavior, making small changes in the task requirements and reinforcing the child for successful completion of each small step. This process, known sometimes as *successive approximations*, is very helpful in teaching new skills across all areas of development (Gulick & Kitchen, 2007). Consider the following example:

Kareem loved watching his mother blow bubbles and running to pop them. The EI provider showed Kareem's mother how to blow bubbles and then wait for Kareem to indicate he wanted more. At first Kareem fussed to indicate more, so the EI provider coached the mother to model saying "bubble." Kareem vocalized "ba" and the EI provider told his mom to blow more bubbles. Kareem and his mom did this for three more turns, and then the EI provider modeled "bubble" more slowly and emphasizing the two syllables with sing-song intonation. When Kareem said "ba," the EI provider again modeled the two syllables and suggested that Mom wait. Kareem was puzzled that he hadn't been reinforced (a behavioral technique known as *extinction*, whereby previously reinforced behaviors are not reinforced) and with a little annoyance in his voice said "buba." The EI provider excitedly said "yes, bubble" and told his mother to again blow bubbles to reinforce Kareem's attempt. Kareem's mother used bubbles and worked on Kareem saying "bubble" almost every day. When the EI provider returned for the next session, Kareem's mother proudly got out the bubbles to show how Kareem was then able to make requests by using the word "bubble."

Prompting is used along with shaping to assist with learning specific skills. Using a prompt hierarchy can systematically help parents and providers facilitate skill development. There are two types of prompt hierarchies: most-to-least and least-to-most. The most-to-least prompt hierarchy involves giving the most intensive prompts needed and progressing to the least intensive to assist the child in completing an activity or following a direction, while the least-to-most involves the opposite, starting with a relatively subtle or less-intrusive cue, and if the child does not "get it," giving him or her a bigger hint. The most intensive prompt involves physical assistance whereby someone helps the child by taking the child's hands or otherwise assisting the body and helping him or her complete the task or follow the direction. For example, if a child is playing with spoons and a bowl and the desired response is for the child to put a spoon into the bowl and he or she does not, one can take the child's hand and help. Next on the hierarchy is showing the child how to complete the task or follow the direction. In order to be successful, the child must be able to imitate the model. For example, the adult would take a spoon and put it in the bowl, then hand the child a spoon, which the child then puts into the bowl. Helping a little less involves giving the child a verbal direction such as "Put the spoon in the bowl." To succeed with this type of prompt, the child must be able to understand the direction and must be able to perform the motor movements needed.

Within these types of prompts are variations that are also hierarchical. For example, when providing hand-over-hand assistance, a caregiver or provider can take the child's hands and completely perform the task and then progress to taking the child's hands to start the task and having the child finish alone. When teaching a child to clap, parents often facilitate this by saying "clap" and taking the child's hands and clapping them. Some children immediately clap in imitation. Others need repeated practice with hand-over-hand help. For the child who requires more prompting, the facilitator takes the child's hands and moves them slightly together, which gives the child the idea to move his or her hands together. Taking the child's hands and moving them part way is known as a *partial prompt* and entails the child being more actively engaged than when the hands are passively moved. The child may later need a touch cue to the hands when hearing the direction "Clap your hands" and may then progress to needing only to hear the verbal direction.

Setting up situations for children to practice answering questions using a prompt hierarchy is also very helpful. For example, when asking a child a question and receiving no reply from the child, the provider or caregiver can consider telling the child the answer so he or she can repeat it (the easiest for the child), give the child a choice of answers, or give the beginning sound as a hint. These three options are in order from most to least prompts on the hierarchy. In some situations the child may need the more intense prompt, but in others he or she may need only the hint of the initial sound. For the child who does not easily imitate words, the provider or caregiver can use physical assistance to help him answer a question using a gesture, can model a gesture, or can say "Show me." These three options also exemplify most-to-least prompting.

Libby, Weiss, Bancroft, and Ahearn (2008) examined which type of prompt to use in what types of situation. They recommended using most-to-least prompting if it is unknown how the child learns best or if errors interfere with learning. They recommended least-to-most prompting when this approach has been successful in the past. They also advocated frequent monitoring of progress to ensure skill acquisition. Though their research was with older children, their advice can also be applied to young children.

Table 3.1 provides an example of a prompt hierarchy given to a mother to help her facilitate her son's independence in the skills targeted in his IFSP. Table 3.2 and 3.3 illustrate examples of prompt hierarchies that can be given to parents and caregivers to help them identify the types of prompts they use and to help them move toward the next level of independence. Using these types of aids not only helps parents and caregivers but also helps EI providers analyze the child's strengths, needs, and the expected behaviors and skills required for specific routines. For example, the authors discovered through this process that children who have difficulty with motor imitation but who follow directions well need very different types of prompting than do children who have difficulties with following directions but who imitate actions well. It is the authors' hypothesis that children who have difficulties with both motor imitation and language processing are likely to need higher levels of prompts than those who do not. Regardless of the type of prompting used, it is imperative that strategies to fade prompts be utilized as soon as the child is ready. For example, a child who requires visual cues to follow directions needs to learn to follow directions by being presented with fewer and fewer visual cues as the child learns to use his or her auditory skills.

THERAPEUTIC AND EDUCATIONAL MATERIALS IN THE NATURAL ENVIRONMENT

Recommended practice in natural environments involves using materials found wherever the child is receiving services, whether at home, child care, preschool, or the park.

Table 3.1.   Sample target and prompt hierarchy

Target:	The child communicates that he wants a cookie.	The child follows the direction "Go get your shoes."	The child gives you his foot to help put on his shoes.	The child initiates requests for "help" or "more."[a]
Prompt:				
Physical assistance for the entire behavior	When you think Jack wants a cookie, take him to the cookie and help him reach for one.	Take Jack to the shoes and help him pick them up.	Take Jack's foot and put it in the shoe	Help Jack hand you an item or use his body to indicate he wants more.
Physical assistance to help the child begin the behavior	Take Jack near the cookie and wait for him to reach for it.	Take Jack to the shoes and hold up the shoes for him to grasp.	Take Jack's foot and put it toward his shoe; wait for him to push his foot in the shoe.	As above, help Jack with the first part of the behavior.
Modeling the entire behavior	Go to where the cookies are and eat some.	Go to Jack's shoes and pick them up.		Hand someone else the item for assistance so Jack can see the effects.
Modeling part of the behavior	Go to where the cookies are and wait for Jack to reach, point, or say "cookie."		Hold Jack's shoe out and wait for him to give you his foot.	
Telling the child what to do	Say "Jack, go get the cookie" and wait for him to do so.	Say "Jack, walk to the door." After he does this say "Jack, pick up your shoes" and after he does tell him "Bring me your shoes."	Say "Give me your foot."	Say "Give me/show me your ___ and I will ___."
Using a gesture / giving a choice/ asking a yes-no question	Ask "Jack, do you want a cookie?" and wait for him to take you to the cookie.	Point to the shoes as you give Jack the direction.		Point, look expectant, ask "Do you want ___?"
Asking an open-ended question	Ask "Jack, what do you want to eat?" and wait for him to take you to the cookie or other food, point to the cookie, sign cookie, or say cookie.		Ask "What do you need to do?"	Ask "What do you need?"

[a]Communication temptations to help Jack initiate activity:
Blow a few bubbles and stop; put the wand on the floor for Jack or put the lid on the bubbles and put the jar down in front of him.
Put snacks in bags or clear containers.
Put only a small amount in Jack's cup at one time.
Put food in sight but out of reach.
Use wind-up toys that Jack likes but are difficult to use.
Use items that need help to be opened or used such as modeling dough, stamps, and markers.
Keep favorite items up high so Jack can see but not reach them.
Put one sock on Jack and stop.
Put Jack's sock on his hand instead of his foot.
Stand at the door without opening it when going outside.

Items Found in the Home versus the Toy Bag

Use of the toy bag, "the icon of the Early Intervention home visitor" (McWilliam, 2010, p. 150), has several problems. Taking in a toy bag sends a message that the early interventionist's interactions with the child and these special toys—rather than the caregivers' interactions between visits— are what lead to improvements. The family is unable to use the same materials between visits, which means they are unable to replicate the strategies modeled by the EI provider. In addition, taking a toy bag implies that the family's materials and toys aren't good enough to help the child

Table 3.2. Most-to-least prompting

Target: *Prompt:*	Behavior regulation and social skills: Cleaning up toys	Cognitive and receptive language: "Give Daddy your shoes"	Expressive language: Ask Mom for more juice (nonverbal child/verbal child)	Gross motor skills: Pulling to stand	Fine motor skills: Pointing with index finger	Self-care/adaptive: Using a spoon
Physical assistance for the entire behavior	Take the child's hands to help clean up each item.	Take the child's hand, helping him or her grasp the shoe and handing it to Daddy.	Help the child pick up the cup and hand it to Mom.	Place the child in half-kneel, with hands on pelvis, shift his or her weight to the side, guide upward to standing.	Tuck the child's thumb and last three fingers to isolate the index finger.	Put the child's hand on the spoon and help guide the spoon to the bowl and then to the mouth.
Physical assistance to help the child begin the behavior (partial prompt)	Help the child pick up and put away several items and have the child finish.	Move the child's hand toward the shoe and wait.	Give the child the cup when near Mom and wait.	When child is in half-kneel, shift weight to the side and wait.	Tap or extend the index finger.	Put the spoon in the child's hand, help him or her scoop, wait for the child to put the spoon in his or her mouth.
Modeling the entire behavior	Show the child how to pick up the item and put it in the container for all of the pieces.	Show the child how to give Daddy the shoe and wait.	Show the child how to pick up the cup/Say "more juice."	Say "Do this" and move from half-kneel to standing.	Say "Do this" and isolate your index finger.	Sit in front of the child with a spoon and a bowl. Pick up the spoon and say "You do." Put the spoon in your mouth and say "You do."
Modeling part of the behavior	Show the child how to pick up and put away several pieces, and then the child does the rest.	Move the shoe toward Daddy and wait for the child to finish the movement.	Show the child how to pick up the cup/say "j___."	Say "Do this" and move from partial standing to upright.	Point to your index finger.	Sit in front of the child with a spoon and a bowl. Pick up the spoon and say "You do." Wait for child to bring spoon to mouth.
Telling the child what to do	Say "Clean up."	Say "Pick up the shoe and put it in Daddy's hand."	Tell the child "Give Mommy your cup"/Tell the child "Say juice."	Say "Stand up."	Tell the child "Use your pointer."	Tell the child, "Get the spoon" then "Scoop" and finally "Put it in your mouth," pausing after each step for child to follow directions.
Using a gesture/giving a choice/asking a yes-no question	Point to show the child what needs to be cleaned up and/or where to put it.	Point to the shoe and/or to Daddy.	If the child picks up the cup, point to Mom.	Point to tell the child to stand up.	Point to the child's index finger.	Point to the spoon or the bowl to cue the child what to do. If the child uses hands, ask "Do we eat yogurt with our fingers?"
Asking an open-ended question	Ask the child what he or she needs to do.	If child picks up the shoes and stops, ask "Who do you need to give them to?"	Ask the child "What do you need to do?"/Ask the child "What do you say?"	Ask "What do you need to do?" giving the child a reason to stand, such as putting a toy out of reach on the sofa.	Ask "How do you show me what you want?"	If the child uses hands, ask the child "How do big kids eat yogurt?"

29

Table 3.3.   Least-to-most prompting

Target:	Behavior regulation/social skills: Walking next to Mom	Cognitive and receptive language: Matching pictures	Expressive language: Pointing to request	Gross motor skills: Jumping in place	Fine motor skills: Releasing objects	Self-care/ adaptive: Taking off socks
Prompt:						
Asking an open-ended question	"Where do you need to walk?"	"Where does that go?"	"What do you want?"		"What do you need to do?"	"What do you need to do now?"
Using a gesture/ giving a choice/ asking a yes-no question	Point beside Mom.	Point to the matching picture.	Ask "Do you want a cookie or a cracker?"		Point to the box.	Point to the child's socks and gesture a motion signifying "off."
Telling the child what to do	Say "Walk next to Mom."	Say "Put the dog on the dog."	Say "Point to the cracker."	"Jump."	Say "Put it in the box."	Say "Pull down your socks and take them off."
Modeling part of the behavior		Move a picture toward the match.	Model isolating the index finger.	Bend your knees.		Remove your socks from your toes.
Modeling the entire behavior	Say "I am walking next to Mom."	Match a picture.	Model isolating the index finger and pointing to an object the child wants.	Jump in place.	Release the item into the box.	Take off your socks.
Physical assistance to help the child begin the behavior (partial prompt)	Physically guide child toward Mom.	Take the child's hand holding the picture and move it toward the match.	Help the child isolate the index finger.	Help the child bend his or her knees.	Stabilize the child's forearm.	Place the child's hands on his or her socks.
Physical assistance for the entire behavior	Hold the child's hand.	Take the child's hand holding the picture and move it to the match.	Help the child isolate the index finger and move it toward the desired item.	Help the child bend his or her knees and jump.	Take the item out of the child's hand and put it in the box.	Place the child's hands on the socks and physically guide him or her to remove the socks.

make progress. One of the authors, when she began working with a family that had two other EI providers who used toy bags, said to the author, "Where is *your* magic bag?"

In addition, taking a toy bag gives the impression that toy play provides the majority of learning opportunities in a child's day. This same family noted that they had gone out to buy the exact same toys that the EI providers used, resulting in unnecessary expenditure of time and money. In addition, because the family thought that "therapy" to help the child talk "was a play-based process," they missed many opportunities within daily family routines to help the child talk. The mother told the author, "I just buy the stuff you guys bring, and play the same games I see you guys do." The use of a toy bag hinders embedding skills in naturally occurring daily routines and limits coaching opportunities. Most people learn best by doing rather than by watching, and watching an EI provider play with special toys from a toy bag offers little opportunity for generalization into functional daily routines. One parent remarked to one of the authors, "The therapists come and play and leave. We don't know what to do." Table 3.4 exemplifies how bringing a toy bag into the home may evoke very different thoughts for providers than for parents and caregivers. In Appendix A, the grid "Substitutions: Using Common Household Items Instead of Bringing Toys" offers practical alternatives to the toys in the bag.

Table 3.4. Differing perspectives on the toy bag

The toy bag may provide:	The provider may think:	The parents or caregivers may think:
Novelty	The toys keep the child's attention during the session.	How can I get my child's attention when I can't get new toys every day or every week?
Carefully selected toys to target skills	They can facilitate specific skill development during the session.	How do I do that at home when I don't have those toys?
A barrier to an equal partnership	I am the professional and it is my duty to lead the session to accomplish outcomes.	I am not sure how to participate when she pulls out the toys during the session. What is my role?
An opportunity to explore new objects	I am providing information about how a child problem-solves and adapts to new objects and generalizes skills.	I am so glad my child can play with those nice toys, even if it is just for an hour, but I hate it when he cries when the toys are gone at the end of the session.
A trigger for some children to demonstrate difficult behaviors	It is difficult when the child keeps getting into my toy bag.	Every time the therapist leaves my child has a tantrum because the toys are gone.
An influence on family routines	These toys facilitate skills that are generalized during family routines.	The therapist uses these toys during therapy. Early intervention is supposed to be routines based. I don't have these toys. I don't know how this is routines based except during playtime with the therapist.
Items for the family to borrow	They can practice this week.	I hope we don't forget about them, break them, or lose them.

Electronic Technology

Electronic technology is often used by EI providers as an educational or therapeutic tool. Electronic technology includes software programs, applications (commonly called "apps"), streaming media, e-books, and the Internet, while noninteractive media include videos, DVDs, and some television shows (NAEYC & Fred Rogers Center, 2012). Technology can enhance early childhood experiences when integrated into the child's routines and used appropriately for the child's developmental level. According to Edutopia (2007),

> True integration occurs when the use of technology and media becomes routine and transparent—when the focus of a child or education is on the activity or exploration itself and not on the technology being used. Technology integration has been successful when the use of technology and media supports the goals of educators and programs for children, provides children with digital tools for learning and communicating, and help improve child outcomes. (p. 8)

The National Association for the Education of Young Children (NAEYC) and the Fred Rogers Center (2012) recommend uses of technology in the position statement *Technology and Interactive Media as Tools in Early Childhood Programs Serving Children from Birth through Age 8.* Their six recommendations are as follows:

1. Select, use, integrate, and evaluate technology and interactive media tools in intentional and developmentally appropriate ways, giving careful attention to the appropriateness and the quality of the content, the child's experience, and the opportunities for coengagement.

2. Provide a balance of activities in programs for young children, recognizing that technology and interactive media can be valuable tools when used intentionally with children to extend and support active, hands-on, creative, and authentic engagement with those around them and their world.

3. Prohibit the passive use of television, videos and DVDs and other noninteractive technologies and media in early childhood programs for children younger than 2, and discourage passive and noninteractive uses with children ages 2 through 5.

4. Limit any use of technology and interactive media in programs for children younger than 2 to those that appropriately support responsive interactions between caregivers and children and that strengthen adult-child relationships.

5. Carefully consider the screen time recommendations from public health organizations for children from birth through age 5 when determining appropriate limits on technology and media use in early childhood settings. Screen time estimates should include time spent in front of a screen at the early childhood program and, with input from parents and families, at home and elsewhere.

6. Provide leadership in ensuring equitable access to technology and interactive media experiences for the children in their care and for parents and families. (p. 11)

Technology can be found in most homes, and most families use technology as part of their lifestyles. Clinical issues concern availability, balance, developmental goals, and motivation and how technology interfaces with families, participation, and IFSP outcomes. Perhaps the most common technology in the majority of homes is the television. While providers need to be sensitive to individual preferences in each family environment, education and discussion concerning the benefits of television (e.g., educational programming, exposure to different cultural representations) and the less positive results (e.g., distractibility, programming with negative content, lack of interaction) can be matched to each individual situation and family.

Many families have apps on cell phones. The following vignette may sound familiar. Braydon was a 22-month-old boy with limited play skills and difficulty engaging in play. During a session, Braydon's father frequently offered Braydon his cell phone to play with. The app he enjoyed had several choices of interaction with a cat, showing cause-and-effect relationships with the press of a button. Braydon was animated and engaged with the app and easily manipulated buttons. This motivated his father to buy more apps for Braydon, as his competency with apps was something his parents took pride in. Braydon's favorite toy was the phone with its apps. Braydon was difficult to engage when playing with apps, preferring self-direction and finding bids for social interaction distracting and unwanted. The EI provider discussed the balance needed between interactive activities and those that did not warrant interaction. In order to achieve his outcomes of playing with more toys in new ways, Braydon also needed to spend time manipulating toys, imitating actions, and problem solving in the environment. Braydon's provider found that the cell phone interfered with Braydon's participation in other daily routines, as well. The EI provider discussed the importance of Braydon's skill acquisition with his parents. Though children may have access to and enjoy apps, these must be balanced with the child's need to interact and engage in a variety of experiences.

Using tablets has become more common in therapy sessions, as well. A physical therapist working with 30-month-old Andrea found that she stood well when the therapist allowed her to use the therapist's personal tablet with apps involving the alphabet. The well-meaning therapist recommended the parent use numbers and letters to motivate Andrea, since the girl liked them so much. The mother was very happy that Andrea was learning letters and numbers and expressed sadness that she could not afford to buy a tablet for her daughter. A few weeks later the mother asked the speech-language pathologist if she had a tablet with which she, too, could work on the alphabet and numbers, and this created an awkward situation for the mother and the pathologist. The physical therapist and the parent were very encouraged by the child's ability to say and recognize letters and numbers, but the speech-language pathologist had concerns about Andrea's lack of a core vocabulary, which typically emerges before labeling numbers and letters. The speech-language pathologist recommended that the parents and physical therapist focus more on core vocabulary and use labeling of numbers and letters on a limited basis—when Andrea needed highly motivating distractions. In addition to the issue of Andrea's need to focus on other language skills, the family did not have access to a tablet and would have been unable to utilize the same strategies used by the physical therapist—using the tablet entailed similar issues as using the items in an EI provider's traditional toy bag. Providers need to balance what motivates the child, what skills need to be facilitated, and what kind of perceptions and priorities families might have when choosing technology used during sessions.

EI providers should review the guidelines for technology use and integration with each family. They should rethink using personal devices if they cannot find ways for families to access the same device through lending libraries or other means. Respect for families and their use of technology, as well as candid discussions about strategies with and without technological support, will assist them in helping the child reach developmental goals.

Knowing general information regarding how to facilitate learning in parents, caregivers, and children is essential for the EI provider in order to teach specific skills to master IFSP outcomes. The following six chapters summarize developmental information and ways to facilitate skill development during participation in common activities and daily routines.

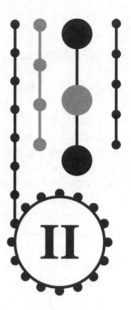

Developmental Progression of Skills

Some EI providers tend to facilitate skills found on evaluation tools that are designed to determine eligibility. Some test items are functional skills that are naturally occurring in a child's day, but others are not. Many gross motor, adaptive/self-help, and communication skills tend to be relevant to a child's typical day. These skills include crawling, walking, jumping, eating, dressing, gesturing, talking, answering questions, and following directions. In the areas of cognition and fine motor skills; however, many test items are not as relevant. For example, many developmental evaluations in the areas of cognition and/or fine motor skills have items such as stacking cubes, stringing beads, folding paper, finding objects under a series of hidden screens, and making a bridge from cubes. These activities are not as commonly occurring in the lives of most infants and toddlers. To help make the leap from test items to functional skills, it is helpful to think about what the test item entails. When one analyzes stacking blocks, required skills include grasping, releasing, shoulder control, using an appropriate amount of force, and eye–hand coordination. Stringing beads requires a pincer grasp, using two hands with one holding and one manipulating, sequencing movements, and eye–hand coordination. Once the skill is analyzed, an EI provider can then consider what daily routines and typical activities require similar sets of skills that will likely be more readily practiced by children and their families or caregivers. Rather than teaching to the test and developing a repertoire of isolated skills, EI providers should be developing functional skills that are relevant to typical routines and activities. Section II provides ways for providers to coach families and caregivers to develop these skills.

Section II also contains skills within the developmental domains of behavior regulation and social skills, cognitive and receptive language, expressive language, gross motor skills, fine motor skills, and self-care/adaptive skills. Each domain has an introduction that describes the developmental progression typically seen in children from birth until 36 months followed by functional skills within each domain. Each functional skill within the domains contains a description, followed by its importance, ways to facilitate acquisition and practice during daily routines and activities, and tips and hints for skill acquisition and practice.

In the subsections that describe the incorporation of skills into daily routines, the language used is that which an EI provider would say to parents and caregivers ("try to," "give the child," and so on). Sample charts for monitoring progress are located in Appendix B. Such charts can be completed by providers or by parents and other caregivers, depending on the situation. Some parents and caregivers are able to collect data between sessions, others have good intentions but find it difficult to do so, and others do not express an interest in documenting progress in written form. As discussed by Buzhardt et al. (2010), "Early childhood programs and practitioners are increasingly required to use evidence-based practices in the services they provide to young children and their families" (p. 201) and these sample charts can assist providers in fulfilling the requirement and help them make important decisions to ensure progress is being made. Parents, other caregivers, or providers can monitor one or multiple skills at a time. Charts can be modified to track levels of assistance or prompting needed for specific skills. They can also be used as coaching tools to describe components of certain skills as well as the progression of skills. During completion of the charts, the provider or the parent/caregiver might notice that a child's performance or participation may vary depending on the routine, which can then help with planning how to further facilitate skill acquisition.

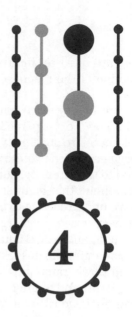

Behavior
Regulation and Social Skills

4

Behavior regulation and social skills are strongly interrelated. When a child is well regulated, he or she is ready to interact and to learn. If a child is dysregulated, he or she has difficulty being calm and organized during daily routines, which affects relationships with parents, other caregivers, and peers as well as the child's ability to learn. Behavior regulation and social skills are also tied greatly to sensory processing. According to DeGangi (2000), "Self-regulation involves the capacity to modulate mood, self-calm, delay gratification, and tolerate transitions in activity" (p. 10). Infants' and toddlers' routines require these self-regulatory skills many times throughout a day: when they are waiting to be taken out of the crib in the morning, accepting movement and touch during dressing and diapering, waiting to eat, and tuning out sounds to go to sleep, to name just a few. As children age and mature, they are better able to wait and understand contingencies such as "After Daddy gets home we can go over to the park" or "First brush your teeth and then we can read that story."

Infants and toddlers learn about their world by taking in information through their senses, and knowledge of the sensory system can help EI providers, parents, and caregivers better understand behavior and learning. Many people remember learning about the five senses early in their school career. Occupational therapists and many others working in EI are well versed not only in the commonly talked about sensory systems (tactile, auditory, gustatory/taste, smell, and visual) but also in the lesser known proprioceptive and vestibular sensory systems. Proprioception is the sense that tells a person about his or her body position. Receptors are located throughout the musculoskeletal system and give feedback regarding orientation in space, rate and timing of movements, and force exerted by muscles. Proprioception is critical to anticipating and planning movements. The other lesser talked about sensory system, the vestibular system, works closely with the proprioceptive system. The vestibular system's receptors are located in the inner ear and give information regarding the force, speed, and direction of head movement. Information from the vestibular system provides feedback regarding muscle tone, balance and equilibrium, ocular-motor control, arousal, attention, and emotions (Williamson & Anzalone, 2001).

Sensory input travels from the various sensory receptors such as those located in the eyes, ears, tongue, skin, muscles, tendons, joints, nose, and internal organs to the brain, where it is registered or perceived. Our brains must "decide" what and how much sensory information to pay attention to and what and how much sensory information to ignore as well as when to pay attention and when to ignore it. Then our brains must interpret the information and give it meaning, which typically comes from past experiences, "decide" on a response (organize the information), and then carry out (execute) the response. Our brains continually receive information from various receptors, and then the information is perceived, selectively attended to, interpreted, and organized so we can execute a meaningful response. The execution of the response often involves a sequence of steps.

There are great individual differences in sensory perception in terms of how much sensation is needed (intensity) and for how long the sensation is needed (duration) before it is perceived. In addition, the location of the stimulus affects one's perception of it, as there are specific types of receptor cells located in various parts of the body. Everyone's sensory perception is quite different, and each person has a unique profile of sensory thresholds related to the intensity, duration, and location of the stimuli. Each person also has a unique pattern of stimuli that he or she prefers and seeks and those he or she dislikes and avoids. Some people are underreactive to certain stimuli and overreactive to other stimuli. At an amusement park it is easy to see a wide range of individual differences among adults. There are those who love movement, auditory stimuli, and visual stimuli and can be found on the roller coaster with the other screaming thrill seekers. In contrast, there are those at the other end of the park on the quiet train slowly rambling through the relative calm and quiet. Individual differences can also be seen in infants and toddlers. There are those who tend to be sensitive to sensory input, easily getting overwhelmed with movement, sights, sounds, and/or touch; those who generally need or seek a lot of movement, touch, and/or noise; and those who are a mixture of the two. Charlie, a 2-year-old who craves movement, touch, and deep pressure, frequently runs around his house, throws himself into others quite unexpectedly, rubs food through his hair at mealtime, and splashes enthusiastically in the tub, whereas his same-age cousin Bradley often sits in one spot looking at books for 15 minutes, fusses during his bath, tends to say ouch when his mother puts lotion on him, and holds on tightly whenever his mother picks him up to put him in the grocery cart. These two boys have very different sensory systems, which greatly affect their daily routines. It is understandable how individual differences relate to self-regulation. For those who are overly sensitive to sensory stimulation, touch during bathing and diaper changes, the lights and sounds at the mall, or the bumpy texture in the food can be quite overwhelming and can greatly affect behavior. Similarly, the toddler who tends to need more sensory input may be crashing into peers at child care settings, climbing on the bookcase and jumping off, stuffing his or her mouth at mealtime, and/or not turning when his or her name is called. The sensory system and its impact on behavior is quite complex. Altering the environment can have great effects on the sensory system. Table 4.1 identifies sensory stimuli that are more likely to calm or more likely to alert and should be considered during daily routines and activities (DeGangi, 2000; Williamson & Anzalone, 2001).

Sensory factors affect all daily routines. Attending to people and objects, moving, eating, sleeping, listening, talking, and brushing teeth all involve extraordinary amounts of sensory

Table 4.1.　Alerting and calming stimuli

Sensory system	Generally alerting stimuli	Generally calming stimuli
Visual	Visual input that is moved at various speeds and in various planes	Visual input that is moved slowly and in one plane
	Bright colors	Soft, muted colors
	"Busy" visual environment	Few distractions
Auditory	Loud sounds	Soft sounds
	Varying sounds (pitch, rhythm, intensity)	Rhythmic sounds
Tactile	Light touch	Firm but gentle touch
	Irregular touch	Maintained touch
	Cooler temperatures	Neutral warmth (close to normal body temperature)
Vestibular	Irregular, fast movement	Rhythmic, slow movement
Proprioceptive	Pulling and pushing with quick changes	Slow, slightly resistive, rhythmic pulling
		Sucking
Taste/smell	Sour, bitter, pungent, spicy	Mild flavors and smells

processing. Such processing is also a factor in the acquisition of many skills that involve praxis, the planning and sequencing of coming up with an idea, figuring out what to do, and carrying out the necessary steps to accomplish a novel motor act (Ayres, 1985). Coordinating the lips and tongue for speech, putting together toys, navigating the playground equipment, following directions to go upstairs and get one's shoes, and getting on and off the sofa all involve sensory processing and motor sequencing. For infants and toddlers who are experiencing difficulties in meeting their developmental milestones or who are having behavior difficulties, EI providers must consider the role of sensory processing.

Being ready to take in information through the senses in different environments, displaying emotions appropriate to situations, playing with toys appropriately, developing independence and the ability to entertain oneself, and interacting with others are skills that cross all developmental domains. Similarly, joint attention, engagement, attention to task, persistence, and frustration tolerance are important in all developmental skills. Learning about rules and consequences as well as ownership, empathy/sympathy, and self-worth all begin in those very early experiences with family and friends.

Parents, caregivers, and EI providers frequently discuss issues related to sensory processing, behavior, and discipline. It is essential that EI providers help parents and caregivers understand development as it relates to behavior. For example, an 8-month-old cannot be expected to clean up toys or wait for a bottle without crying when extremely hungry, nor can a 1-year-old be expected to sit quietly during a 2-hour church service or sit in a highchair in a restaurant for 30 minutes before the food arrives.

Many caregivers have questions about how to discipline children who have delays or disabilities, while others struggle with how to manage children's behavior. Parents have expressed concerns, including "I don't know if he understands" and "I don't want him to be upset," during discussions about consequences to inappropriate behaviors such as hitting or tantrums. In the authors' experience it is difficult for parents to set limits when their children have significant health-related issues such as frequent hospitalizations or surgeries or when the child has significant sensory processing and/or communication challenges. According to Smith (2004), "Young children are constantly engaged in exploration and discovery of the world around them, within which they learn to understand that there are boundaries" (p. 29). Smith reviewed the literature and found that parenting practices associated with positive outcomes include parental warmth and involvement; clear communication and expectations; induction and explanation; rules, boundaries, and demands; consistency and consequences; and context and structure. For children who have significant behavior challenges, caregivers often struggle with the practices Smith associated with positive outcomes. Caregivers may need to learn how to implement strategies beyond those gleaned from their personal experience or general parenting resources such as magazine articles or well-child doctor visits. Teaching caregivers principles from ABA can be very helpful in their efforts to decrease challenging behaviors. According to Gulick and Kitchen (2007), looking at the function of behavior is the most important consideration when developing a system for changing behavior, yet it is the most ignored.

Most, if not all, behavior has at least one of the following functions: to get something such as attention, a toy, food, or drink; to avoid or escape from something; and/or to give oneself stimulation, known as *automatic reinforcement*. An example of the importance of looking at the functions of behavior can be seen in a toddler who bites. Behavioral strategies need to be different for children who bite for different reasons: one child bites because it makes the gums feel better (automatic reinforcement), another bites to communicate "no" (to escape something), and yet another bites to make a child playing nearby drop a toy (to get something). For the child who bites because it feels good, giving him or her teethers, gum massage, or chewy foods may be appropriate. For the child who bites to escape a demand, such as when Mom takes the child's hands to help him or her clean up the blocks, he or she needs to learn the replacement behavior of saying "no" instead of biting, and the child also needs to learn to follow directions to clean up his or her toys. The child who bites to get a toy from a peer needs to learn to ask for the toy and to learn to wait until the other child puts it down, both replacement behaviors for the biting.

Behavior is very complex, and it often takes observation, analysis, time, and fortitude to change undesirable behaviors. Sometimes the function of the behavior is difficult to ascertain, and if a parent, caregiver, or EI provider doesn't think about the function or guesses wrong as to the function, the behavior may get worse. For example, if a child throws food when he or she is done eating, having the child get out of a chair and telling the child he or she cannot have any more or giving the child a time-out is likely to increase the incidence of throwing because the child is getting the result he or she desires. Sometimes behaviors get worse before they get better. If a child is not receiving reinforcement for behaviors that were previously reinforced, the parents, caretakers, and providers may see an escalation in the behaviors, called an *extinction burst*. For example, Julie screamed in the grocery store, so her mother gave her candy so she would be quiet. Julie learned that screaming in the store had a good outcome for her: candy. When her mother realized Julie was screaming to get candy, she decided she would no longer give the girl any candy. The next three shopping trips were quite embarrassing for the mother as Julie screamed louder and louder and even started to hit. This extinction burst was not a surprise to Julie's EI provider. Together, she and Julie's mother developed a plan to give Julie small bites of crackers during the shopping trip when she was behaving appropriately and not screaming. Julie's screaming in the store disappeared after two subsequent trips, and then the provider showed her mother other ways to reinforce Julie's appropriate behavior so she no longer needed to be given food to get through the store.

Many EI providers have some knowledge of sensory processing and behavior; however, the expertise of someone with specialized training may be needed for children who have behavior difficulties that result in significant disruptions in daily routines such as eating, sleeping, or participating in group child care settings. Jack is an example of a child who has significant challenges that required an EI provider with specialized training. Jack is 2 years old and had significant reflux and poor weight gain as a very premature infant. Whenever he cried, he vomited. His parents understandably tried to keep Jack from crying whenever they could, and when he did cry, his parents stopped the crying by giving Jack what he wanted. When Jack's reflux diminished, his parents asked the EI provider for help, as Jack slept in his parents' bed at night and for naps and during the day constantly demanded attention, food, and drink—behaviors they wanted to change. The EI provider helped the parents develop positive behavior strategies that reinforced Jack for small steps toward the goals of requesting in appropriate ways and going to sleep in his own bed with less and less support. They gradually taught Jack new skills, and the family's quality of life greatly improved.

This chapter contains milestones in the area of behavior regulation and social skills. Each skill is described, its importance discussed, ways to incorporate its development in daily routines and activities are examined, and tips and hints to further its development are offered. The reader is reminded that the language used is that which an EI provider would say to parents and caregivers in order to coach and support them.

BEING CALM AND REGULATED

Infants and toddlers rely on others, first, to help them be calm and ready to take in information from the environment and, then, to develop the ability to self-regulate.

Importance: According to Dale, O'Hara, Keen, and Porges (2011), "Successful development during the first year of life is dependent on the infant's ability to regulate behavioral and physiological state in response to unpredictable environmental challenges" (p. 216). If an infant or toddler is having difficulty with regulation, the child is potentially missing learning opportunities, and the likelihood increases that child, parents, and caregivers also struggle with difficulties such as bonding, sleep deprivation, and mood difficulties. Regulatory processes refine greatly during the first 2 years (DeGangi, 2000).

How to Incorporate into Routines:

 Bath Time: Because the temperature of the water can affect a child's regulation, try warm temperatures to soothe a very active child or to help prepare a child for bedtime. For the calmer child, provide a slightly cooler bath to help alert him or her and help with learning readiness for an activity after bath time.

 Bedtime: Follow a bedtime routine with calm activities just before the child goes to bed. Some children need a longer time of calm activities than others, and if bedtime is difficult, a longer calm-down period may be needed.

 Book Time: For active children who have difficulty sitting for books, try talking about the pictures and making book time very short. Gradually increase the amount of time spent on the book and gradually progress to reading very short books with few words per page to longer books with more language. For group story time, incorporate movement or vocal participation to assist with maintaining attention.

 Community Outings: The success of community outings is often related to a child's regulation. Some children get very overstimulated at the park, at the mall, or in other public places. For those children, schedule very short outings and gradually increase the duration. Watch for signs of overstimulation and try to leave before the child "falls apart." To soothe a child, try going for a walk or taking the child for a ride in a wagon, stroller, or wheelchair. For the child who tends to be underreactive, go outside for a fast ride in a stroller or run around the yard to help alert him or her.

 Diapering and Dressing: It is important that the child's behavior or regulatory state be addressed before attempting to dress or diaper him or her. Calm the very active child by reading a book before diapering or quietly singing a song before or during diapering. For the child who tends to be very sensitive to touch, use firm rather than light pressure when helping to put arms in a sleeve or rub cream on a diaper rash, tell the child what you will be doing, and have him or her help as much as possible.

 Mealtime/Snack Time: For children who tend to get overstimulated easily, provide food at warm temperatures to see if the warmth is calming. Provide opportunities to suck from a bottle, sippy cup, or straw depending on the child's skill level. For those children who tend to be underaroused, try colder temperatures of food to see if the coolness alerts them. Try stronger flavors (e.g., tart fruits or cinnamon added to applesauce) to see if the child tends to be more alerted.

 Playtime: If the child is demonstrating low arousal or sluggishness, play active games such as bouncing, Peekaboo, chase, and other fast-paced activities to alert him or her and help to facilitate interaction and participation. For children who are very calm but then tend to get overstimulated quickly, follow active play with activities that are more calming such as songs or books. Watch the child closely for cues that the activity level is optimal. For children who tend to be very active, start interactive playtime with calming activities such as a quiet song. Gradually increase the stimulation, but again watch for signs such as increased activity, decreased eye contact and engagement, irritability, or aggression, which indicate the need for more calming. Often it is helpful to schedule active play followed by more calm play throughout the day.

Tips and Hints

If a child is under- or overaroused, mealtimes can be challenging. The underaroused child may take a long time to eat, may appear very sleepy, or may have difficulty coordinating chewing and swallowing. The overaroused child may also have a difficult time coordinating eating but may also be resistant to sitting for mealtime or may eat too fast.

The timing of the active/calm play can be crucial to encouraging successful routines such as mealtime and bedtime. For children who have difficulty with over- or underactivity or reactivity, the advice of an occupational therapist with expertise in sensory processing should be sought.

INITIATING AND MAINTAINING EYE CONTACT

Eye contact occurs when a young child looks at the eyes of another person. It may be brief, but as the child develops it will gradually increase for longer durations. Eye contact can be elicited by others, for example, through touching, by making sounds, or by calling the child's name. Eye contact also can be initiated by the child, for example, by looking at another person's eyes to request attention or more of an activity.

Importance: Eye contact is an important component of social interaction and communication. Looking toward the eyes of others is an important foundation for initiation of sounds and facial expressions, for understanding emotions, for back-and-forth interactions, for requesting, and for commenting.

How to Incorporate into Routines:

Bedtime: When putting the child to bed, move your face close to his or her eyes when saying goodnight.

Book Time: When reading the child a story, point out something specific in the story and point to the picture being talked about, then comment about it. For example, when reading a book such as *Brown Bear, Brown Bear, What Do You See?* (Martin & Carl, 2010), physically point to the bear and say, "Look! He's furry." Wait for the child to gaze toward you to share the discussion, then continue to read, repeating the cycle to help the child shift gaze toward the speaker and back to the book and referent being discussed.

Community Outing: When taking walks with children who are in strollers or wheelchairs, turn the child so he or she can see your face, if possible, as you comment about what you see and what the child is doing.

Mealtime/Snack Time: When holding the bottle for or breastfeeding the child, softly talk to him or her to encourage looking toward your eyes. When the child is eating in the highchair, booster seat, or at the table, when giving him or her the food, give a few pieces and then pause so the child will look up at your face to indicate "more."

Tips and Hints

Holding objects up to your face when talking to a child who is not looking can help the child shift his or her gaze to your face.

For the child who does not frequently demonstrate eye contact, when participating in familiar routines such as singing or bouncing, sing or bounce several times and pause. As soon as the child looks at you, resume the activity.

ENCOURAGING INDEPENDENT PLAY SKILLS

Independent play skills may include exploring with the senses, playing with containers, looking at books, putting toys together, or pretend play.

Importance: When a child is able to safely play independently, caregivers are able to accomplish routines they need or want to do.

How to Incorporate into Routines:

Bath Time: Give the child some time to play with cups, bowls, and bath toys when time allows. If needed, show him or her ways to play and then allow time for the child to explore the items independently.

Book Time: Provide books the child can look at safely without supervision; for example, avoid lift-the-flap books for children who tear pages.

Playtime: Find a balance between having structured play with "teaching" and giving the child time to play independently.

Tips and Hints

Arranging the environment with toys that motivate the child will encourage independent play.

Slowly increase space between the child and caregiver to encourage the child to feel comfortable playing independently.

Using natural breaks such as going to the bathroom or getting the laundry, while ensuring the child is safe, can initially help ease the transition of spending time independently.

GAINING ATTENTION

Young children gain attention by crying, by vocalizing, by using gestures (e.g., pulling, tapping, hitting, pointing, extending items to show) and by using words.

Importance: The ability to gain attention is integral to initiating communication and seeking help or information.

How to Incorporate into Routines:

Book Time: Place one or more books near the child and sit close by to encourage the child to point to or hand you the book to signify a request to read the book.

Community Outing: When the child points and/or vocalizes spontaneously, respond by commenting on what the child is trying to communicate.

Mealtime/Snack Time: When the child is finished, look for signals that he or she is done or wants more.

Tips and Hints

When children have difficulty gaining attention—or gaining attention in appropriate ways—model the desired behavior using prompts if necessary; for example, give hand-over-hand assistance to tap someone or model the needed word for the child to repeat.

PLAYING SOCIAL GAMES

Young children first respond to social games by smiling, then by laughing. Next they respond to the words and the gestures and imitate the action involved. Later, children initiate by using the word or gesture and look at others for the anticipated response.

Importance: Early social games involve awareness of others, turn taking or reciprocity, and imitation. According to Caimaioni and Laicardi (1985), social games occur regularly in everyday activities, are a marker of social and cognitive development, and help with the mastery of the rules of language.

How to Incorporate into Routines:

Book Time: Read some of the many available books that incorporate social games such as Pat-a-cake and Peekaboo. Play Peekaboo with any book: hiding behind it and reappearing with a playful "peekaboo!"

Diapering and Dressing: Play This Little Piggy and "I'm going to get your belly" and watch for the child to anticipate the routine and ask for more either nonverbally or verbally.

Playtime: Incorporate "so big" into play to encourage imitation.

Tips and Hints

To encourage participation, perform part of a familiar social game and pause with an expectant look to see if the child finishes the action.

For children who are difficult to engage and tend to play alone, use a lot of affect and excitement to facilitate interaction.

For a child who is hypersensitive to sounds and dislikes a lot of stimulation, use low volume and a calm tone of voice and gradually increase the affect and excitement.

USING OR SHOWING "MINE" AND DEFENDING POSSESSIONS

Saying or demonstrating "mine" and defending possessions can be seen when a toddler grabs a toy from someone else, when he or she fusses or cries when someone takes away a toy, or when a verbal toddler says "mine." Verbal children may also say their name and the name of the item, such as "Cassidy's ball."

Importance: According to Ross, Vickar, and Perlman (2010), early conflict such as fighting over toys reflects a transition in social-cognitive development, just as does cooperative interaction. Defending possessions involves coordinating attention to play objects and attention to other children as well as understanding others' intentions. Sometimes this results in a child's use of physical force or aggression. Many parents appear embarrassed by their young children's inability to share, not realizing that this skill takes many years to develop.

How to Incorporate into Routines:

Diapering and Dressing and Mealtime/Snack Time: Playfully taking a child's food, sock, or toy and saying "mine" may elicit a toddler doing the same.

Grooming and Hygiene: Brush teeth at the same time as the child and show him or her your toothbrush and his or her toothbrush.

Playtime: When one child takes a toy away from another, model the word mine or say "my _____" for the latter child.

Tips and Hints

Children at first do not defend their possessions but later do so enthusiastically. Many caregivers struggle to help a child balance the social skills of defending possessions and sharing; however, looking out for one's own interest develops before understanding others' perspectives.

PEER INTERACTION

Children first watch their peers and later interact with them. Howes (1980) describes five levels of toddler play: 1) parallel play whereby children are within 3 feet of each other and engage in similar activities without acknowledging each other; 2) parallel aware play whereby children exhibit eye contact; 3) simple social play in which children engage in the same or similar activities and interact by talking, smiling, and giving and receiving toys; 4) complementary and reciprocal play whereby children have roles that they exchange, such as when playing Peekaboo or chase; and 5) reciprocal social play, which involves more complex and interdependent exchanges.

Importance: Playing with peers is an important skill for developing and maintaining social relationships and is the beginning of learning to cooperate, collaborate, lead, and follow, skills that are necessary for all ages.

How to Incorporate into Routines:

Book Time: Look at books with a child on each side of you and direct your attention to one child then the other. Look for the children to acknowledge each other.

Community Outing: Parks have many naturally occurring opportunities for watching and interacting with peers. Climbing, sliding, swinging, and playing in the sand box facilitate observation of and interaction with peers.

Mealtime/Snack Time: To facilitate peer interaction, structured activities such as eating lunch together or having a snack during a play date provide the opportunity for peer interaction within a structured framework.

Playtime: When playing with the child, act as if you are a peer and model sharing of materials and taking turns across coloring activities, puzzle pieces, songs, running and chasing, simple games, and other shared activities. When a child is with a peer or sibling, comment about what the other child is doing. Model ways to interact by giving and trading items with the other child.

Tips and Hints

When a child exhibits behaviors such as grabbing or hitting because he or she wants a toy, teach the child replacement behaviors along with giving an appropriate consequence. For example, if a child grabs a toy, model for the other child to say "mine" and redirect the "grabber" to a different toy.

Using a more skilled sibling or peer to help a child learn skills can be a good strategy for generalizing and relieving, in small part, the caregiver of all responsibility for teaching. Coaching the caregiver to coach an older or more skilled sibling or peer to interact in a way that facilitates a skill is a good strategy for teaching (e.g., "Show Brian the truck. Ask him to make it go-go-go. If you say, 'Go go go,' he may say it too."). Be sure to praise siblings and peers when they demonstrate these skills.

TESTING LIMITS/BECOMING INDEPENDENT/ACCEPTING LIMITS

Toddlers frequently test limits by participating in behaviors for which they have been repeatedly told "no." There are many rules to learn and follow as they develop the ability to accept limits from a variety of people in their lives.

Importance: Most parents, caregivers, and service providers recognize that certain look when toddlers are about to touch something they know they are not supposed to touch or to engage in an activity they know is forbidden. Sometimes this is a way a toddler seeks attention, but it also appears to be a way the child learns rules and finds out how important the rule is. Caregivers' philosophies regarding rules and discipline fall on a continuum from very lenient to very strict, and children and EI providers must adapt to the rules of the environment. As stated by Forman (2007), "Both the direction of the toddler's motivated behavior and the parent's desire to limit it follow from the multiple rapid changes in capacity seen in this developmental period" (p. 291).

How to Incorporate into Routines:

Bath Time: Be consistent with safety rules, such as sitting rather than standing and keeping the water in the tub, as children learn the expectations and test them to be sure.

Bedtime: When a child begins to delay bedtime by one more story, one more drink, crying to go downstairs with Daddy, and other tactics, try to anticipate the child's stalling by making sure he or she has had a drink, said goodnight, and had a set number of stories or songs. Be consistent with the rules.

Community Outing: For a child who tends to resist hand-holding or riding in a stroller, give choices such as "Walk next to me or I will hold your hand" or "Hold my hand or get in your stroller." Give snacks and treats while shopping when the child is being good rather than after he or she starts crying, screaming, or demonstrating other unwanted behaviors.

Diapering and Dressing: Provide a goodie bag of something fun to hold during diaper changes. Sing songs, talk about something the child likes, and provide other distractions before the child begins to display undesirable behavior.

Grooming and Hygiene: Allow the child to help, but finish the toothbrushing and washing so they are done thoroughly.

Mealtime/Snack Time: Provide choices of foods and snacks but avoid becoming a short-order cook by limiting the number of options. For children who tend to throw food, determine if they are throwing for attention or to signify "all done." The function of the behavior determines the correct consequence.

Playtime: For the child who refuses to clean up, make the task easy to complete by first having the child pick up only a few items and over time increase the expectations. Sing a cleanup song to help make the task more enjoyable and to provide a predictable auditory prompt.

Tips and Hints

See "Tips for Toddlers: Encouraging the Behavior You Want" in Appendix A.

TURN-TAKING AND SHARING

Turn-taking is a skill that has various levels of difficulty, from rolling a ball back and forth with one partner to waiting at circle time for each member of the class to put his or her picture on a poster. Taking turns requires the ability to wait, awareness of others, and awareness of the common goal. Brownwell, Ramani, and Zerwas (2006) found that toddlers ages 19 months, 23 months, and 27 months all had some difficulty taking turns, even after being specifically trained to do so. Sharing requires understanding that another person has a need, and this understanding has rarely been observed in studies of children younger than 25 months; in most of the instances in which it did occur, the sharing was in response to a request (Dunfield, 2010). Most studies of sharing behaviors in infants and toddlers, such as those discussed and investigated by Dunfield, Kulmeier, O'Connell, and Kelley (2011), appear to have focused on sharing with an adult rather than with peers, and, as many EI and child care providers can attest, toddlers are more likely to share with adults than with peers. Turn-taking involves learning to wait for a turn and learning simple rules.

Importance: Turn-taking and sharing are important skills within peer interactions that begin to emerge but are not strongly developed in the early years of development.

How to Incorporate into Routines:

Book Time: Reading to the child and a friend or sibling provides a cooperative opportunity for taking turns, responding, and establishing the same activity for shared attention. Waiting for each other to respond will help the child learn to take turns. If the book has flaps to lift, the children can take turns lifting the flaps. The children can each pick out a book to read, helping each share in the other's preferences.

Mealtime/Snack Time: Model sharing of snacks with a sibling or peer by sharing items one at time, back and forth, across the children at the table. Saying "one for you, one for you, one for you" will label the equality of turns. Waiting as the snack is provided and watching equal allotment sets the stage for regulation while waiting and taking turns across snack distribution during a "group" activity.

 Playtime: When in the yard or driveway, play simple back-and-forth games such as racing, throwing a ball, or pushing toys to provide structure for turn-taking and sharing.

Tips and Hints

Young children usually are able to share from a large group of materials more readily than when there are only a few items.

To help a child learn to wait, have the child clasp his or her hands together and say "waiting hands." Verbal prompts such as "Show me waiting hands!" can help the child focus on a behavior while waiting.

When the child has to wait for a turn, a small diversion may help with the waiting process, such as a holding a toy, singing a song, or counting. Having a child sing the ABC song or count to 10 can ease the child's difficulty in waiting.

At first, keep turns very short and limit the number of turns.

Warning the child first, such as "One more minute, then it's Suzan's turn," may help with transitions.

Trading toys may ease difficulty sharing.

Gestural indicators may add communication skills within turn-taking, such as tapping one's chest and saying "my turn" and then helping the child tap his or her chest to indicate "my turn" when appropriate.

Prior to a play date, involve the child in a plan for isolating very special toys that would be difficult to share. Put the highly desired toys away during a play date.

Make rules for sharing that reflect the family values. For example, some families allow particular toys to be one child's possessions and do not allow the sibling to play with them without permission, and other families have sharing as a rule across possessions.

If a child has a tantrum while waiting or while being helped to share, be sure that the child does not get what he or she wants while screaming or he or she will learn that tantrums have beneficial results.

When distributing toys with pieces, such as puzzles, blocks, or shapes for a shape sorter, saying "one for you, one for you, one for you" will label the equality of turns and facilitate waiting.

Holidays and birthdays that involve new gifts can be especially challenging times for sharing. Having rules about sharing may facilitate the process. One family an author worked with allowed a 24-hour "new toy rule," whereby the child did not have to share something new for one day. Asking families how they handle these issues and collecting solutions may benefit providers in assisting other families.

Setting a timer for 1–2 minutes is helpful: when the timer goes off the other child gets a turn with the item.

To help teach turn-taking and sharing, it is helpful to start with an adult who gets a very short turn compared with the child's longer turn. The next helpful step is that the turns become equal in length followed by turns between two children. To facilitate the turns between the children, counting to 10 for each turn helps both children anticipate how long before the exchange occurs.

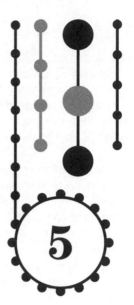

5 Cognitive and Receptive Language

Most evaluation and assessment tools separate cognitive and communication skills; however, cognition and receptive language are closely related. Thus, in the context of daily routines and participation in very young children, it is helpful to classify them together. Evidence exists to support the interrelatedness of cognitive and receptive skill development, including that conceptual development shapes linguistic development (Snedeker & Gleitman, 2004) and receptive understanding of words affects conceptual development (Casasola, 2005; Gentner & Goldin-Meadow, 2003; Gumperz & Levinson, 1996; Levinson, 1997; Lupyan, Rakison, & McClelland, 2007). Listening and paying attention are critical for development of both understanding and cognition. Childhood cognition, while partially dependent upon the child's ability to attend and listen, is also dependent on active exploration (Bruner, 1973; Gopnik & Meltzoff, 1997). In part, children's own actions lead to conceptual and cognitive discoveries (Kushnir, Wellman, & Gelman, 2008).

Cognitive and receptive language skills develop as children understand the world around them. Sensory information from what children hear, see, and feel is very important to early cognitive and receptive language skills: Children look around, visually track objects and people, turn to sounds, and are aroused by touch and movement. Children then begin learning about their world, exploring more actively as they mouth, shake, and bang. This leads to understanding about cause-and-effect relationships: They discover that hitting a toy produces a sound, using their voice produces a smile from a caregiver, or extending backward results in being put down on the floor. Around this time, object permanence develops, signaling that the world has a representation whether or not it is seen. Imitation, a pivotal skill for learning, begins with imitation of simple actions and sounds and progresses to more complex sequences that are the foundation for manipulating play materials as well as using phrases, clothing, and utensils. Children demonstrate understanding of the world around them by using familiar objects the way they have seen others do: brushing their hair, drinking from a cup, or putting a phone to their ear. This leads to multiple steps in pretend play, which can be seen as children put together several steps such as feeding a stuffed animal and then putting it to bed.

Understanding of language also blossoms during the first years, as children begin to respond to their names and demonstrate understanding of the names of objects and people around them. Comprehension of many concepts, such as number, size, position, shape, color, and gender develop, in the toddler years, and these mental representations organize experiences and provide important structure for learning. Children begin to follow directions during the toddler years, beginning with single-step and progressing to two-step directions that are related (e.g., "Get your cup and give it to me") and then to directions that contain two unrelated steps (e.g., "Go get your shoes and put your cup in the sink"). Another gateway to understanding and cognition is found in preliteracy skills. Children begin to gain knowledge through their experiences with text as parents and caregivers talk about pictures in books and then read stories. Cognitive and receptive language skill development in the early years is the foundation for life-long learning. Parents and other caregivers can greatly affect this process by modifying many of their existing daily routines.

Sometimes children may be demonstrating certain skills in daily routines but do not generalize the skills during EI sessions. Consider the following example. Amanda's EI provider was working on matching and sorting skills, and Amanda was not very interested. The provider showed Amanda's mother how to facilitate these skills in daily routines and also tried to teach Amanda to match and sort during structured play, but Amanda showed little interest over the span of several months. One day during a session, Amanda was having a snack of breakfast cereal and her mother commented on how Amanda was sorting out a certain color of the cereal to eat it first. The EI provider knew that meant Amanda had the ability to visually discriminate, the skill needed to match and sort. She asked the mother for two bowls and showed the toddler how to sort her cereal into the containers. Amanda did this quickly and enthusiastically, quite a change from previous presentations of matching and sorting. The EI provider was then able to progress to sorting objects, pictures, colors, and shapes during the next several sessions. Using what was motivating and familiar to the child was a great starting point from which to teach the child new skills, and the provider learned a valuable lesson: to ask caregivers questions about eating to help determine if this routine might be a good way to introduce sorting and matching. It is helpful for EI providers not only to use natural routines but also to have an understanding of the complexity of cognitive skills. Many cognitive skills have motor components, attention components, visual-perceptual components, and language comprehension components. If one looks at cognitive skills on various evaluation tools, the interrelationships of the skills can be seen. For example, stacking blocks can be found on the cognitive section of one assessment and the fine motor section of another. This skill involves hand skills, imitation skills, visual-perceptual skills, and an understanding of the function of objects.

This chapter contains milestones in the area of cognitive and receptive language skills. As in the chapters on other skills, each skill is described, its importance considered, ways to incorporate the skill's development into daily routines and activities are presented, and tips and hints for further developing the skill are offered. The reader is reminded that the language used is that which an EI provider would say to parents and caregivers in order to coach and support them.

ENCOURAGING LISTENING AND ATTENTION

Listening skills involve learning to hear and to distinguish important auditory stimuli, such as environmental sounds, speech, or key words. Both listening and attention involve attending to salient stimuli. Listening begins with localizing sounds, for example, turning toward a barking dog. According to Richards, Reynolds, and Courage (2010), "The development of attention in the infant can be characterized by changes in overall arousal (attentiveness) and by changes in attention's effect on specific cognitive processes (e.g., stimulus orienting, spatial selection, recognition memory)" (p. 41).

Importance: Listening and attending to sounds in the environment are prerequisites to skills that develop later, such as attending to speech.

How to Incorporate into Routines:

 Bath Time: Splash water, bringing the child's attention to the sound. Name body parts while washing to help the child attend to important words.

Book Time: Look at a book with the child. When the child loses interest, playfully insert the request "just one more page" to help expand attention skills. While the child is enjoying the book, point to pictures and ask the child to point to things too—the child will have to listen to your words to point to what you name.

Mealtime/Snack Time: When the child is eating, talk about the different foods on his or her plate. Notice whether or not he or she looks up at you and back at the food you are commenting on. Point to the food. See if he or she attends to your point, looks to the food, and then looks back at you. Sit across the table from the child so you are face to face, as this will help the child attend to your face, to your point, and to the words you say.

Tips and Hints

Hide a toy or object that makes sounds, such as a musical toy. Wait for the child to find it by looking or moving to get it. Start with the item in view and progress to hiding it under a cloth, under a table, and then in another room.

Starting games with a predictable sound that alerts the child can help the child attend to the initiation of a game (e.g., "Aaaaaaaah," "Peekaboo," "I-I-I-I'm … gonna get you!")

Call attention to relevant environmental sounds, such as phones ringing, trucks going by in the street, airplanes flying outside, or squeaky swings.

Add associated information when appropriate to sounds (e.g., "I hear the garage door! Daddy's home!" "The phone is ringing. That's Grandma!").

Accompany sounds with gestures to provide more information (e.g., "birdy singing" along with pointing to the bird, saying "airplane!" along with hand gestures like an airplane taking off).

Label a sound along with its emission (e.g., while squeaking a squeak toy, say "squeak, squeak, squeak!").

Key words in directions can be accompanied by gesture or emphasis (e.g., "Give it to *Daddy*" accompanied by pointing to Dad).

Directions can be demonstrated and labeled and then compliance can be prompted as a chain that may help the child learn to follow the direction. For example, the provider demonstrates giving a block to the child's father by saying, "This is giving it to Daddy," and then handing over the block and saying, "Give it to Daddy."

CAUSE AND EFFECT AND USING MOVEMENTS TO CONTINUE AN ACTIVITY

Cause-and-effect skills develop when young children discover that their sounds and their actions elicit a response and they then purposefully use the sounds and actions to get the response they desire. They use their bodies to indicate they want more of something by doing a movement that represents the movement that has stopped or by touching another person to communicate more. Examples include making a bouncing movement after a dad stops bouncing the child on his knee, extending the foot after a tickle to the toes stopped, or pulling a mother's hand back to the body after she stops a massage.

Importance: Cause-and-effect skills are pivotal to communication and general learning. When children understand they can affect objects and people and influence their environment, new opportunities abound. As stated by Sobel and Kirkham (2007), developing an understanding of the world is dependent on organization of information into a representation of "causal structure" (p. 298). Using movements to indicate a desire for more is one of the first ways children communicate other than by crying or vocalizing. It is the beginning of showing intent to communicate a specified request and also is a demonstration of early problem-solving behaviors. Turn-taking in familiar routines or games within the family is facilitated when children have this skill of expressing intent. Affective respond-ing (happiness, laughter) and affective matching (both the caregiver and the child are sharing happy feelings with smiles and laughter) are increased by a child's competent turn-taking within enjoyable games and strengthens social responding within families.

How to Incorporate into Routines:

Bath Time: When the child is being dried off and wrapped in the towel, pull him or her into your lap and give a playful bear hug. See if the child leans closer for another play-ful hug. When the child is being dried off, give the child a playful lift to "fly up to the sky." See if the child pulls or reaches to continue the activity.

Book Time: When reading a book with the child, find ways that actions in the book can be used in play with the child. If the character is walking, playfully use two fingers to "walk" across the child's toes, up the leg, and to the head. When you stop, see if the child signals more walking by reaching or offering a body part to signal "more." If the book character is swinging, gently lift the child to engage the body in a swinging motion. Stop. See if the child indicates the desire to continue. If the character says something funny or silly, say the phrase or sentence playfully against the child's cheek, neck, or into his or her hand. Stop. See if the child indicates the desire for continuation.

Diapering and Dressing: While dressing or undressing, play This Little Piggy with the child's toes. See if the child offers the other foot to continue the game.

Mealtime/Snack Time: Use predictable cues to signal it is time to eat (e.g., shake the bottle, say "time to eat," or put the child in a highchair) so the child can associate these with eating. Look for cues the child is using to communicate and put words to those actions. For example, if the child turns his or her head or throws the bowl when fin-ished, model saying "all done" and begin to work on replacement behaviors such as saying or gesturing all done by modeling or helping the child. When feeding the child from the spoon, on occasion stop with your hand by the child's mouth. See if the child pulls your hand or the spoon toward his or her mouth. The same can be done with a cup or bottle.

Playtime: Give early learners items that make noise when the child shakes them, such as sealed plastic bottles filled with rice or beans. Play games such as Peekaboo so the child learns that, when he or she pulls the barrier, someone reappears and joyfully says "boo." When the child makes a sound, make a sound in return to teach the child the cause-and-effect component of vocal turn-taking. Use a lot of enthusiasm and be playful so the child learns that his or her actions result in fun. For example, if he or she drops a toy on the floor, react in an exaggerated manner, laughingly saying "uh-oh," so the child is likely to drop an object again. Play repetitive games with "Row, Row, Row Your Boat" and Ring Around the Rosy or by flying the child up on your legs like an airplane. Stop. See if the child indicates continuation with a movement similar or related to the game.

Tips and Hints

For children who love cause-and-effect toys but who struggle with social communication, it is beneficial for caregivers to become the cause-and-effect "toys" by using a great deal of affect, animation, and repetition so that the child will look for the response from the person rather than the toy. For example, if the child is pushing buttons to hear the alphabet or a repetitious phrase, say what the toy "says" in a tone and volume the child will likely attend to and find more motivating than the toy.

Use pause time and expectant looks to cue the child that a message is necessary.

When the child uses body movements to indicate more, use such phrases as "Oh, you want more ____."

At first, if the child does not use movements to request continuation of an activity, prompt the child with hand-over-hand assistance. Fade the full prompt to a partial prompt and then to no prompt over time.

OBJECT PERMANENCE

Object permanence was a term used by psychologist Jean Piaget in the 1950s, and much research has been done on the concept (Munakata, McClelland, Johnson, & Siegler, 1997). Object permanence refers to the understanding that when something is hidden or out of sight, it still exists. Preliminary research on this topic relied on reaching; however, later research has focused on looking and has found that very young infants do hold representations in their minds (Baillargeon, Spelke, & Wasserman, 1985). Children first search for partially hidden objects, and later they search for objects that are fully hidden. Searching for partially hidden objects requires that the child recognize that part of the object belongs to the whole object. Before children demonstrate this skill well, they often play with the material used to cover the object instead of searching for the object itself. The child's motivation is also a factor in object permanence, as a child typically will not search for an item he or she does not find interesting or useful at that particular time.

Importance: Object permanence relates to exploring and problem solving. In order to search for something that is hidden, a young child relies on his or her memory and must use a motor response to search, whether it be uncovering a toy hidden under a blanket or crawling to find a family member who is in another room. When children cry because Mom or Dad leaves the room, they are showing the ability to understand object permanence. Thus, object permanence is also related to social development.

How to Incorporate into Routines:

Mealtime/Snack Time: For children who have favorite snacks and foods, playfully hide the food in your hands, under a napkin, or under a bowl and have the child search for it. This works best when the child is not excessively hungry but hungry enough to want the item!

Playtime: To encourage the understanding that objects out of sight still exist, playfully hide a child's favorite toy under a blanket, in a box, or behind a book and see if the child looks for it. If not, try having a portion of it visible. Allow the child to see you hide the item at first and progress to having the child look for an item that he or she did not see hidden. Play hiding games where you hide under a blanket or behind a wall or furniture and have the child find you. At first you may need to be only partially hidden, and you may need to give the child a lot of auditory cues such as "Come find me" to help the child locate you.

Tips and Hints

If the child does not like to have his or her face covered to play Peekaboo, hold a small towel or blanket in front of the child's or your face for the child to pull off or look around.

Hide objects that are highly motivating to the child to ensure the child has a reason to look for them.

TURNING TO NAME

When the child's name is called, the child turns toward the person who called the name.

Importance: A child's name is a specific reference to that child, and, therefore, is a key word to alert the child to attend, look, or prepare for an important message. The child demonstrates an important listening skill when he or she turns toward the sound of his or her name being called.

How to Incorporate into Routines:

 Community Outings: When outside at a park or in the yard, call the child's name to alert him or her that you will be sharing items of interest.

 Household Activities: When cooking, call the child over to see, smell, or help. When cleaning, call the child over to show him or her something of interest. When folding laundry, call the child's name to show him or her something of him or hers that you are folding.

 Playtime: Finding games that involve calling the child's name, such as Peekaboo or Hide and Seek, helps the child practice listening for his or her name.

Tips and Hints

Call a child's name only when it is appropriate to do so, such as when giving him or her something or when being playful. Calling a child's name to gain attention with no functional reason teaches the child that turning to name is not always important and may result in a child turning to his or her name less frequently.

Some caregivers typically call a child's name only when the child is doing something wrong, and the child consequently hears his or her name followed by a reprimand. To prevent or remedy this, it is helpful to call the child's name and then present a preferred item or activity.

When a child has difficulty turning to his or her name, the child may need to hear the name several times, may need to be touched to gain attention, or may need an increase in volume. The child may need to learn first to attend to sounds that are less specific. These may include environmental sounds such as the doorbell, the telephone, the toilet flushing, birds singing, or a truck going by.

DEMONSTRATING UNDERSTANDING OF WORDS

Over time, the number and types of words that children understand increase.

Importance: Understanding words is necessary to follow spoken directions, to learn many new skills, and to participate in conversations.

How to Incorporate into Routines:

Book Time: Reading with the child gives the child access to words across categories, events, characters, and themes. Pointing to pictures and saying the names helps the child learn vocabulary words. Naming a word and asking the child to show what was named helps the child match the word to the representation and show knowledge of the word. Allowing the child to pick favorite books will incorporate motivation into learning.

Diapering and Dressing: Name the child's body parts, clothes, and actions being used (lay down, leg in, pull up, zip, button) to teach functional vocabulary related to diapering and dressing.

Mealtime/Snack Time: Label the foods the child is eating, the utensils, and the temperature of the food. Talk to the child while he or she eats, using words that describe the food or the child's actions (e.g., *cut, chew, yum*).

Tips and Hints

Label the child's actions and describe or present what he or she is paying attention to using nouns, verbs, adjectives, and other words.

Use words often to describe everyday events. Learning the words for objects, actions, and descriptions that seem ordinary to adults is important to the child's development of a core vocabulary. Simple, everyday words such as *sit, couch,* and *pillow* are as important to teach as *circle, square,* and *triangle.*

IMITATION OF ACTIONS WITH OBJECTS AND WITH THE BODY

Young children imitate actions with objects, such as banging a toy, and imitate actions with their bodies, such as clapping and blowing a kiss.

Importance: Imitation is an important foundation for learning; without it, a child has "little chance for the agile acquisition of behaviors" (Cooper, et al., 2007, p. 413). Young children learn by imitating both adults and peers to develop social, motor, problem-solving, communication, and self-help skills. According to Stone, Ousley, and Littleford (1997), children can first imitate actions with their bodies when they can see their imitative action. Ledford and Wolery (2011) advocate that teaching object imitation should occur before teaching gestural imitation for children who are not yet imitating. In addition, they recommend that targeted behaviors should be "familiar, frequently occurring in the natural environment, and functional" (p. 253).

How to Incorporate into Routines:

Bath Time: Model actions such as pouring water on different body parts or from one cup to another; washing; squeezing the washcloth, sponge, or tub toy; splashing gently; and blowing bubbles in the water (as long as the child can safely do so without choking!) and wait to see if the child imitates the actions. If not, provide physical assistance to help the child.

Diapering and Dressing: When time allows, be silly with clothing by putting a sock on your head and letting it fall several times, then handing it to the child to see if he or she imitates you. When getting the child dressed, add a silly motor component. For example, after putting on a sock, take the child's foot and pat it on the floor saying "stomp, stomp, stomp." Wait to see if the child imitates the action on his or her own, and if not, help the child do the action you modeled.

Grooming and Hygiene: Brush your teeth as the child brushes his or her teeth. Show the child how to move the brush back and forth over the teeth. Wash hands with the child to model each step of the process for the child to imitate.

Mealtime/Snack Time: Model imitating feeding others and feeding dolls or stuffed animals. Blow on a warm bowl of soup or oatmeal in an exaggerated fashion to try to elicit imitation from the child.

Playtime: For early learners, model banging objects on a surface and, later, banging an object in each hand, at the mid-line of the body. Use pots and pans and a spoon to model and elicit imitation of banging. Play Peekaboo with a small towel or blanket and pause to see if the child imitates. Be silly by putting something on your head, pretending to sneeze, and making the object fall while saying "ah-choo," as this often elicits giggles and encourages engagement and imitation. Make objects walk, jump, run, or slide down a book to encourage imitation. When playing house, rock the baby, comb the baby's hair, and cook a meal, embedding familiar routines for the child to imitate. When playing with blocks, model building, knocking over, and lining up for the child to imitate.

Tips and Hints

For beginning imitators, use actions with objects such as banging, shaking, throwing, and pushing.

Early imitative actions with the body include waving, blowing kisses, tickling, and clapping.

Larger movements are more easily imitated than smaller, finer movements. For example, for most children, clapping is easier than wiggling the fingers, and opening the mouth is easier than wiggling the tongue.

Familiar gestures are easier to imitate than novel ones.

It is easier to imitate actions the child can see. For example, patting the leg (a visible gesture) is easier than patting the head (an invisible gesture).

Often a child will be more ready to imitate actions with the mouth (and even sounds or words) when eating, because the same muscles are used for eating as for talking.

Children who have difficulty relating and communicating often find it easier to imitate actions with objects and develop the ability to imitate actions with the body later.

Some children show a pattern of delayed imitation whereby they imitate after a time delay rather than immediately. It is beneficial to practice getting faster imitation with actions that are most easily imitated.

Sometimes it appears that children are imitating an action but they may be following a direction, or vice versa. It is beneficial to make sure a child can imitate actions without having been given a direction. For example, clap or pat your stomach and say "You do" or "Do this" and see if the child can imitate. This is different from saying "clap" and modeling clapping, as in that case one cannot discern if the child is following the verbal direction or imitating the visual model.

To elicit imitation of a new action, sound, or word, model two that are in his or her repertoire for the child to imitate. Then, model the more difficult action, sound, or word. A quick series of three, with two easy ones first, often elicits imitation of the more challenging action, sound, or word.

USING GESTURES WITH SONGS AND RHYMES

Gestures that represent ideas, objects, or movements are embedded within a familiar song or rhyme.

Importance: Gesture use in songs and rhymes signal that the child is imitating, listening to key words associated with the gesture, and using gestures to represent ideas, objects, or movements.

How to Incorporate into Routines:

Book Time: Some books have familiar songs or rhymes as the story. When reading to the child, model the actions represented by the pictures and the text. Adding motivating gestures such as petting an animal, popping pictured bubbles, or making characters "walk" down the stairs with tapping may motivate the child to imitate.

Diapering and Dressing and Grooming and Hygiene: Use songs and rhymes associated with body parts during diapering and dressing and grooming and hygiene ("If You're Happy and You Know It"; This Little Piggy; or Head, Shoulders, Knees, and Toes.)

Playtime: Use songs as a way to play together, practicing songs regularly so that the child can learn to imitate gestures in familiar songs such as "Twinkle, Twinkle, Little Star," "Row, Row, Row Your Boat," and "Five Little Monkeys."

Tips and Hints

Many videos exist that picture children modeling gestures to familiar songs and rhymes. Watching the videos can help the child imitate, or they can be used as one more way to expose the child to songs, rhymes, and gestures.

If a child does not imitate gestures in songs, help him or her by using hand-over-hand prompting.

FUNCTIONAL USE OF OBJECTS

At first, children explore objects by banging, shaking, mouthing, and turning, and later they begin to use specific objects for their inherent purposes. For example, a hat may be put on the child's or another person's head, a phone may be put to the ear, or a remote may be aimed at the television (rather than being mouthed or banged!).

Importance: Using objects for their intended purpose demonstrates that the child recognizes the object and the object's function. This skill involves visual discrimination and imitation. This skill is very important as it is necessary for participation in activities across all daily routines from toddlerhood to adulthood.

How to Incorporate into Routines:

Bath Time: During bathing, hand the child a washcloth and encourage him or her to wash body parts.

Diapering and Dressing: When helping the child put on clothes, pause to see if the child moves the body part that goes into a particular item, such as moving his or her foot toward the shoe. If the child does not, tap on the body part and give the child a verbal cue, such as "Shoe … I need your foot."

Grooming and Hygiene: Give the child his or her comb, brush, and toothbrush before using them on him or her and see if he or she puts the item to the correct area of the body. If not, guide the child's hand and tell him or her what the object is used for, by saying such things as "We brush our hair."

Mealtime/Snack Time: Provide a spoon for the child to hold while being fed and ask him or her for a real or pretend bite of food.

Playtime: Provide opportunities for the child to play with common objects such as cups, spoons, hats, and no longer used or toy telephones and remotes. Show the child how to use these objects during play routines and then hand the toy to the child to try.

Tips and Hints

Children typically show understanding of the function of objects with objects they see their parents caregivers use multiple times a day. Thus, spoons, phones, and remotes are good items to target first in many homes.

PRELITERACY

According to Lawhon and Cobb (2002), "The growth of literacy, including reading, writing, speaking, viewing, and listening, is a life-long process that begins during prenatal development when voices and music are heard and remembered" (p 113). Preliteracy skills refer to both a child's knowledge of and experience with text and oral language. Enhancing a toddler's opportunities to interact with books and other items with text and to hear spoken language with intonation, rhyme, and/or rhythm helps build important language skills related to literacy. Some toddlers know their letters, recognize the sign of their favorite fast food restaurants, and show an interest in a street sign, all of which are the beginnings of literacy.

Importance: Very young children acquire important experiences from books that lead to literacy skills later in their development (Dodici, Draper, & Peterson, 2003). Children's concepts about print often predict later skills in reading, spelling, and writing (National Institute for Literacy, 2008).

How to Incorporate into Routines:

Bath Time: Provide plastic, waterproof books for the tub.

Bedtime: Establish a nightly routine that incorporates a bedtime story to expose a child to listening to text, intonation, repetitive words, and sentence structure. Allow the child to choose the books for the bedtime story.

Community Outings: Visit a bookstore or library and help the child pick out books. If applicable, associate the book and activities. For example, after picking out a book on leaves, collect leaves on the way to the car or when walking home. When the child begins to show an interest, point out signs such as stop signs and those that represent familiar destinations. Enroll the child in a toddler story time at a local library. Provide small books for car rides.

Playtime: Provide early learners with soft cloth, plastic, or cardboard books. Use rhymes from familiar books within play activities (e.g., Pat-a-cake; One, Two, Buckle My Shoe).

Tips and Hints

Consider the child's attention span and ability to process language when deciding what book to look at and read. Choose books with topics that are motivating for the child (e.g., trucks, trains, favorite characters), books that are developmentally appropriate in theme, and books that have features the child finds interesting, such as flaps, textures, or sounds.

Teach about text from the print found within daily routines. Use text from everyday items the child knows and ask the child to "read" what it says. For example, when pouring the child's milk, show him or her the word *milk* and ask "What does this say?"

When a child knows a story well, ask him or her to "tell" the story, fill in the blanks, or fill in a word.

Exaggerate intonation while reading, in order to emphasize key words.

Expand themes in the book by relating them to everyday themes; for example, if reading *Brown Bear, Brown Bear, What Do You See?* (Martin & Carle, 2010), relate animals to the child's experiences.

Relate books to the child's experiences (e.g., "Daddy is going fishing. Remember the story we read about the fisherman?").

Leave books out in the environment for the child to explore.

Combine gestures with text (e.g., shaking a finger and frowning when reading *Five Little Monkeys Jumping on the Bed* [Christelow, 1998]) or moving the hands up when reading aloud "up-up-up!"

Have the child sit in your lap for daily looking at pictures and reading books.

Provide sturdy books for the child to use independently while the caregiver is busy or the child is engaged in independent play.

Ask questions about the pictures when reading with the child.

Read while the child is playing or reading, in order to provide a model.

Use books for ideas for crafts, games, or activities to teach children that books can be a resource.

PRETEND PLAY

According to Barton and Wolery (2008), the definition of pretend play varies significantly in the literature; however, across definitions pretend play involves a representation of actions, roles, and themes. According to Bergen (2002),

> Pretend play requires the ability to transform objects and actions symbolically; it is furthered by interactive social dialogue and negotiation; and it involves role taking, script knowledge, and improvisation. Many cognitive strategies are exhibited during pretense, such as joint planning, negotiation, problem solving, and goal seeking. Make associated changes. (n.p.)

Children first demonstrate pretend play with real objects, such when they are pretending to talk on the actual phone, and then they expand to using representative objects such as a block as the phone. Children pretend first using a single step and later they are able to sequence several steps, such as feeding a doll, taking it for a walk, and putting it to bed or putting a man in a car, driving the car to the park, and then having the man go down a pretend slide.

Importance: Pretend play gives children ways to rehearse and practice events happening around them, which aids in their understanding of the world. Pretend play involves understanding the perspective of others, an important foundation for social skills such as empathy. Linguistic competence and problem solving are also interrelated with pretend play (Bergen, 2002). Imitation skills are necessary before a child will demonstrate pretend play. Pretend play can be a strong motivator to help young children practice developmental skills, such as jumping like a frog, crawling like a puppy, or saying "choo-choo" like the train.

How to Incorporate into Routines:

Bath Time: Suggest that the child pretend to be swimming or pretend to be a fish while in the tub.

Book Time: Ask the child to pretend to do what the characters in the book are doing.

Household Activities: If a caregiver is involved in household chores that are not safe for the child to participate in, give the child a safe item with which to pretend to do the chores. For example, if the child is not able to safely control a watering can, he or she can pretend to water the flowers. Similarly, if Grandma is cooking at the stove, the child can stir his or her pot on the pretend stove.

Playtime: Incorporate familiar routines into play, such as pretending to eat, pretending to sleep, or pretending to talk on the phone. First, use real objects in the pretend play (e.g., a bowl when pretending to eat) and then show the child how to use other objects to represent the play item. Once the child is pretending with everyday routines, introduce familiar themes into pretend play, such as going to the doctor, going to school, and going to the store. As the child's repertoire grows, introduce figures into the play, such as having the teddy bear or the doll be Mommy or the child.

Tips and Hints

Pretend play can be used to rehearse what will happen to a child before the actual situation occurs in real life, such as going to the doctor, getting blood work, or going to the dentist. This may help prepare a child. In addition, some children like to reenact unpleasant experiences, as these to help them understand them.

If a child is using one step in pretend play, model two steps to help expand ideas.

MATCHING AND SORTING

Matching refers to putting an object with a like object. Sorting refers to putting like objects together. First, young children will pick up like objects from a group, such as picking up all the cereal and leaving the green peas from their high chair tray or taking all the balls out of the toy box and leaving the other toys. Later they are able to put objects into groups, such as putting all the blocks in the block box and all the toy cars in the toy garage. Later, children sort and match by color, shape, and size.

Importance: Sorting and matching activities represent the young child's abilities to reflect a new level in the "early understanding of the world in terms of *kinds* or conceptual categories, ones in which proximity in space ostensibly represents categorical similarity" (Courage & Howe, 2002, p. 263). Sorting and matching activities are necessary for cleaning up toys in an organized manner, playing with puzzles and shape sorters, and using other similar developmental toys. As children get older, sorting and matching are necessary for many academic and household tasks.

How to Incorporate into Routines:

Community Outings: When grocery shopping, have the child find matching items such as apples or grapes by holding up one and asking him or her to find another. Have him or her sort items into bags, such as putting green apples in one bag and red ones in another.

Dressing and Diapering: Give the child one shoe or sock and put the matching item among other items that do not match. Ask the child to get the matching item.

Household Activities: When putting away clothes after doing the laundry, have the child find all the socks from the pile, find matching pairs of socks, or sort all Daddy's socks and all of sister's socks into two piles. When putting away dishes, have the child help put all the spoons in one place and all the forks in another.

 Mealtime/Snack Time: Point out similar objects and foods when the child is eating. If the child did not eat all he or she was given, encourage him or her to put the unwanted items in several piles, sorting by type of food, or give the child bowls to sort the unwanted items into. Have the child sort fruit snacks or snack mixtures by snack type, by color, or by shape.

 Playtime: During playtime with multiple identical items such as blocks, encourage matching by picking up one item and saying to the child "Here's one, where is the other?" At first, provide a small field of objects, such as two or three, and then progress to a greater number of items from which the child can choose. Encourage sorting by giving the child bowls or baskets and have the child sort by object, size, shape, color, or function, depending on the child's skill level. Have the child help clean up by putting all the blocks in one box and all the cars in another.

Tips and Hints

It sometimes appears that children have matching skills when they are actually relying on the spoken word for the item. For example, if someone holds up a ball and says "Find another ball," it is possible for the child to find the ball without looking at the item being held up as the model; he or she hears "ball" and looks for the ball. However, if someone holds up a ball and says "Find one of these," the child must look at the ball and find something similar. This would be true visual matching. It is possible for a child to match without knowing the name of an item.

Children often match during play or other routines but not in structured situations, as they may not understand what is being asked. This is seen in children who eat only the marshmallows in their cereal or eat only the green fruit snacks or only wear their red hat. In formal testing or during structured activities, these children may not make matches, but in everyday situations they are visually discriminating and matching. They have the skill, but they may not have understood what is being asked of them.

PROBLEM SOLVING

Problem solving involves the ability to plan for and execute the steps to achieve a goal (Daehler, 2008). Ahola and Kovacik (2007) describe how mental maturation and experiences allow children to process and store information to use at later times to solve problems. They describe eight stages that lead to problem solving: 1) connections made from feeling reflexive acts, 2) accidentally making something happen, 3) purposefully repeating an action, 4) using a tool, 5) exploring using trial and error, 6) experimenting based on a hypothesis, 7) testing a hypothesis, and 8) applying past cause and effect relationships to new situations.

Importance: The ability to solve problems is needed for learning new skills and feeling competent. Problem solving also leads to increased independence.

How to Incorporate into Routines:

 Dressing and Diapering: Be silly and put the child's sock on his or her hand, which often results in a look of confusion before the child figures out he or she must indicate that the sock goes on the foot. He or she likely will put out the foot or point to the foot. For a toddler who can answer questions, when getting ready to go outside, ask questions like "What do we need to put on your feet?"

 Mealtime/Snack Time: When the child requests a drink or a snack, playfully sabotage the situation to encourage problem solving. For example, occasionally give the child an empty cup when he or she asks for a drink so he or she will have to hand it back to you. For the child who can answer questions verbally or by pointing or gesturing, ask questions such as "What do you need now?" if he or she does not tell you when you give him or her a bowl of applesauce and no spoon.

 Playtime: There are many ways to foster problem solving during play. Provide various sized containers with lids to encourage motor problem solving and visual perceptual skills as the child uses trial and error to place the lids on the containers and gradually learns to recognize the shape and size to fit them easily. Place desired objects slightly out of reach so the child will learn to move to get them, to use a tool such as a stick or stool, or to ask for help. Pretend that you do not know what the child needs and encourage him or her to communicate in new ways. Occasionally put desired items in a clear box or bag to encourage the child to hand the item to another person. Put desired objects into old purses or bags with zippers to encourage the child to ask for help and/or use both hands to unzip—two different methods of problem solving. Provide toys or household objects that require sequencing, such as toys or objects that require several steps be taken for an action to occur. Common toys include shape sorters, pop-up boxes, cause-and-effect toys that require several actions, and puzzles that have pieces that fit in only one way.

Tips and Hints

Problem solving can be facilitated in many ways, such as by asking questions, by setting up the environment so obstacles need to be overcome, by providing only portions of what is needed for an activity or routine, by doing something unexpected, or by partially completing activities or routines.

Setting up the environment so the child does not have access to all his or her favorite items is a good way to work on communication problem solving. Putting items within sight but out of reach, using clear storage containers the child cannot open, activating a toy the child cannot activate independently, giving only a small amount of food or drink so the child has to ask for more nonverbally or verbally, and doing a portion of a familiar routine and then stopping and waiting for the child to indicate the next step are all ways to facilitate problem solving related to communication.

Motor problem solving can be facilitated by playfully blocking a child so he or she has to go a different direction to reach a desired object or person. Obstacle courses of step stools to climb on, tables to crawl under, an adult's leg to step over, or a chair to crawl under are useful to work on motor problem solving.

Children first solve problems with their bodies and then learn to use words. For example, children grab before they learn to ask for something, push before asking someone to move, and some try to bite open a bag before asking for it to be opened. Modeling and helping the child with the more mature way to solve a problem is helpful; however, it is important to help caregivers understand that solving the problem comes first and manners develop later.

CONCEPT DEVELOPMENT

Early important concepts include number (one, all, two), size (big, little), position (in, out, on, off, under, next to), color, shape, and gender. Size concepts are utilized in nesting and stacking toys. Children understand and use size words such as *big* and *little*, often first referencing these to food, such as wanting a "big" cookie. Children will first match, then sort, identify, and finally say shape and color words.

Importance: Early concept development is the foundation for later academic learning and represents the ability of the child to organize information.

How to Incorporate into Routines:

 Book Time: Books can be used to supply visual cues for concept formation. Counting books may help number development. Provide books that present opposites and themes that contrast sizes—for example, a dinosaur as a pet and a new baby in a household with older family members. Books that feature looking for hidden objects may include words related to position. Many books exist that discuss color. Gender can be discussed relative to a main character or narrator of a story.

 Community Outings: When shopping at the grocery store, discuss numbers of items, such as one box of cereal or two apples. Compare boxes or fruits by size (pudding/cereal, grape/watermelon). Talk about the position of the child and items relative to the cart (in or out). Help the child find colors and shapes such as the round top of a can or yogurt container and the green grapes. The gender of other shoppers, those depicted on boxes, or the cashier can be referenced.

 Household Activities: When doing laundry, talk about big and small items, the color of clothes, and the location of items in the dryer, in the washer, or in the basket.

Tips and Hints

Emphasize developmentally appropriate concepts.

When opportunities for illustrating concepts occur, teach the concept to the child through both demonstration and repetition.

Many songs have concepts within them and provide a theme that ties the concepts together.

The more the child can experience the concept, in general, the more easily the child may learn: A child may learn *in* more easily when he or she is in a tent rather than putting blocks in a box.

Because conceptual knowledge precedes word knowledge, be sure the child can identify the individual members of a concept; for example, knowing *circle* and *square* is important prior to knowing *shapes*.

FOLLOWING DIRECTIONS

Directions are sentences that contain meaningful words the child must attend to in order to complete a task successfully. Over time, children can understand and comply with increasingly difficult directions, first those that have just one step (e.g., "Give it to me"), then two steps that go together (e.g., "Get your shoes and socks"), and after that, two steps that are unrelated (e.g., "Give Nana the paper and come eat your lunch").

Importance: Directions are important messages that indicate what the child should do for behavior compliance, safety, helping in the house, manipulation of toys, learning steps of an activity, and participation in games.

How to Incorporate into Routines:

Household Activities: Use simple one-step directions such as "Give it to me," "Take it," "Shut the door," "Open the door," "Throw it away," "Get down," and "Get up" when the child is helping with chores.

Playtime: As the child plays with toys, provide such directions as "Push it," "Put in," "Put it in here and then push it," "Take the pen and draw," "Push the button and catch them," and "Stack them here and get your cars." When playing simple games, give directions such as "Your turn to run," "Throw it," or "Give it to Sissy."

Diapering and Dressing: Asking the child to help will encourage his or her ability to follow directions. Phrases such as "Get a diaper," "Find the wipes," "Give it to me," "Lie down," "Put your leg in," and "Pull your pants up" are just a few directions related to dressing routines.

Tips and Hints

The easiest directions to follow are those paired with an action the child would do anyway. For example, when a child goes into the garage and reaches up to pull the door closed, say "Close the door" (which the child was going to do anyway) so the child learns how directions are related to actions.

Children will often do well with very familiar directions that are part of a predictable family routine, for example, "Get your shoes" when going outside.

- Prompting while giving the direction may be necessary for children to comply when the direction is not well understood.

- Use repetition of familiar directions to provide multiple opportunities for practice.

- Pair visual prompts with verbal direction when necessary.

- Use functional directions within contexts to motivate and help with success.

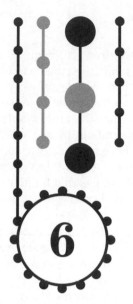

Expressive Language

Although expressive language is often associated with first words, the foundation skills for talking begin at birth, well before those highly anticipated first words. Being able to communicate effectively with others is a result of many interrelated developmental skills. Communication skills have an impact on all areas of a child's life. Communication allows the child to obtain basic needs such as food or comfort as well as desires such as toys, activities, or people and is a critical skill for effective social interaction.

Babies begin making sounds very early in life, and in addition to making sounds they also develop gestural communication, for example, reaching and pointing (Paul, 2007). Three main stages of communication occur between birth to 18 months of age, and these stages lay the foundation for expressive language skills: 1) preintentional communication, 2) intentional communication, and 3) symbolic communication (Rowland & Schweigert, 2004).

The first stage of expressive language development, the preintentional stage, is a time when the infant's behavior occurs without the infant having an idea or intention in mind. Infants cry, look, or turn, and those actions are responded to with interpretation by the caregiver. For example, the baby may cry to signal a state of discomfort reflexively, and the caregiver checks a few solutions—whether or not the baby wants to be held, needs a diaper change, or wants to be fed. At this stage, the baby does not have the intention of communicating, even though its cry is met with the fulfillment of needs.

In the next developmental stage of expressive language, the intentional stage, children learn to use gestures (e.g., reach and point), body movements (e.g., making a motion with their hands to get Mommy to play Peekaboo again), and facial expressions to communicate what they want and to comment on things in their environment. Gestural communication, in part, begins to lay the foundation for symbolic communication, because use of gestures is one of the first ways the child begins to represent or symbolize what he or she wants to say or request. There are many studies that document how gestures link to later-developing language skills (e.g., Carpenter, Nagell, & Tomasello, 1998; Capirci, Iverson, Pizzuto, & Volterra, 1996). Gesture use is one of the earliest and most consistent signs of children's communicative intent (Thal & Bates, 1988). According to Crais, Watson, and Baranek (2009), gesture use should be documented, because gestures are the first signs of communicative intent, are an early means of communication, and, for children with communication delays, are used more than verbal language for an extended period of time.

In the third stage, the symbolic communication, children use words as symbols. Children who have difficulties with speech production may use picture or object exchanges or other alternative or augmentative strategies to communicate. Typically developing children will begin to represent what they need or what they are thinking about with words. This is the stage when words begin, and if a child is nonverbal, this is when he or she is able to use picture symbols, object exchange, and other alternative or augmentative strategies to communicate. The precursors for being able to use words, pictures, symbols, or objects to represent what the child wants come from the skills learned in the prior stages. When a child begins to use symbols, usually words, the child has begun the process of being able to communicate specifically (e.g., *juice, cereal, bird*) and is able to reference things that do not occur in the here and now (e.g., saying "Daddy work"). A typical progression of expressive language goes through predictable stages that build upon the previously acquired skills: Reflexive responding gives way to sounds and prelinguistic gestures. Prelinguistic gestures develop prior to intelligible words. As first words develop, conventional gestures to support those words develop too, for example, waving bye-bye or hi, putting arms up for "up," and pointing to make choices (Rowland & Schweigert, 2004). Cooing and vocalizing are the first sounds babies make, and after a time, children begin to approximate words and then perfect word use (Paul, 2007).

Children begin to combine words after much practice using single words. Many sources, including Rescorla and Achenbach (2002) and Van Tatenhove (2007), discuss a relationship between a core vocabulary of 50 words and two-word combinations. Along with the increase in the number of words used and combined, the function of language expands to include changes from the here and now and what is tied to physically present events, actions, people and objects. It grows conceptually across functions such as commenting, asking, protesting, refusing, and initiating. Early two-word combinations consist of nouns, adjectives, and verbs that enable the child to talk about actions, people, objects, locations, and possession (Bloom & Lahey, 1978).

After words are combined, grammar will emerge as children begin to use verb tense, plurals, possessive markers, helping verbs, and prepositions. Evidence from children learning English suggests that grammar is learned in a fixed order. Brown (1973) studied the acquisition of 14 English grammatical pieces, known as morphemes, and found, for example, that children learned the /ing/ of the present progressive (jumping) before they learned the plural of nouns; they learned plurals and possessives of nouns before they learned the articles (the, a); and they learned articles before they learned the regular past tense of verbs. Helping verbs (e.g., is, are) were developed much later. He also found that children learned some irregular past tense forms, like broke and went, before they learned regular past tense. Children learn to ask and answer questions as vocabulary, phrases, and sentences grow (Bellugi & Brown, 1964). By the age of 3, most children can be understood the majority of the time by both familiar and unfamiliar listeners. Lynch, Brookshire, and Fox (1980) provide intelligibility guidelines. Familiar listeners, including parents and caregivers, should understand 25% of what the child says at 18 months, 50%–75% at 24 months, and 75%–100% at 36 months. For listeners who do not know the child well, intelligibility changes from 50% at 24 months to 75% at 36 months.

As children begin to talk, they begin to use speech sounds in combination with vowels to make syllables. Early developing sounds are /m/, /n/, /h/, /p/, /f/, /w/, /b/, /ng/, and /y/. Sounds mastered after age 3 are /k/, /g/, /l/, /s/, /r/, /ch/, /v/, /z/, /dz/, /sh/, and /th/ (Sander, 1972). The exact age of acquisition varies, but the order is fairly standard. For example, /m/, /n/, /h/, and /p/ are early-acquired sounds, and /v/, /z/, and /th/ are later-acquired sounds.

Along with knowledge of family priorities, knowledge of the progression of expressive language skills is helpful, if not imperative, in making clinical decisions. Careful consideration of the child's profile of development will be fundamental in making decisions about intervention. Because skills in child development have significant variance when they emerge, the decision about whether or not a child is showing a delay may be difficult to discern.

This chapter contains milestones in the area of expressive language skills. Each skill is described, and its importance considered. Ways to facilitate skill development in daily routines and activities as well as tips and hints are presented. The reader is reminded that the language used is that which an EI provider would say to parents and caregivers in order to coach and support them.

COOING AND VOCALIZING

The first sounds a child makes are crying, fussing, vegetative sounds such as burps or feeding sounds, sighs, grunts, vowel sounds, trills, clicks, friction noises, and sounds that are similar to the consonant sounds /k/, /h/, /g/, and /y/ (Marshalla, 2001).

Importance: Cooing and vocalizing are the foundational skills for later speech-sound development, control of phonation and respiration, learning about how the mouth moves, establishing back and forth sounds with a caregiver, and other skills that lead to the first words. Cooing and vocalizing will often elicit a response from caregivers, which reinforces the development of sounds.

How to Incorporate into Routines:

Diapering and Dressing: Playfully cover your face with an item of the child's clothing or bring the box of wipes or a diaper in front of your face to play Peekaboo. Say "peeka-boo" with high affect, vary tone and intonation, and wait for the child to get excited by the game, your face, and your attention. Respond to the child's vocalizations by using an animated tone of voice to make sounds back to the child.

Mealtime/Snack Time: Prolong words and sounds, for example, "Ooooh, yummy yummy milk. Yum, yum, yummy!" Pause. See if the child will vocalize in return. Hold the child close during bottle- or breast-feeding to provide face-to-face interaction, which helps the infant attend to face and sounds.

Playtime: Use rhythmic repetition of strings of speech and vocal patterns with high affect to help children alert to speech and attend to sounds. Very often children will coo and vocalize in response to this type of speech. For example, you might try saying, "Oh, you are such a big boy. Such a big boy! Ah-hah! Big boy!" Then pause and see if the child responds.

Tips and Hints

Increasing animation in response to cooing and vocalizations may help the child to respond more. Adding pauses after vocalization may also help the child respond.

Playfully and gently touch noses, nuzzle, and/or blow raspberries on the child's belly to encourage vocalizations.

Children may be more likely to make sounds during activities and routines that they find particularly enjoyable. Finding activities that excite the child, like bath time or rough and tumble play, may elicit more vocalizations. Using these times of days to practice back and forth sounds may help facilitate the child's use of sounds.

MAKING VOWEL AND EARLY CONSONANT SOUNDS

The first vocalizations later develop into strings of consonants and vowels, often marked with intonation patterns that sound like the adult speech the child hears. At first, syllables begin with just a few consonants and vowels. Sound development continues and more consonants can be heard in the child's syllables, such as /p/, /b/, /w/, /n/, /h/, and /m/ (Velleman, 2003).

Importance: Early sounds represent increased control of phonation, vocalization, and the parts of the mouth used to make sounds, such as the lips, the back of the throat, or the tongue. The sound combinations create early syllables, that is, patterns of consonants and vowels. These early patterns are the foundation of word approximations and word development. Using a variety of early sounds is a signal that speech is progressing developmentally.

How to Incorporate into Routines:

Bedtime: Rhythmic repetition of words and sounds embedded into routines can help children learn sounds and words practiced in the same way, at the same time, and repeated. Repeating sounds and words during routines encourages children to repeat them and also helps them associate their meanings. For example, as you say "night-night," over time the child may begin to try to imitate, responding with "ni-ni." Another example of a phrase that might be embedded into bedtime routine is "I love you." Perhaps a song such as "Rock-a-bye Baby" might be added into the bedtime routine.

Book Time: Read books that have simple text that repeats. The high predictability of a simple book is a good way to encourage early developing sounds.

Community Outings: During errands, say "Let's go bye-bye. Bye, bye, bye!" to capitalize on early developing sound sequences. To elicit imitation, use single words to describe actions. For example, while getting into the car seat, label by saying "up," "in," "click," or "snap" to provide simple consonant-vowel patterns for the child to hear and imitate.

Grooming and Hygiene: When brushing teeth, saying "ch-ch-ch" to label the sound can become part of the routine. Label "water," say "brush-brush-brush!" or look in the mirror and say "That's you!"

Playtime: Narrate what the child is doing, using single words to pair the child's actions with words; for example, model by saying "walk, walk, walk!" when walking outside or back and forth to a toy box. As with errands and bedtime, using single words to describe gives a simple speech model that can be easily imitated over time, such as *cook, hot, eat, carrots,* and so forth.

Tips and Hints

Imitate sounds the child makes to encourage him or her to make the sound back. This helps the child learn to make the sound again.

Use exciting activities to encourage the child to use more sounds and syllables. Some examples are bath time, pool play, rough and tumble games, running and chasing, and other physical activities. For many children, the more active and exciting an activity, the more sounds a child will make.

- Laughter is also a way to strengthen the muscles involved in phonation.

- Very often children will be quiet when play requires concentration, such as activities that involve fine motor coordination. These are times when vocal play may not be easily elicited.

USING GESTURES

Gestural communication develops along with sounds and words. Gestures are early forms of communication and have a predictable developmental sequence. Many gestures occur before words. Gestures develop across communication functions (reason). To protest, first the child will use his or her body to signal refusal or protest (arch away) and push away. Later the child will learn to shake his or her head no, and then say "no." To ask for objects, first the child will look at the object, then to the adult, then back to the object again (or vice versa). Later, the child opens and closes his or her hand to request objects. To request actions, the child will reach while opening and closing his or hands (e.g., to be picked up), give an adult and object for help, point to get an adult to do something, and then take the adult's hand to do something. To seek attention, the child will bring objects to get attention, use consistent body motion, grab an adult's hand, or show off by making silly faces or sticking out his or her tongue. Representational gestures develop first by showing the function of an object, then hugging an object, clapping for excitement, dancing to music, shrugging shoulders for "I don't know," blowing a kiss to others, signaling "shh" with fingers to lips, nodding "yes," pretending to sleep, and giving a high five. Joint attention to comment is represented by showing or giving, then pointing to an object, and then pointing to an object in response to an adult's request. A child will later use a gesture as a clarification, for example, the child says "ka" and points to a cup. Gestures to request information include pointing to a picture or object to gain information (Crais, Watson, & Baranek, 2009). Later, gestures complement spoken forms, and later still, children increase pointing in combination with spoken words (Capone & McGregor, 2004).

Importance: The development of prelinguistic communication (communication with gestures rather than words), in part, sets the stage for children to represent their intentions in symbolic ways later. The development of gestures also supports the ability to talk about the things that are in the here and now, prior to having words to do so. The use of gestures signifies that the child understands that communication is socially mediated with others and that using gestures helps get his or her message understood. Gestures often augment spoken language for children and adults, providing emphasis or aiding understanding of the message.

How to Incorporate into Routines:

Bedtime: When the child is waking and needs to be lifted up from the crib, hold your hands to model "up," and help the child show "up" with his or her arms too.

Community Outings: Model pointing to items and actions of interest and label them to help the child learn the meaning of pointing. When taking a walk, ask the child which way he or she wants to go. Show the child how to blow a kiss to loved ones when leaving the house.

Mealtime/Snack Time: When cleaning up, ask the child where things go to elicit a point.

Playtime: Sing songs with gestures such as "The Wheels on the Bus" and "Itsy Bitsy Spider."

Tips and Hints

Putting things out of reach but in view can set the stage for reaching to communicate. For example, if bubbles are a favorite toy, place them on the top shelf in view but out of reach so the child will have an opportunity to request with a reach or point.

Encourage the child to use a gesture to continue an action by stopping the action and waiting to see if the child uses his or her body to indicate more. If needed, model the action. For example, when pushing a child on a swing, stop the swing and wait to see if the child wiggles or rocks to indicate more swinging.

Placing toys, snacks, or other desired items into clear containers that the child is unable to open can encourage the child to hand them over for help or point at the desired object.

Exaggerate gestures when interacting with the child; shrug your shoulders when you do not know something. Playfully shake your head yes and no in an exaggerated manner during play and other routines. Exaggerate facial expressions and gestures when describing feelings and actions such as hot, cold, and crying.

MAKING CHOICES

The child makes a decision about a preferred item or activity from a set of options.

Importance: Making choices is important for children in order to exercise intent in preferences, and it may also help with behavior regulation when the child is an active part of choosing. Children benefit from the opportunities they receive to respond to questions and assert choices. These skills influence initiating and completing tasks within the environment (Van Tubbergen, Warshcausky, Birnholz, & Baker, 2008).

How to Incorporate into Routines:

Bath Time: Hold up bath toys and ask the child which one he or she would like to play with: "Do you want the duck or the boat?" Help the child show you with reach or point and then model the name of the toy. Ask the child which color towel he or she wants. Ask "More tub or all done?" if the child truly has a choice.

Diapering and Dressing: When time allows, give the child choices of clothing items, where to get dressed, or what to put on first.

Mealtime/Snack Time: Offer choices of foods and beverages when appropriate.

Tips and Hints

Presenting choices of two objects will allow a child who is not yet talking to point to indicate a selection.

At first, children have the most success choosing from a field of two. Some children will make choices with their eyes before they use a reach. After children become proficient at choosing from a field of two, they are able to select from larger arrays but may become overwhelmed when there are more options.

Using visual cues can help children who are not yet responding easily with only words or who learn well with supporting visual cues. Rather than saying only, "Do you want the blue block or the green block?" also show the blue block and the green block.

It is helpful to set up the environment so the child needs to communicate what he or she wants. For example, when playing with a puzzle, put the pieces within the parent's, caregiver's, or provider's reach but not within the child's reach. If giving food choices, be sure the child cannot take the food him- or herself.

Drawing attention to a choice you name by shaking an item slightly can help the child look at both choices.

Giving word choices is helpful for children who have difficulty recalling the words needed. For example, saying "which one?" might make it more difficult for the child to retrieve the word and/or sounds that go with the choice, but saying "Milk? Juice?" provides a word model to facilitate imitation.

USING FIRST WORDS

At first, the child uses increasingly varied, more speechlike vocalizations and approximations of single words (Proctor, 1989). First words are often *mom, dad,* and *baba* for bottle. The child begins to use sounds and sound patterns that begin to sound like words and/or are early words.

Importance: Children begin to understand the power of spoken language when they can request by using a word or when they comment and someone comments back.

How to Incorporate into Routines:

Community Outings: When going on errands, children may be approximating a word, for example, "car" by saying "da." Encourage the child by saying "Yes! Car!" so that the word approximation is reinforced. Adding more describing words to the child's comment (e.g., "We ride. Bye-bye.") helps the child expand word use. If the child can approximate a word, provide opportunities for the child to use words, for example, "Time to go to the store. Ready, set......." (child provides "go!"). Pointing at favorite foods in the grocery store and naming the items provides a simple model the child can imitate when ready. When shopping at a store for household goods, stopping in the toy aisle will provide high motivation for labeling and naming.

Diapering and Dressing: While getting the child dressed, model names of clothing items and body parts, for example, "Off. Shoes off. Toes! Toes, toes, toes!"

Playtime: Respond to the child's approximation, for example, if the child wants to go outside and taps on the patio door, saying "ah-ah." Label "out" and add "outside. Sure. Open. Open door." Wait for the child to express his or her desire for play choices. For example, when the child goes to the swing, pause and allow the child to name "swing" or "up." When the swing slows down, rather than pushing right away, wait for the child to indicate "more" or "push."

Tips and Hints

Modeling words for the child to use will help the child learn how to use words instead of crying ("You don't want to get out of the tub! You can say, 'no.'").

An important strategy for encouraging first words is to say many single word descriptions about what the child is doing and focusing on. With this strategy, experiential information is encoded into words so that the child can then learn which words go with which experience.

Make a brag book by taking photos or using magazine pictures and allow the child to "read" the book to important people such as Grandma, a baby sitter, or other significant people in his or her life. This helps a child gain confidence in his or her attempts to say words and provides practice in being communicatively competent.

When children are not saying many words, the use of single word models is best. For example, the child may be playing with his or her cars and not saying words. Use of single words to describe what the child is looking at and doing will follow his motivation and pair a verbal model with actions and attention. For example, as the child pushes the car, model "Push!" As the car goes down a hill, model "whee" or "fast!" Fun sounds such as "brmmm!" can be particularly enticing.

USING DIFFERENT TYPES OF WORDS

When children begin to use first words, different kinds of words, for example, nouns, verbs, and adjectives, emerge as development progresses.

Importance: Various types of words lead to more complex exchanges and conversation. A span of ideas represented by different words is important and partial evidence that language is developing as it should.

How to Incorporate into Routines:

Community Outings: To help the child learn to mark verbs, saying "go," "shop," and "drive" when out running errands helps the child learn more actions words. To help the child learn possession, talk about his or her and the caregiver's clothes or body parts while riding in a shopping cart (e.g., your shoes, your nose, my nose, my hair, my buttons). As two-word combinations emerge, model a variety of meanings when combining words. For example, when outside for a walk, verbally use descriptions like "pretty butterfly," "pop bubble," "cold water," splash water," "water flowers," and "Mommy's flowers."

Diapering and Dressing: Describe actions by saying "on" and "off" during dressing.

Playtime: Look at things that come in different shapes and sizes, such as a "big rock" and "little rock" or a "bumpy stick" and "smooth leaves." Express common actions such as "boom" for falling or "pop" for bubbles.

Tips and Hints

When the child repeats the same word types frequently (e.g., nouns) or uses a restricted repertoire of word types (e.g., calls "mom," says "this" often to the exclusion of other kinds of words), help the child imitate more words that expand vocabulary. Model the word and prompt the child to repeat to encourage practice of new words.

USING PHRASES AND SENTENCES

As children begin to combine two or more words together, they do so for a number of different communicative reasons. Children will develop words to call attention (e.g., Mommy! Look); make requests (e.g., more milk, shoe off, that mine?); protest (e.g., no, not truck, no night-night); comment (e.g., stuck, broke, ball, cookie); greet (e.g., hi, bye); answer (e.g., replies to "What's that?"); and acknowledge (e.g., "yes"). Children then begin to incorporate grammar into their phrases and sentences, such as plural endings, possession, pronouns, and verb tense markers such as *ing*. Sentence structure of the native language is marked, for example, in English, using adjectives in front of the noun.

Importance: Using phrases and sentences allows children to communicate more complex ideas to get their needs met and to navigate the complexities of social interaction. As phrases develop into sentences, children are able to convey thoughts about associations and reasoning and ask more complex questions than single words allow.

How to Incorporate into Routines:

Bath Time: While in the bath, use phrases to describe, for example, *hot water* or *all clean.*

Book Time: Use books to talk about what is happening on the page or in the story to help children learn sentence structure and descriptive sentences, for example, "The tiger is hungry. He is eating." Emphasize the *s* at the end of words when multiple items are represented, such as in a counting book (e.g., "Look! Leaves. Butterflies. Birds. Cars. Swings.") Describe actions with *ing* (e.g., throwing, walking, and running), to teach *ing* verb endings. Use present tense verbs to help teach verb tense forms (e.g., "I like books. I want to read.")

Community Outings: When the child comes on errands, model verbs with tense markers. For example, if the child says "Daddy go," model "going, going, going." To incorporate possession, model context-based possession such as "Daddy's car" and "Trey's seat." Summarize the outing to model past tense, for example, "We went to the store. Daddy bought paint."

Mealtime/Snack Time: Describe foods for the child during meals to help him or her learn to comment on foods (e.g., "yellow corn and white potatoes").

Playtime: Ask questions to help the child practice giving answers, for example, "Who is under the blanket? Is it Grandma?" The child might respond, "No! It's me!" Add comments to help the child expand his or her vocabulary (e.g., "That was fun!" or "I'm tired!").

Tips and Hints

Systematic expansions can help build sentences with grammar and syntax. When the child says one word, add one more (e.g., the child says "cookie" and you say "Want cookie. Sure you can have a cookie."). When the child uses two-word sentences, model three-word sentences. Add small grammar pieces to the child's sentences, such as a plural /s/, an *a, the,* or *ing*. Some examples follow: The child says "kitty chair." The caregiver can model "kitty *on* chair." The child says "it book." The caregiver can model "it *a* book."

Slight overemphasis on the part of speech being modeled can help the child listen for the piece of the sentence being taught—for example, for helping verbs, "The book *is* on the chair" or for plurals, "cat*s*."

ANSWERING QUESTIONS

Children learn to respond to questions they are asked with answers. Questions contain a word that signals the type of information necessary: yes/no, what, what (are you) doing, who, when, how, and why. Listening skills are important for learning the key word to respond to, and children have to answer within the requested category (e.g., *when* requires a time response, *where* requires a place response). Questions can also be open ended, meaning that they do not elicit a simple word choice but rather require phrases or sentences, for example, "What do think about our trip to the zoo?" or "What kinds of things do you like when Grammy visits?" (Paul, 2007).

Importance: Questions require the child to know how to answer. The ability to answer questions indicates growth within predictable, sequential developmental responses to questions.

How to Incorporate into Routines:

Bedtime: Ask questions about activities done during the day. This will help the child be part of a conversation. For example, ask or say "We went to the zoo today?" "Which animal did you like?" "Then we came home for snack," "Did you like the zoo?" "Who went with us to the zoo?" and "We had popcorn. Do you like popcorn?"

Diapering and Dressing: Talk about where you are placing a clothing item to help the child answer questions about body parts and location, for example, "Where should I put your shirt?" or "Where do your socks go?" Ask "What is that?" to elicit naming of clothing.

Mealtime/Snack Time: Embed questions into the routine, for example, "Mom is going to make dinner. What should we eat?" "What does Mommy need to stir?" or "What is this?" (holding a pan). Practice verb answers by asking "What am I doing?" when stirring, washing dishes, or cutting vegetables.

Tips and Hints

When children do not answer a question, model the answer to help them learn to respond appropriately over time. For example, if you ask "Who is that?" and the child does not answer, model "It's Grandma!"

Be sure to ask developmentally appropriate questions. Sometimes children do not answer because the question is too difficult for their level of understanding.

In order to answer open-ended questions without prompting, children must have more sophisticated expressive language skills than those needed to answer yes-no questions. Thus, one must match the type of question to the child's stage of language development.

Adding visual cues can be very helpful when a child is learning how to answer questions.

Holding up items or objects or looking at pictures supports the questions being asked.

Use questions in a balanced way. Because questions elicit an answer, providers and caregivers who ask a lot of questions may feel that the child is practicing language well. Check to be sure the child also uses language spontaneously. Using too many questions can lead to prompt dependency for talking and can mask a situation where increasing spontaneous word use might be a priority.

ASKING QUESTIONS

Children begin to ask questions by using a rising intonation to mark a question, for example, "Mommy?" or "Hot?" and move to asking yes/no and *wh* forms of questions next (Brown, 1973).

Importance: Questions are a form of communication that helps a child gain information. Using questions is an important use of language for learning information from others or obtaining needed information.

How to Incorporate into Routines:

Book Time: Encourage the child to ask a sibling or caregiver which book the person wants to read.

Community Outings: Encourage the child to ask you what you liked about experiences, for example, after a trip to the zoo. Model the question, for example, "What did you like?" Accept imperfect grammar; at this age it is common for children to leave out *did*, resulting in "What you like?" or "What like?"

Mealtime/Snack Time: When providing snacks, give just a few items so the child will have an opportunity to ask for more.

Tips and Hints

Model questions across opportunities and encourage the child to repeat by prompting, "You say____."

Embedding questions into a game can provide opportunities for the child to practice, for example, calling to a sibling "Where are you?" during a hiding game or asking "What's in there?" when playing a game to hide objects in a box or bag.

BEING UNDERSTOOD

When the child attempts first words and develops early expressive vocabulary, he or she will use words that have incorrect sounds, sound omissions, or syllable omissions. Later, the child's speech progresses into mature forms of the word. Intelligibility at age 3 ranges from 71% to 80% (Weiss, 1982), meaning that by that age most of what children say is understood.

Importance: It is important to help children develop speech sounds so that they can be understood successfully.

How to Incorporate into Routines:

Bath Time: When taking a bath, the child might say words without all the sounds, for example, "ha" for "hot." Reinforce the child's efforts with, for example, "Yes! Hot!" and emphasize the missing sound. This helps to shape sound development by providing clear speech models.

Mealtime/Snack Time: When offering the child a snack or mealtime food choices, give him or her two options and ask the child which option he or she wants. Should the child point to the preferred option and pronounce the word incorrectly—for example, the child points to cheese and says "dee"—comment as if she said "cheese" appropriately by saying, "Cheese! I love cheese too," and be sure to model the word cheese slowly and clearly, slightly emphasizing the /ch/ and the end sound.

Playtime: When playing with toys, say simple, short word models to help the child learn about sounds in a word. For example, when cooking at a play stove, the caregiver can model "egg" and repeat "egg." When the child repeats "eh" the caregiver can model "egg!" emphasizing the last sound in egg so that the child can hear the speech model.

Tips and Hints

Provision of a clear word model will often help the child imitate more accurately than a prompt without a word. For example, "Cat. You say, cat" may be more helpful than "What is this called?"

Modeling sounds of words slowly and clearly helps the child pay attention to the word and its sounds.

Slightly overemphasizing the sound that the child should listen to can help imitation. For example, if the child says "dod," model "Do*g*. Yes, do*g*!"

In general, it is always a good idea to ensure that no medical issues, such as fluid in the ears or a hearing loss, interfere with speech development. These issues are usually addressed at regular doctor visits; however, asking the caregiver whether or not medical contributions have been ruled out will ensure that the provider defines whether or not health issues may be a factor in speech development.

Be sure that the word or sound expected is within developmental range. Requesting clear pronunciation of words outside of the child's expected development will lead to frustration and unrealistic expectations.

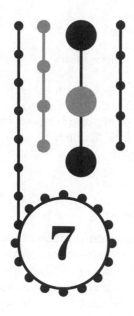

Gross Motor Skills

7

According to many theorists, gross motor development typically develops from the head to the toes (cephalocaudal) and from the center of the body to the outside of the body (proximal to distal) (Cowden & Torrey, 2007). The development of head control in a variety of positions is a critical skill, as it is the prerequisite for many other motor skills. Rolling, sitting, and moving from one position to another are all dependent on voluntary changes in head position. Since the institution of the Back to Sleep campaign by the American Academy of Pediatrics in 1992, it has been noted that some parents do not put their infants on their bellies for playtime, and this has affected the rate of gross motor skill acquisition (Salls, Silverman, & Gatty, 2002; Zachry & Kitzmann, 2011). Playing on the stomach (in prone) is an extremely important routine that EI providers should be facilitating, as spending time in this position is a prerequisite for the development of other early gross motor skills, including head control, rolling, and crawling. For infants and toddlers who may have experienced reflux or abdominal or cardiac surgeries and for those who dislike the sensation of being on their bellies, time must be spent to gradually increase tolerance of this position so other milestones may occur.

Using motivating play activities or using desired objects often helps young children learn to tolerate less preferred positions and learn to move in new ways. Once children are mobile, using preferred activities and daily routines gives multiple opportunities to practice. For example, for children who are just beginning to roll, having them roll to get to their parent or their pacifier lying nearby may help decrease hesitation to move. For children who are just beginning to walk with two-hand support, having them take a few steps to their highchair and gradually progress to walking across the room to the highchair gives multiple daily opportunities presented at a child's pace. Once children are walking, numerous opportunities exist in natural routines within multiple environments to practice walking on a variety of surfaces, climbing, jumping, and balancing.

Gross motor development is influenced by a variety of factors such as muscle tone, sensory processing, experiences, and neurological status. Children who have lower tone have difficulty moving against gravity while children with higher tone often have difficulty coordinating various muscle groups. If a child is uncomfortable with movement, he or she is not going to be motivated to move until movement becomes more pleasant. Similarly, children with visual impairments must be given motivation to move toward an auditory or tactile goal to understand that movement can serve as a means to an end. Children who have neurological difficulties such as hemiplegia or brachial plexus injuries have developmental challenges necessitating both remedial and compensatory skills. EI providers often face the challenge of working on the next steps in gross motor development when children have difficulties imitating and/or following directions.

Gross
Motor

Early interventionists must have a good understanding of these influences in order to best help the families and caregivers facilitate progress in gross motor skills.

This chapter presents milestones in the area of gross motor skills. As with the skills presented in other chapters, each skill is described and its importance presented. Ways to facilitate skill development in daily routines and activities are noted, along with tips and hints for encouraging development. The reader is reminded that the language used is that which an EI provider would say to parents and caregivers in order to coach and support them.

TUMMY TIME

Lying on a surface with the belly on the floor is also known as prone positioning.

Importance: Spending time on the belly is very important in early development. First an infant must tolerate this position and then learn to turn the head to clear the airway. Then head control begins to further develop as the child lifts his or her head to look around. The neck muscles become stronger, and then muscles lower on the neck and spine begin to work. Head control on the belly is an important prerequisite to rolling, sitting, crawling, standing, and walking. Once head control develops, the child begins to use the arms and is able to bear weight on forearms and then extended arms, eventually getting onto hands and knees.

How to Incorporate into Routines:

Diapering and Dressing: After changing diapers or clothes, roll the child to the belly for a few seconds. Gradually increase the time before moving the child to a new position.

Playtime: Place favorite toys or a mirror on the floor for the child to look at and touch. At first, place the child to the side of where he or she is looking. Encourage head turning to the other side by moving the toys there. Lie on the floor with your head next to the child's head and make funny sounds, sing songs, and talk to the child to help increase tolerance of this position. As head control improves, place the toys so the child will need to pick up his or her head to look at them. As the child gets stronger, his or her head will be higher and higher off the floor.

Tips and Hints

Children who have very high or very low muscle tone may need help to turn their heads when on their bellies to ensure they are able to breathe well.

Many infants tolerate being on their bellies over an adult's lap better than on the hard floor, and this is a good position with which to begin. It is often helpful for an adult to sit in a chair and put a stool under one foot to make one leg higher than the other. The child then lies across the legs with the body lower than the head. This decreases the influence of gravity and takes pressure off the chest or belly. For children who have gastrostomy tubes or colostomy bags, the adult can slightly spread their legs and the appliance can be in this space, relieving pressure. Similarly, placing the child on a wedge with the arms over the front so the hands are resting on the floor is helpful. A wedge can be made by taking a couch cushion and putting a pillow under part of it.

This position is very helpful for children with tracheostomy tubes. When on his or her belly, a child will first put weight on the forearms and later on extended arms. To reach while on forearms, he or she will first slide his or her arm along the floor, and later, as more control develops, he or she will lift his or her arm off the floor to reach out in space.

SIDELYING

Sidelying refers to lying on either the left or right side and maintaining this position for rest or for play.

Importance: The ability to stay on one's side involves the balance of stomach and back muscles and good alignment of the spine (Liddle & York, 2004). This position allows for the hands to touch each other and allows both hands to be seen more easily at once. Reaching for toys in front is easier in this position than it is when the child is on his or her back or belly because gravity has less of an influence. Once in the sidelying position, it is easier for the child to roll to either the belly or to the back.

How to Incorporate into Routines:

Book Time: Look at pictures in books or read stories to the child when he or she is on his or her side.

Playtime: At various times throughout the day, place the child on his or her left and right sides. Lie next to the child and play Peekaboo or sing songs. Place favorite toys the child may look at and reach toward near the child's hands, and as reaching in this position improves, move the toys slightly out of reach to encourage reaching, grasping, and rolling.

Tips and Hints

If the child does not like being on his or her side, try placing a rolled-up towel or pillow behind him or her for support. Depending on the style of the sofa, the child may be able to lie on his or her side with his or her back to the bottom of the sofa. Once the child tolerates this position, remove the support so he or she can learn to roll. Remember to never leave the child unattended when you are using supports such as pillows or the back of the sofa in case he or she wiggles under them!

PLAYING ON THE BACK

Lying on the back, or supine, is a position for many play routines.

Importance: Lying on the back is a common position for play and for sleeping. While on their backs, infants have a stable base from which to move their eyes for tracking and move their limbs. At first, infants learn to move their heads from one side to the other, and later they begin to move against gravity as they reach into space to bat at or grab toys, and later still they move their legs against gravity, bringing hands to knees, hands to feet, and feet to mouth. This position also brings hand-to-hand, hand-to-foot, and foot-to-foot play, which prepares the hands and feet for other sensations as well as weightbearing.

How to Incorporate into Routines:

Diapering and Dressing: During diapering, bring the child's legs up and help him or her grab the knees. Once this is done easily, help the child grab the feet. As these skills develop, playfully bring the feet toward the mouth.

Playtime: Use motivating toys to encourage the child to reach up against gravity. To encourage the hands to knees, hands to feet, and feet to mouth during play, help the child bring the feet up and rub, tickle, and play social games such as This Little Piggy to encourage the child to lift his or her legs.

Tips and Hints

It is important to make sure a child's position is changed frequently to avoid flattening of the back of the head or muscle asymmetry, especially if the child is not yet able to change positions independently. For children who tend to turn their heads to one side more than the other, it is necessary to position them to encourage head turning to the nonpreferred side by placing interesting objects on that side. Similarly, it is crucial to hold the child or lay him or her so he or she has to look toward the nonpreferred side to watch family or peer activities.

For children who use one arm or hand more than the other, it is sometimes helpful to put a small towel roll under the nonpreferred shoulder to help them bring the arm forward to reach.

ROLLING

Rolling from the belly to the back usually occurs before rolling back to belly, but some children do roll back to belly first. Children who do not like being on their bellies are often motivated to move off their bellies and begin to roll when placed on their tummies.

Importance: Rolling is usually the young child's first means of moving independently from one place to another. Being able to move on one's own is very important in terms of independence and having the ability to explore new places, textures, sounds, or tastes. Rolling stimulates receptors in the brain that are connected to the inner ear, part of what is known as the vestibular system. The vestibular system gives us important information about our bodies, helps us with balance, and helps us to coordinate our eyes.

How to Incorporate into Routines:

 Diapering and Dressing: At the end of each diaper change or after getting the child dressed, roll the child to his or her belly, providing less assistance over time.

 Playtime: Playfully roll the child from belly to back and back to belly on a firm but soft surface such as a bed or a carpeted floor. Encourage rolling to the right and to the left, from the back to the belly, and from the belly to the back.

Tips and Hints

Place the child on his or her side, show him or her a favorite toy, and slowly move the toy so that the child's head movement tracks it (visually and/or auditorally), which will encourage a roll. If the child does not roll, gently place your hands on the child's hip and help him or her roll.

If the child prefers only rolling to the right, spend more time encouraging rolling to the left, and vice versa.

SITTING

Learning to sit happens gradually, as children first sit with a lot of support and then progress to sitting independently. Sitting requires the balance of muscles on the front and back of the body. There are many stages in between sitting with maximum support and sitting independently. At first children use their arms to help balance by placing their hands in front of them on the floor, on their legs, or on a surface such as a box and later progress to sitting without using their arms. To sit safely, children must be able to catch themselves using their arms (protective reactions) to the front, to the side, and, much later, to the rear.

Importance: The ability to sit enables a child to see the world from a different perspective and allows for increased interaction with others and the environment. Sitting allows the child to use the hands in new ways.

How to Incorporate into Routines:

Bath Time: To help a child sit in the tub, provide a bath seat or plastic laundry basket to sit in.

Book Time: Prop the child on the corner of the couch or on your lap to "read" stories and "talk" about the pictures.

Diapering and Dressing: Dress the child in a sitting position, providing support if necessary. This enables a child to more easily use his or her hands to help.

Playtime: With the child on your lap or on the floor, place one hand on the child's chest and one hand on the child's upper back so his or her head is steady. As head control improves, support the child lower down on his or her body. Once the child is able to sit for brief periods, place pillows nearby so that if the child falls he or she will land on a soft surface. As sitting balance improves, place items nearby for mouthing, banging, and exploring.

Tips and Hints

To help a child learn to sit, it is helpful to begin providing support high up on the chest, and as head and trunk control develop, the supporting hands can be positioned lower and lower.

To optimize using the muscles related to eating, it is important that children be well supported while they eat. Mealtime is not a good time to practice having the child work hard on sitting, because he or she won't be able to concentrate on coordinating the lips, tongue, or cheeks. Ideally, the hips, knees, and ankles should be at 90 degree angles, and the edge of the seat should be just behind the child's knees. This is often very difficult to achieve with booster seats and high chairs, which are made to fit children for an extended period of time. Using rolled towels may be helpful to keep the child from leaning, and if the child's arms don't reach the tray well, sitting on a small phone book may be useful. In addition, adjust the seatbelt so that the child's lower back and pelvis are flush against the back of the seat to allow for optimal motor control.

COMMANDO CRAWLING

Commando crawling or army crawling is characterized by the child pulling the body using the arms, with the belly and legs on the floor.

Importance: Commando crawling requires arm strength and head control and also further develops the strength in the upper body. Commando crawling enables a child to move from one place to another to explore. Though rolling is typically the first method of moving around, commando crawling allows a child to get to a target fairly quickly and to keep the target in sight.

How to Incorporate into Routines:

Mealtime/Snack Time: Place the bottle, sippy cup, or snack container just out of reach to motivate the child to move forward. As soon as the child touches the bottle, cup, or snack package pick up him or her to position for eating or drinking.

Playtime: Place interesting objects just out of reach, first to the side to encourage circular pivoting and then to the front to encourage commando crawling. Position yourself on the belly in front of the child so he or she will move to get you. At first, position the objects and yourself just out of reach and gradually increase the distance needed to crawl.

Tips and Hints

Reaching for objects of interest, first from one side and then from the other, helps the child practice shifting weight from one side to the other, a prerequisite to crawling.

Before commando crawling, children swivel on their bellies so their heads end up where their feet were. This is known as circular pivoting.

Children often crawl backward for a short time until they figure out how to move forward.

Sometimes it is beneficial to help the child get a sense of how to push off by blocking the feet with the hand or by gently pushing the feet downward so the child learns to push off the floor.

Put a couch cushion on the floor with a favorite toy on it, out of reach, to encourage the child to pull up on the cushion. This increases arm strength and helps facilitate a hands-and-knees position.

CRAWLING ON HANDS AND KNEES

Before learning to creep or crawl on hands and knees (quadruped), children often remain stationary on hands and knees when placed that way and later get into a hands-and-knees position independently. Before learning to move forward, most children rock back and forth in this position.

Importance: Crawling on hands and knees involves using the left and right sides of the bodies with newly found coordination; as the right arm moves forward, so does the left leg, and vice versa.

How to Incorporate into Routines:

Playtime: Hold favorite toys or objects above the hands and then gradually move the items a few inches away. Once the child is able to move forward a few inches, gradually move desired items a little farther away.

Tips and Hints

Practice having the child reach first to one side and then the other to help the child develop the ability to shift his or her weight from side to side, which is necessary to move forward. If the child has difficulty staying on hands and knees, make it a little easier by placing the child in this position over your legs as you sit on the floor.

You may find that the child first moves backward, as this is common until children figure out the necessary motor pattern to move forward.

Children often love having siblings, parents, or peers crawl across the floor using the same method they are using.

MOVING IN AND OUT OF SITTING

Moving in and out of sitting is the change of position from hands and knees to sitting and from sitting to hands and knees.

Importance: Typically, children purposefully first move from sitting to their bellies or hands and knees and then later are able to move from their hands and knees to sitting. Some children make the transition from sitting to hands and knees and vice versa after they begin to move forward on their bellies and hands and knees. The ability to change to and from these positions requires coordination and strength as well as rotary movements.

How to Incorporate into Routines:

Diapering and Dressing: After changing the child's diapers or dressing/undressing them, rather than picking up and pulling the child into a sitting position, rotate the child to the side and help him or her push up into a sitting position.

Playtime: When the child is sitting, place favorite toys and objects just out of reach to the side and gently guide him or her to the side to get the toys. When the child is on the belly, hold favorite toys or objects so that the child needs to move into sitting to get the coveted item.

Tips and Hints

To help the child move from hands and knees to sitting, present a toy in front of him or her and slowly move it to the left side toward his or her left hip to encourage the child to shift his or her weight to the right and rotate into a sitting position. Similarly, when the child is on hands and knees, move the toy from in front of him or her toward the right hip to encourage the child to shift his or her weight to the left and rotate into sitting on the other side.

To help a child move from sitting to hands and knees, help him or her put the left hand on the floor on the left side and help him or her reach with the right hand to get a toy or favorite object placed to the left. Similarly, place interesting items on the right side and encourage weightbearing on the right hand with a reach to get the toy with the left hand. As the child gets proficient with this, begin to move toys farther away to motivate the child to reach a greater distance. Soon the child will be moving from sitting to the floor using rotation and will then be able to move from sitting to a creeping position.

PULLING TO STAND

Pulling to stand involves putting the hands on a surface such as a chair or a sofa and moving into a standing position. Usually the child moves from a sitting position on a raised surface such as a stool or an adult's leg or from a high kneel to a half kneel (bearing weight on one lower leg and the other foot).

Importance: Pulling to stand typically comes before cruising and walking with support or walking independently. It requires strength in the legs and in the arms as well as the coordination of the leg muscles. Practicing moving from sitting to standing further strengthens leg muscles.

How to Incorporate into Routines:

Playtime: Sit the child on a small stool or on your thighs while you kneel with your buttocks on your heels. Put favorite toys on a chair or sofa in front of you and encourage the child to stand to reach them. After he or she learns to pull to stand from your lap, have the child kneel at the sofa and entice him or her with favorite objects just out of reach until he or she stands.

Tips and Hints

Removing couch cushions is sometimes very helpful and makes pulling up on the couch a little easier, as the supporting surface is lower to the ground.

If the child is on your lap and is having trouble moving to standing, slowly move into high kneeling, which will raise the child to his or her feet.

To help a child move from high kneeling to standing, hold the child at the pelvis and gently tip the child to the side. This will likely encourage the child to bring the leg on the opposite side of the tilt into a half-kneeling position and then up into standing.

CRUISING

Cruising occurs when a child moves sideways while holding onto a stable surface such as a sofa.

Importance: Cruising helps develop strength and coordination in the leg and hip muscles, which are later used for independent walking. Cruising is often one of the first upright movements a child makes without needing the help of an adult.

How to Incorporate into Routines:

Playtime: When the child is standing at a sofa or low table, place a favorite toy or object on the surface, just out of reach. Encourage the child to move his or her legs, first the one closest to the toy and then the other, taking a step to move sideways. Place toys to the left and to the right so the child develops the ability to move to both directions.

Tips and Hints

If the child has difficulty moving the first leg, gently place the hands on his or her pelvis or hip area and gently tip him or her a little to the direction away from which he or she needs to move. This will unweight the leg and allow the child to move it toward the toy. As the child gains control, move the toys farther away until the child is able to cruise the entire length of the couch or table.

STANDING UNSUPPORTED

Standing unsupported entails the ability to stand for indefinite periods without needing to hold onto a person, furniture, a wall, or another object for support.

Importance: The ability to stand unsupported is needed before a child can be a safe walker, because it is necessary to be able to maintain balance when one stops walking to interact with others or with the environment.

How to Incorporate into Routines:

Book Time: Present a book to the child while he or she is standing. Have the child hold the book with two hands to encourage the child to balance.

Diapering and Dressing: Have the child stand up with support during dressing activities to develop balance skills.

Grooming and Hygiene: Have the child stand on a step stool and hold onto the sink while brushing teeth, washing hands, or brushing hair. A low mirror may help maintain interest in these activities.

Playtime: Have the child stand and hold on to a variety of supports while playing with toys, while singing, or while watching television to give him or her experiences that challenge balance.

Tips and Hints

Have the child stand with his or her back against a wall or sofa to develop comfort without a surface in front of him or her. Once he or she is able to do this, encourage him or her to lean forward to get a desired item.

WALKING

Walking independently entails the ability to move from one place to another in an upright position without the need for support. Before being able to walk independently, a child first walks with two-hand support. The child progresses to walking with a push toy or by pushing an object such as a stool or large box and then is able to walk with an adult holding just one hand. Standing balance is often progressing at the same time, which enables the child to safely walk a few steps without falling. Children often take one or two steps and quickly progress to being able to walk several steps, then a few feet, across a room, and then around the house. Once a child is able to walk on a flat surface, he or she then progresses to being able to walk from one surface to another, such as from carpeting to a bare floor, and then later can walk on uneven terrain such as a yard or playground.

Importance: Walking independently gives a child a new sense of independence and the ability to explore from a new height. The world looks different from an upright position, and the child is able to look around, find a destination, and then move to interact.

How to Incorporate into Routines:

Mealtime/Snack Time: Have the child walk to his or her highchair or booster seat each time he or she eats, which will give the child many opportunities to practice this skill each day. At first, provide two-handed support, and, as the child's balance improves, change to one-handed support.

Playtime: Provide large boxes and laundry baskets filled with clothes or toys for extra weight for the child to push. Have the child stand with his or her back against a wall and encourage him or her to first lean forward and, once comfortable with that, walk one step to get to outstretched arms for a hug or a favorite object or treat. Once he or she can walk one step, move back to encourage two steps, then later three, and so forth.

Community Outings; Diapering and Dressing; Grooming and Hygiene: When changing locations to participate in these routines, practice walking with support to give multiple opportunities for practice. Provide needed support until the child is comfortable and gradually decrease the amount of help provided.

Tips and Hints

Sing songs, count, or blow bubbles to help distract and/or motivate the child who is hesitant to stand and take steps.

RUNNING

Running develops after a child is skilled at walking, and it begins as a hurried walk. In order to run a child needs to coordinate both sides of the body at a faster speed than is necessary for walking.

Importance: Running is often an activity done in early interactions with peers. It is a necessary skill in many sports and is also a skill that helps one escape from danger.

How to Incorporate into Routines:

Bath Time: Playfully race the child saying "Hurry, hurry, run, let's go take a bath"

Community Outings: When going to the store, for a walk, or to the park, run for short periods of time and gradually increase the child's endurance.

Playtime: Play chase with the child or playfully say "I'm going to get you" when coming toward the child to tickle him or her.

Tips and Hints

Hold the child's hands or have him or her run while pushing a toy.

At first, have the child run where falling will be safest, such as on a carpeted area or a flat grassy area, rather than on an uneven hill.

RIDING TOYS

Riding toys include various types of wheeled vehicles. Often, children first use their feet to move a vehicle backward and then figure out how to move forward. To move forward, children may first move both feet at the same time and then alternate feet, while others alternate from the start. After being able to alternate feet to move forward, children then are able to pedal, which involves greater coordination of both sides of their bodies.

Importance: Being able to move riding toys often gives children a sense of independence as well as a new way to explore and move. Also, this is often the first step in a leisure activity (bike riding) that may last for many years. Some children master riding toys before walking and others master walking first.

How to Incorporate into Routines:

Playtime: To encourage moving forward, hold out a favorite snack or favorite toy a few inches away and help guide the child's feet forward, giving the favorite item as soon as he or she reaches you. Gradually increase the distance needed to reach the item.

Tips and Hints

For children who are hesitant to get on a riding toy, first have them push it with a stuffed animal sitting on it. As they become accustomed to this, have them do favorite activities such as watching a show or eating a snack while sitting on the riding toy. Gradually introduce movement as the child's tolerance increases.

When the child is ready to learn to pedal, placing two different stickers on the child's shoes can be useful so you can give verbal cues such as "Push with (sticker name). Now push with (other sticker name)."

NAVIGATING STAIRS

Crawling up a step or two and then a full set of stairs typically occurs before crawling down the stairs. Some children crawl down backward while others thump down the stairs in sitting position, while still others slide down feet first. When learning to walk up stairs the typical progression is walking with both hands held by a caregiver, then holding on to an adult's hand and a railing or wall, then walking independently holding a rail or wall, and finally walking up without support. At first, children walk up stairs "marking time" by putting one foot then the other on the same step and then progress to step over step or an alternating feet pattern characterized by one foot on each step. Walking down the stairs is typically more difficult due to the need for greater balance, and the progression is similar to walking up the stairs, but often children use a more mature pattern to ascend before that pattern is used to descend the stairs.

Importance: Going up and down stairs by themselves gives children a great deal of independence and a feeling of accomplishment. Strength, balance, and coordination of both sides of the body are required to successfully walk up and down the stairs.

How to Incorporate into Routines:

Bath Time; Bedtime; Diapering and Dressing; Grooming and Hygiene; Household Activities; Mealtime/Snack Time: If the child is in a home or child care setting where a bathroom, bedroom, and kitchen are on different floors, walking up and down the stairs for diapering, eating, tooth brushing, or dressing gives many opportunities for practice.

 Community Outings: If the home or child care center has stairs, have the child walk up and down them rather than carrying him or her whenever possible and feasible.

 Playtime: Place a favorite object on the second step to encourage the child to crawl up to get it. Once the child can climb two or three stairs, place the favorite object on the fifth or sixth step and encourage him or her to crawl to reach the target. Once he or she is able to crawl up, begin to work on having the child walk with two-hand support, then one-hand support, and then progress to having him or her walk independently while holding the railing. Encourage the child to crawl down one or two steps and then progress to three or four, then five or six, and finally a whole flight by having preferred objects or favorite people at the bottom and by assisting with leg movements. Once the child is able to crawl down, repeat the same technique with walking down, first with two-hand support, then one-hand support, and then with the support of a wall or railing.

Tips and Hints

Some families prefer to have a child hold someone's hand on the steps and are very cautious about safety, preferring that the child not be independent on the steps. In this situation or when there are no steps in the home or child care setting, boxes, phone books, or stepstools can be used to practice stepping up and down.

If the child is hesitant to crawl up the stairs, place a desired object on or have someone sit on the second or third step from the bottom.

BALL PLAY

Ball play in infants and toddlers includes rolling, throwing, and kicking. Catching skills also develop during the toddler period as children first catch balls by trapping them with their arms and body and later developing skills to catch using only their hands.

Importance: Young children first explore balls by mouthing and then soon experiment with the visual and auditory effects of throwing and rolling. Later, after developing the ability to release objects, rolling and throwing become an important social game that involves both motor coordination and reciprocal play or turn-taking. Ball play helps develop more refined coordination as children learn to throw with aim toward people and objects and greater balance as children learn to kick from a stationary position.

How to Incorporate into Routines:

 Playtime: For the early learner, provide balls of varying sizes and textures to explore by mouthing, rolling, and throwing. Sit across from the child and roll a ball back and forth with him or her, starting very close and progressing to farther away to develop aim and the ability to use the appropriate amount of force. Similarly, stand nearby when playing a game of catch and gradually move farther back as the child learns to throw with aim and later to catch. Once a child is able to walk independently on a variety of surfaces, model kicking a ball and provide one-hand support, if needed, to help the child shift his or her weight in order to kick the ball forward.

Tips and Hints

Balloons or light-weight inflatable balls such as punch balls (which should be used under close supervision, as they are unsafe for young children if they pop) are helpful to use when teaching catching, as they are a good size and can be thrown very gently and slowly to give the child more time to coordinate his or her movements.

Provide rolled-up socks for practice throwing with aim into boxes or baskets.

Provide boxes or laundry baskets to develop aim and control for throwing.

Empty large plastic bottles and/or boxes are good targets for a modified game of bowling to practice rolling, throwing, or kicking with aim.

JUMPING

Jumping involves moving while keeping both legs and feet together. Jumping in place, a short distance forward, and down from a low surface are skills enjoyed by many toddlers.

Importance: Jumping involves coordinating both sides of the body at the same time. Often when children first try to jump, they have difficulty keeping both legs together and lead with one foot. Children often jump from a low surface such as the bottom step or from a low stepstool or jump in place before being able to jump forward a distance.

How to Incorporate into Routines:

Bath Time; Bedtime; Diapering and Dressing; Grooming and Hygiene; Household Activities; Mealtime/Snack Time; Playtime: Have the child jump from one activity to another, providing support as needed.

Playtime: Pretend to be rabbits or frogs. Have the child jump down from stools and phone books, jump in place on pillows, or over a string on the floor.

Community Outings: Have the child jump over cracks in the sidewalk, providing two-hand support and then no support.

Tips and Hints

For a child who is not bending his or her knees when attempting to jump, show him or her how and, if needed, help him or her to bend by gently rotating the legs outward from the thighs.

For a child who is jumping by leading with one foot, hold both of the child's hands to encourage him or her to coordinate both sides of the body.

An old phone book, taped to keep the pages from separating, is a great way to encourage jumping from a low surface as the short distance to the floor makes it easier for many children, especially those who may be a bit fearful.

Take turns jumping with the child to give the experience of waiting and a good model for jumping.

If two people are available when taking walks, many children enjoy holding hands and jumping down the street.

CLIMBING

Climbing involves using the arms and legs to pull the body onto a higher surface, such as a chair, sofa, or a sliding board.

Importance: Climbing involves strength, planning, and coordination. Some toddlers are very comfortable testing gravity and attempt to climb out of their cribs while others are not as adventurous, depending on their personality and/or sensory processing.

How to Incorporate into Routines:

Playtime: To encourage the child to climb onto the couch, try taking off the cushions and placing a favorite item just out of reach toward the back of the sofa. If the child has difficulty pulling himself or herself up, allow him or her to stand on a phone book, stepstool, couch cushion, or your lap. Gradually decrease the height of the helping step and any hands-on help you provide.

Community Outings: Help the child climb onto playground equipment such as slides and spring toys by shifting his or her weight onto one leg by gently placing your hand on the child's hip or shoulder and transferring the child's weight to the leg that will be the anchor. This unweights the leg that will step up or over. As the child shows progress, decrease the assistance until he or she is independent.

Tips and Hints

Children should be taught how to climb safely off furniture by helping them to turn around and slide down feet first.

For children who are hesitant to climb, gently expose them to movement and heights at their pace to increase their comfort level.

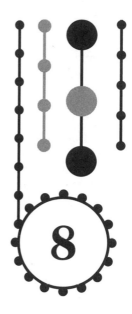

Fine Motor Skills

Fine motor skills are those that require small muscle movements, and they are generally hand skills. Fine motor skills are very much influenced by the larger muscles, which provide a stable base from which the smaller muscles can work (Case-Smith, Fisher, & Bauer, 1989). For example, for the hands to work best, the shoulder muscles must be working well. Posture also very much influences the smaller muscles. If a child is expending a great deal of effort to hold himself or herself up in a chair or on the floor, the hands may not be free to manipulate items well. Even if the child is not propping on the arms, the arms may not be in an ideal position. For example, if a child does not have adequate sitting balance, he or she may compensate by retracting the shoulder blades, which may result in elbow flexion and difficulty reaching forward. When working on new fine motor skills, it is helpful to have the child positioned as stably as possible so he or she can work on the hand skills without having to work hard at maintaining an upright position.

Fine motor skills are very much influenced by visual skills. For most fine motor skills, the eyes direct the hands. Visual attention, visual tracking, and visual pursuits greatly affect fine motor skill acquisition. Cognitive skills also very much influence fine motor skills, and one can find the same type of activity, such as stacking blocks, in both the cognitive and the fine motor sections of developmental assessments. The understanding that blocks can be stacked is a cognitive skill in terms of understanding the function of objects, and the fine motor skill is the ability to use the eyes and upper extremity together. The higher the block tower, the greater the coordination needed. Shoulder, arm, and hand stability; grasping patterns; visual skills; direction following; imitation skills; and, of course, impulse control greatly affect the ability to stack blocks.

One particular child comes to mind to further illustrate the complexity of fine motor development. A physical therapist and a teacher of the deaf and hard of hearing were providing services to a young child who has a diagnosis of Down syndrome. During the annual evaluation, they found that the child did not release items into a container, and they requested a consultation from an occupational therapist to recommend activities to help the child learn to use his hands better to release. The occupational therapist found that the difficulty was not with the child's hand skills, per se, but were more related to difficulties with his cognitive skills. He could actively let go of objects, as he dropped his bottle when done and he dropped objects to pick up other objects. He did not see a purpose in releasing into a container. This child was at a sensory level of play, and it was found that when releasing resulted in sensory feedback he was more likely to release into a container. The occupational therapist helped him release into a container and then made the objects in the container spin to stimulate and reward the child's visual and auditory systems, along with enthusiastically cheering him for his great effort. Over time, this behavior was shaped until the child became independent and was able to put a variety of objects into a variety of containers. Though those working in the field of child development often classify skills in one of the developmental domains, many skills have components of more than one domain.

Many times EI providers who are working on skills in other domains can also address a child's fine motor skills. Sometimes, however, consultation or direct service from an occupational therapist may be needed. If a child has a very strong hand preference and uses the nonpreferred hand very little or not at all, such as when a child has hemiplegia or a brachial plexus injury, the assistance of an occupational therapist and/or a physical therapist should be sought. If an older toddler has difficulty sequencing fine motor actions such as using a fork, playing with toys that have multiple steps, or imitating complex actions, an occupational therapist should evaluate the child's motor planning skills.

This chapter presents milestones in the area of fine motor skills. Each skill is described and its importance discussed. Ways for providers to coach caregivers to facilitate the skill's development in daily routines and activities are also presented, as are and tips and hints for furthering the development.

VISUAL FIXATION AND ATTENTION

Visual fixation occurs when the eyes focus on an object or a person.

Importance: Visual fixation is one of the first visual skills to develop and is a prerequisite for tracking and coordinated reach and grasp. As discussed by Columbo (2001), visual attention includes four functions: alertness, spatial orientation, attention to object features, and attention to one stimulus while inhibiting attention to another. It is easiest for some children to focus on and attend to reflective objects such as mirrors or aluminum foil.

How to Incorporate into Routines: During all routines, when using objects such as the washcloth during bathtime, pajamas when getting ready for bed, the bottle during mealtime and snack time, the brush during grooming, and the rattle during playtime, present the item in front of the child's eyes, shaking it to draw attention to it. In addition, during all routines, talk to the child in a sing-song cadence to encourage him or her to look at your face.

Tips and Hints

If it is difficult for the child to pay attention to faces, make silly sounds and funny faces to help get his or her attention. Wearing brightly colored lipstick, funny glasses, or a sticker on the nose may also help draw attention to a caregiver's face. Minimizing distractions helps the child to focus on specific visual targets.

Some children attend very well to visual stimuli but have difficulty shifting their attention from one stimulus to another. Children with autism sometimes appear to "get stuck" on patterns or forms. Eye movements involving quick shifts from one stimulus to another, known as saccades, are good to practice by having a child look from one person or object to another. To facilitate this, it is helpful at first to use shaking or other movements or auditory cues such a silly sounds to encourage shifting of attention.

VISUAL TRACKING

Visual tracking, called *smooth pursuits* in some developmental assessments, is characterized by the eyes following visual stimuli such as toys or faces that are moving. Tracking skills include tracking to mid-line, across mid-line, and up and down.

Importance: Tracking helps a child understand what is going on in the environment. Following people who walk into and out of a room, grasping a toy that is moving, and grabbing a ball that is rolling are most successful when good tracking skills exist.

How to Incorporate into Routines: Tracking can be incorporated into any routine or activity. With the child in supported sitting such as in a swing, on a lap, or in a bath seat, move toys slowly from one side to another, several inches in front of his or her eyes. Once the child is able to watch the objects without losing focus, try moving toys up and down. When talking to the child, move your face slowly in front of the child to encourage the eyes to follow you. At mealtime, encourage the child to watch you move the bottle or spoon.

Tips and Hints

A child can best use his or her eyes when the head is stable. For children who have difficult tracking, first practice with them lying on their backs and progress to supported sitting.

BATTING AND REACHING

Reaching toward or batting at toys with the hands typically occurs before a child is able to grasp. In sitting, children usually reach using both hands and then later usually use just one hand, the one closest to the object.

Importance: Batting and reaching help develop eye–hand coordination and are often some of the first movements that begin the process of learning about cause and effect. When the child discovers that when he or she hits a toy and it moves or makes a sound, he or she begins to understand that hand movements make things happen, an important cognitive skill. Reaching requires control of the shoulder, and practicing these movements strengthens shoulder muscles, which give a stable base for more refined movements of the hands, which develop later. Reaching in all positions is important for functional skill development.

How to Incorporate into Routines:

 Bath Time: Hold out toys for the child to bat at so they will fall in the water and splash.

 Bedtime: Present books, your face, and bedtime comfort objects nearby for a child to touch.

 Diapering and Dressing: Place a clean diaper or clothing item above the child's eyes to bat away to play Peekaboo. Tickle or rub the child's arm or hand and then stop with your hand near the child's. When the child reaches and touches your hand, begin again.

Mealtime/Snack Time: Playfully encourage the child to reach for the bottle or the cup as well as snack foods.

Playtime: Place toys that make sounds within the child's reach when the child is on the floor.

Tips and Hints

If the child uses one hand more than the other—for example, a child who has a brachial plexus injury or hemiplegia due to cerebral palsy—place highly desired objects near the nonpreferred side to encourage the child to move that hand.

PVC pipe or cardboard wrapping paper tubes can be used to suspend spoons, rattles, or other objects using short pieces of ribbon during close supervision.

GRASPING

Grasping occurs when the fingers are used to hold a toy, a finger, or another object. At first the grasp is reflexive, and later it comes under voluntary control. A child is able to hold a toy for only a short length of time when grasp is first developing. Children first grasp objects placed on or near their hands, and once they are able to do this, they are able to combine reaching and grasping. When the wrist is in an upward position (extended), grasping is easier, as the fingers are more likely to close on an object. Children are first able to grasp lightweight, narrow, or thin objects such as plastic links, bracelets, and socks. They will be more likely to grasp items that make sounds they like, those they find visually appealing, and/or those that have a texture they like.

Importance: Grasping is important for the development of play skills, thinking skills, and self-care skills such as eating, dressing, grooming, and practicing hygiene. After a child can grasp, he or she can explore objects in various ways.

How to Incorporate into Routines:

Bath Time: Provide sponges, washcloths, empty small plastic bottles, and toys such as rubber duckies for the child to grasp.

Diapering and Dressing: Have the child reach for your hands, a diaper, or a toy after diaper changes.

Mealtime/Snack Time: Gently help the child hold the feeder's fingers as he or she is bottle fed or breast fed. For babies who take a bottle, encourage them to hold the bottle by gently and playfully taking their hands to the bottle. As the child begins to finger feed, place soft pieces of food on his or her tray.

Playtime: Provide a variety of shapes and sizes of toys for the child to hold, starting with lightweight and thin rattles and rings, and progress to heavier and more varied shapes.

Tips and Hints

For children who have increased muscle tone, it is helpful to relax the child's body before working on grasping activities. Rhythmic movements and gentle stretching performed before presenting the item to be grasped may assist the child.

Having the child's forearms on a surface such as a highchair tray often helps provide stability, which makes grasping easier.

For children who have visual impairments, using colors that contrast with the surface on which the items rest will help the child find the objects to be grasped.

TRANSFERRING FROM HAND TO HAND

Transferring refers to moving an object from one hand to another. Before children transfer hand to hand, they often transfer from one hand to their mouth and then to their other hand.

Importance: Very young children often practice transferring from one hand to another as they explore an object using vision, touch, hearing, and taste. Transferring from one hand to another also occurs if one hand gets tired, if it is necessary to push a hand through a sleeve and a large item is being held, if one hand is more skilled than the other and the nondominant hand needs to hold while the dominant hand performs a skilled movement, or if the dominant hand needs to reach and it is holding an object. Transferring helps a child refine grasping, releasing, and coordinated use of two hands.

How to Incorporate into Routines:

Diapering and Dressing: Have the child hold a relatively small toy (but not so small that it is a choking hazard). When it is time to push the child's hand through a sleeve, help the child move the toy to the other hand.

Mealtime/Snack Time: Give the child two food items, presented one at a time to the same hand to facilitate a transfer. Present both items to the right hand and then later to the left, or vice versa.

Playtime: Place a bowl, basket, or box of easily held toys in front of the child. At times place the container near the right hand and at other times, near the left hand. As the child takes them out, he or she may move the items to the other hand.

Tips and Hints

Children who have a strong hand preference, such as those who have a brachial plexus injury or hemiplegia, often transfer from the nonpreferred to their preferred hands long before they transfer in the other direction. Practice transferring into the nonpreferred hand helps the child practice grasp and release in a way that is meaningful for him or her.

Fine Motor

RELEASING

Releasing occurs when the fingers and thumb open or extend, resulting in loss of grasp of an object.

Importance: A child must learn to actively release objects in order to be successful with many activities, such as handing items to others, self-feeding, and putting items away. Babies are able to grasp before they are able to actively release. Infants often use their mouths to help pull items from their hands. When children are learning to release objects, they often use the surface (an adult's hand, a highchair tray, or a bowl) against their palms and fingers to assist with letting go of the object. After much practice, they can release without the assistance of the surface. Releasing large items such as rattles and pacifiers is easier than releasing small items such as small pieces of food. Releasing into a large target such as a bowl requires less eye–hand coordination than does releasing into a container with a small opening.

How to Incorporate into Routines:

Bath Time: Provide plastic tub toys, cups, and bowls to make bath time fun facilitating practice of release.

Mealtime/Snack Time: Give the child small pieces of finger food to practice releasing into the mouth. As a child gains more of a skilled release, provide containers first with large openings and then progress to smaller openings for him or her to put the food into.

Playtime: Provide a variety of containers to practice release. Children often love to put things into holes and slots. (See "Container Play" later in this chapter.)

Diapering and Dressing: Have the child hand you the diaper, wipes, lotion, and other types of supplies to help with release. At first it may be necessary to gently tug to help the child release, but over time the child will be able to drop the item into a waiting hand. Have the child throw the dirty diaper in the trash and put worn clothes in the hamper.

Tips and Hints

The position of the wrist affects releasing objects. When the wrist is flexed or bent, release is easier because the fingers generally open.

For children who use one hand more than the other, such as children with hemiplegia or a brachial plexus injury, presenting objects to the nonpreferred side necessitates a transfer to the preferred hand and gives a lot of practice for release from the nonpreferred as the dominant hand naturally tugs at the item.

Some children, often those who have increased muscle tone, throw objects when they have difficulty releasing. Using the technique of gradually reducing the pressure of the tug to fade the assistance is often helpful in facilitating an active release.

GRASPING PATTERNS

Grasping patterns change as children gain control of their fingers and use their eyes and hands together. At first, the infant uses a grasp reflex and then he or she gains voluntary control. Early studies and many developmental assessments such as the Hawaii Early Learning Profile (Parks, 1992–2011) and the Erhardt Developmental Prehension Assessment (Erhardt, 1994) refer to the little finger or the ulnar side being the most active during early grasping. This pattern is based on early work by Halverson (1931); however, Lantz, Melén, and Forssberg (1996) refuted Halverson's research, finding that the index finger is quite active early as infants use all their fingers to grasp. In either case, objects are generally first held in the palm, and over time the fingertips become more active, allowing the child to hold toys and other objects with the tips of his or her fingers and thumb without using the palm. Next the child begins to be able to pick up smaller items such as little pieces of food using the thumb and index finger. This is known as using a *pincer grasp*. The pincer grasp often changes from the earlier forms of the thumb being on the side of the fingertip and the thumb pad being on the fingertip pad to the more mature form of the fine pincer grasp, which is when the child uses the tip of the thumb and the tip of the index finger (see Photos 8.1–8.3).

Importance: The use of mature grasping patterns with control of the fingertips and the thumb allows for refined movements involved in many activities, including eating, playing, using writing implements, dressing, and hygiene.

How to Incorporate into Routines:

Mealtime/Snack Time: Have the child hold teething biscuits and, as eating skills improve, have the child pick up pieces of finger foods.

Playtime: Provide a variety of shapes and sizes of toys and objects for the child to hold. Progress from placing them in the child's hands to having the child combine reach and grasp. If the child does not readily reach for the item, touch the child's hand with the item and wait to see if he or she grasps it. If so, gradually move the object a little farther away from the child's hand.

Tips and Hints

Use contrasting colors for children who have visual impairments.

When facilitating a pincer grasp, hold items to be grasped in your fingertips, which will help the child use his or her fingertips. Providing support at the child's forearm or having the child's forearm on a surface will provide extra stability that often helps facilitate a pincer grasp. As the child's skills improve, decrease the amount of external support; progress from holding the small bit of food in your fingertips just above the surface to presenting the food bit in your outstretched hand above any surface.

For children who are unable to eat small bits of food but whose fine motor skills are ready for facilitation of a pincer grasp, have them feed others or use small bits of food for sensory play or container play.

Small empty plastic bottles are often a good size for grasping and are very helpful for children who have increased muscle tone. They are often just the right size to help position the thumb so it is rotated toward the little finger.

Fine Motor

USING BOTH HANDS

Using both hands together, also known as bilateral coordination, encompasses holding a larger object with both hands, holding an object in each hand at the same time, and using one hand to hold and the other to manipulate.

Importance: Babies often begin to hold a toy using both hands at the same time and then progress to being able to hold a toy in each hand at the same time. After they are good at those two skills, they begin to use their hands for different purposes, with one hand stabilizing or holding while the other hand manipulates. Many activities that children and adults perform require

Photo 8.1.

skilled use of both hands. Drawing and writing when the nondominant hand holds the paper, using a cell phone, cooking, cleaning, opening a container, putting gas in a car, and unlocking a door are common bilateral activities that adults perform daily. These bilateral hand skills likely were practiced as young children while dressing a doll, putting together interlocking blocks, stringing beads, and scraping the last bit of yogurt from the container, just a few of the many daily tasks done with both hands.

How to Incorporate into Routines:

 Bath Time: Show the child how to splash with both hands. Have the child hold small bath toys in each hand. When the child is ready to help with bathing, have him or her hold the washcloth and help put on the soap.

 Book Time: Hold the child on your lap when reading to him or her. Have the child help hold the book with both hands.

 Diapering and Dressing: In the early stages, children can help hold a diaper in one hand and the tube of cream in the other to assist in the diapering process. For children who are ready to assist with dressing and undressing, have them help pull their shoes and socks on and off and pull their shirts and pants on and off. Have the child help zip and button when they are proficient at easier dressing tasks.

 Grooming and Hygiene: During toothbrushing, have the child help unscrew the toothpaste lid while holding the toothpaste and have the child help put the toothpaste on the toothbrush while holding the toothbrush. Before washing the child's face, have the child hold the washcloth and pump the liquid soap or rub the soap on the cloth.

Mealtime/Snack Time: Once the child is able to grasp toys, place his or her hands on the bottle and gently help him or her hold it. If the child is resistant and seems to think it is your job, try putting the bottle near, but not in, the child's mouth, which hopefully will result in the child grabbing the bottle and placing it into the mouth. If you let go, he or she may decide to hold it! Provide sippy cups with two handles to encourage the use of both hands. When children are beginning to use a spoon to self-feed, help them to hold the bowl/plate with one hand while they scoop with the other. When giving the child snacks such as cookies or crackers, give two items, one for each hand.

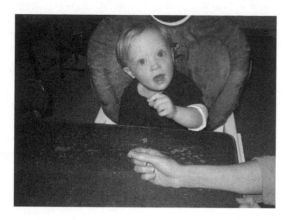

Photo 8.2.

Playtime: Place socks, rattles, and other toys in both of the child's hands. For children who no longer put items in their mouths, have them put tape or stickers on a paper towel tube, raw ziti pasta on a straw or on an unsharpened pencil, and bits of cereal in an empty bottle to encourage using two hands together to complete a task. When looking at a book, have the child hold the book with one hand and turn the pages with the other. Cardboard or plastic books are easiest and the most durable for young children. Sing songs with hand motions such as "Itsy Bitsy Spider" and "The Wheels on the Bus" to encourage two hand use.

Tips and Hints

If the child prefers to use one hand more than the other when quite young, encourage the non-preferred hand to be more active by tapping, gently shaking, or massaging it often; children under a year generally do not show a strong hand preference.

For children with a strong hand preference and a strong nonpreferred side, provide opportunities for the nonpreferred hand to hold objects for the preferred hand to manipulate. This is much easier than having the dominant hand hold and the nonpreferred hand manipulating.

Rattles that have moving parts often encourage a young child to hold with one hand and manipulate with the other.

Empty plastic spice bottles are often a good size for toddlers to hold and are useful for emptying and filling as well as putting on and taking off lids, all two-handed activities.

BANGING OBJECTS AND CLAPPING

Children first bang objects on a surface such as a high chair tray, and later, after being able to hold a toy in each hand, they bang objects together. Generally, clapping occurs around the same time as banging objects together at mid-line.

Fine Motor

Importance: Banging objects on a surface and at mid-line helps a child learn about cause and effect and is a fun way to practice gaining control of the upper body and of coordination of the eyes and hands. Clapping is a fine motor skill that has great social consequence as the child cheers for him- or herself and for others to show approval and pride.

How to Incorporate into Routines:

Playtime: Provide blocks, rattles, plastic containers, small boxes, and similar household objects for children to bang. Clapping can be modeled and encouraged during all routines to show happiness and praise. Clapping can be done with songs that are sung or listened to. Give the child lids to pots and pans to bang to music when sitting, walking, or marching.

Tips and Hints

Children with hemiplegia or who have a brachial plexus injury often move their dominant hand toward the nonpreferred hand when banging and clapping. Gently holding the dominant hand may facilitate movement of the nonpreferred hand toward the dominant hand.

POKING AND POINTING

Poking and pointing involve isolating the index finger. Children usually first begin to use their index fingers to poke (often in their mouths and noses!) and then later to point. When they first begin using their index fingers they don't tuck their other fingers, but as their skills progress, the index finger extends while the thumb and other fingers flex or tuck into the palm.

Importance: Isolating the index finger to poke and point helps develop motor coordination for activities such as picking up small items, activating toys with buttons, and, later, buttoning clothing. Though the ability to isolate the index finger is a fine motor skill, using the index finger to point is also an important component of communication. Pointing for communication involves showing and requesting.

How to Incorporate into Routines:

Bath Time: Have the child point to the body part for you to wash next.

Book Time: Have the child point to pictures you name as well as to pictures he or she wants you to talk about.

Mealtime/Snack Time: Give the child a small container or a cleaned foam egg carton with bits of cereal or other finger food in them to encourage the index finger to scoop out the food. Hold out choices of food or drink for the child to point to in order to make a selection.

Playtime: Provide empty containers such as plastic bottles with relatively narrow openings and playfully help the child isolate his or her index finger and place it into the opening, making a silly noise. Provide pudding or ketchup for finger painting and show the child how to draw with the index finger. Sing a modified version of "Where Is Thumbkin?" changing the words to "where is pointer?" until a child can isolate the other fingers and thumb, a later developing skill. Ask the child to point to your nose, playfully saying "beep-beep" to motivate the child to do this again.

Photo 8.3.

Tips and Hints

Children who have Down syndrome often use their thumbs to point and sometimes need physical assistance (gently holding fingers, except for the index, into a fist while extending the index finger) to help them learn to isolate their index fingers.

CONTAINER PLAY

Container play involves first taking out and then putting in.

Importance: Container play helps a child practice grasp and release and is the beginning of cleaning up, putting shapes in a shape sorter, and putting pieces in a puzzle.

How to Incorporate into Routines:

Bath Time: Provide empty plastic bottles, plastic bowls and cups, colanders, spoons, and ladles for filling and pouring.

Diapering and Dressing: Have the child help put dirty clothes in the hamper, wet diapers in the trash can, and clean clothes in the drawer.

Household Activities: Have the child help clean up at the end of activities or at the end of the day, putting items in bins, boxes, bowls, and other containers.

Mealtime/Snack Time: Give the child small containers to put small bits of cereal or other foods into.

Fine Motor

Playtime: Containers such as bowls, pots and pans, plastic storage containers, and empty spice containers make great toys to fill and dump.

Tips and Hints

Some children are hesitant to put their hands into deep containers, so it is beneficial to use shallow ones to encourage them to take things out. Piling many items into deeper containers such as bowls can be helpful, especially if favorite or desired objects are put on the top. Once children are good at taking items out of shallow and deep containers they then begin to put items in.

At first children put in and take out repeatedly, and then they begin to put in many items before taking any out. Initially children need large openings such as bowls and pots, but later they progress to being able to put objects into containers with small openings.

Empty milk jugs, juice bottles, or detergent bottles are great for filling. Small, thin items such as pieces of straws are easier to put in the holes than larger items such as clothespins, unsharpened pencils, or long straws, as the latter group requires more motor coordination and planning.

Many toddlers enjoy filling and dumping. For children who put items in their mouths, use dry cereal, and for children who do not, try dried beans, rice, popcorn, and/or raw pasta under close supervision. Children can use their hands, or if they are ready to use utensils, provide a spoon. Some toddlers who are easily overstimulated find this activity to be calming.

Having a small container for unwanted bites of food often stops a child from throwing items on the floor.

Some children are hesitant to touch modeling dough. Many children who do not want to play with it often are willing to clean it up and put it back in the container. This is often a good first step to feeling comfortable playing with it.

TAKING APART AND PUTTING TOGETHER

Children first are able to take toys apart and later put them together.

Importance: Children develop eye–hand coordination, visual-perceptual skills, and understanding of size relationships by taking apart and putting together objects. See the section in Appendix A called "Substitutions: Using Common Household Items Instead of Bringing Toys."

How to Incorporate into Routines:

Household Activities: During meal preparation, have the child sit at the table, highchair, or booster seat and help open and clothes lids of containers needed, such as taking the lid off the butter or margarine tub.

Mealtime/Snack Time: Have the child put lids on ketchup bottles, plastic storage containers, and other similar items.

Playtime: Provide various sizes of plastic containers with lids and shoeboxes with tops; provide toys that go together easily such as those with hook and loop fasteners, progressing to toys that easily slide together and then to toys that snap together. If the child scribbles using markers, have him or her help put the cap on when finished with each one. Provide the child with two nesting bowls, measuring cups, and boxes to fit one inside the other, and, as skills increase, increase the number of items to be nested.

Tips and Hints

When children have difficulty putting together toys and household objects, the EI provider must carefully look at the child's strengths and needs to figure out the cause, as these activities have many prerequisites, including eye–hand coordination, bilateral hand coordination, visual perception, and planning and moving the body in order to solve problems (motor problem solving).

Taking apart toys comes before putting them together. Many families have some commercially available toys, and the progression usually seen is that children initially take apart items starting with pulling rings off a ringstack, pulling apart pop-beads, and pulling apart interlocking blocks. After they are good at taking things apart, the progression of putting toys back together usually involves putting rings on the ringstack and putting together blocks that easily slide together and need little manipulation to line up the two pieces. Strength is a factor that may need to be addressed if children have difficulty pulling apart or pushing together.

For children who have difficulty stacking blocks, use small cans such as those containing tuna. As one clever mother did, cut a picture into four pieces and adhere each piece to a can so a picture appears once the cans are stacked (see Photo 8.4).

Puzzles are often a favorite of children who have strong visual skills. Children first take pieces out of puzzles and then are able to put them in. Successful puzzle completion is dependent on many variables, including the shape, size, and number of the pieces, whether there is a matching picture on the board, and the child's grasping patterns. The more irregularly shaped the pieces, the more difficult they are to place. For example, circles are easier to fit into the puzzle because they do not need to be turned a certain way. Young children typically progress from having the ability to complete a simple puzzle, such as a circle in a formboard, to puzzles with other shapes and simple familiar pictures with matching pictures, to irregularly shaped pieces without matching pictures, and finally to interlocking pieces with increasing numbers of pieces. Once a child memorizes where the pieces fit, the opportunities for motor problem solving decrease. In addition, the child's grasping patterns should be matched with the puzzle. For example, a child who is not yet using a pincer grasp will likely have difficulty using a puzzle with tiny knobs.

Success with shape sorters also follows a developmental progression. First children are able to insert circular objects, as no orientation is needed. The more irregularly shaped the piece, the more it needs to be turned correctly. The more slots to choose from, the more visual discrimination is needed. The more sides to the shape sorter, the more sequencing is needed.

Nesting is another skill that necessitates a lot of motor problem solving and also involves cognitive skills. The child must have a sense of size in addition to being able to sequence the motor acts of placing the cups, boxes, or figures inside each other. Because of their regular shape, cups are easiest, and the fewer the number of pieces, the easier the task.

PREWRITING

Prewriting skills progress from imitating making marks; scribbling; imitating circular, vertical, and horizontal strokes; and making circles and crosses or *ts*.

Importance: Prewriting skills are the foundation for learning to write one's name, the letters of the alphabet, and words. Opportunities to use a variety of writing tools help develop the hand skills and eye–hand coordination needed for a mature grasp needed for good handwriting. When experimenting with writing, children often begin to establish a hand preference and practice using two hands together with one hand holding the paper and the other hand "writing." Coloring and drawing are independent activities that many children find rewarding as they get older.

Photo 8.4.

How to Incorporate into Routines:

Bath Time: Put liquid soap, soap finger paint, or foam soap on the side of the tub for the child to draw with, using the index finger. Model circular scribbles, lines, dots, and other simple figures for the child to imitate.

Playtime: Place pudding, ketchup, and other foods on a cookie sheet, on the highchair or booster seat tray, or on another safe surface and show the child how to make dots, lines, and circles. Use action words while modeling for the child to help with imitation. For example, say "dot, dot, dot" while modeling dots, "around, and around, and around" while modeling circular scribble, and "down, down, down" when modeling vertical lines to give the child extra cues to help master the activity. Use chunky chalk, markers, paint brushes, and crayons progressing to thinner ones as hand skills improve to help develop control of the small muscles in the hands. Provide large surfaces at first and progress to smaller ones as the child gains more coordination and control. Give the child opportunities to paint cardboard boxes with water.

Tips and Hints

For children who do not show an interest in using crayons or markers, it is sometimes helpful to add more sensory feedback to the activity by putting the paper on top of corrugated cardboard. As the child scribbles, he or she feels the bumps, which may add motivation. Vibrating pens also help some reluctant scribblers.

Give children a variety of pencils, pens, chalk, and crayons to teach them how to regulate the amount of pressure needed for different writing implements.

TEARING AND CUTTING

Tearing paper requires using two hands and helps to develop the skills needed for cutting with scissors. Once young children are ready for blunt, small scissors, they first make little snips on the edge of paper, then are able to cut across a piece of paper, and finally can cut on a short, bold line.

Importance: Cutting paper requires coordinated use of two hands, and as children reach preschool and elementary school they need more advanced eye–hand coordination to cut shapes and pictures.

How to Incorporate into Routines:

Mealtime/Snack Time: When making a salad, give the child lettuce to tear.

Playtime: Provide newspaper or paper for recycling for the child to tear and put into a basket or box. For older toddlers, try cutting modeling dough and heavier paper such as cardstock. Some toddlers enjoy helping to cut out coupons and pictures, but they don't yet have the skills to do so very accurately.

Tips and Hints

For toddlers who are having difficulty snipping with scissors, using a small pair of tongs such as toaster tongs to pick up objects to release into a container. This practices using the same hand movements as scissors but takes less precision and coordination.

HAND PREFERENCE AND HAND DOMINANCE

Children begin to use one hand more than the other after much experience with reaching, grasping, and manipulating using both hands. Fagard and Marks (2000) discuss how the research literature as to when hand dominance develops is quite diverse and contradictory due to factors such as the difficulty in measuring the trait.

Importance: Using both hands together is necessary for many activities, and as children develop it is important that one hand becomes more skilled than the other. There are some individuals who are truly ambidextrous, but there are some who don't develop a hand preference due to difficulties crossing the midline of their body. Very young children (younger than 1 year) should not show a strong hand preference, as this indicates a lack of regard for one hand and/or difficulty with its coordination. Some children frequently switch hands when one hand gets tired.

How to Incorporate into Routines:

Playtime: Place toys to the child's left and right. When the child is playing on the floor, encourage rolling and reaching to both sides. After the child is able to sit independently, as before, place toys to the left and to the right. In addition, place toys in the center to encourage the child to make a decision of which hand to use.

Mealtime/Snack Time: Place food directly in front of your child as well as to the sides. If the child is beginning to use a spoon, place the spoon in the middle of the tray or eating surface to encourage him or her to select a hand regardless of which one is closer.

Fine Motor

Tips and Hints

If a child neglects one hand, he or she should be encouraged to use the nonpreferred side as much as possible by placing items to the side the child does not use as frequently. When the child is eating, playing, or participating in other motivating activities, gently hold the preferred hand for gradually increasing time increments so he or she will have success using the nonpreferred hand.

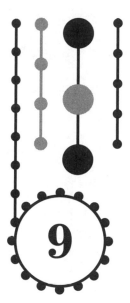

Self-Care/Adaptive Skills

9

Adaptive skills in this book refer to self-help skills that are relevant to infants and toddlers. These include eating and drinking, dressing, hygiene, and sleeping. Eating skills in infancy and toddlerhood progress from sucking successfully to taking food from the spoon. Children first eat smooth purees, then purees of more texture and mashed foods. They progress to ground and chopped textures and then to finger foods; the latter require a child to have enough eye–hand coordination to move the food from a surface to the mouth and enough coordination of the oral structures to successfully chew and swallow. Many children in EI have difficulties making the transition to solid foods due to a motor coordination problem, sensory challenges, a history of medical problems such as gastroesophageal reflux, or a combination of these. Having a child who does not eat as expected is very challenging for many parents, as it is very stressful when a child does not easily participate in an activity that is so fundamental to bonding and to sustaining life. When working with children who have eating challenges, it is imperative that the process be positive for the parents and the child.

EI providers who address eating and drinking should be very familiar with signs of aspiration and should coach parents and caregivers to implement techniques to ensure the chin is pointed slightly downward when the child is presented with food and drink. Aspiration occurs when food or liquid enters the airway, and its signs can include coughing, gagging, wheezing, bouts of pneumonia, color changes around the eyes, watering eyes, apnea, and/or a wet vocal quality (Weir, McMahon, Barry, Masters, & Chang, 2009). If signs of aspiration occur, it is necessary for medical specialists to be consulted quickly to ensure the health of the child.

Undressing and dressing skills are often not a high priority for families; however, when children assist they have opportunities to develop greater independence. Many children who tend to resist dressing and undressing become much more cooperative when they actively participate. Dressing and undressing routines can be used for many language opportunities. In addition, dressing and undressing routines are influenced by sensory and motor processing skills as well as social factors. These routines can be used to facilitate motor sequencing, body awareness, and social interaction.

Sleeping, like eating, is a very important aspect of a family's daily routine. Sleep deprivation in children and in adults can have serious consequences, ranging from mood and behavioral changes to learning difficulties (Jan et al. 2008). Many excellent resources are available to help children get to sleep and stay asleep. There are methods for parents who want to avoid crying at bedtime (Pantley, 2002, 2005) as well as more traditional methods that accept crying as a possible part of the process (Ferber, 2006), and those somewhere between on this continuum (Waldurger & Spivack, 2008;

West & Kenen, 2010). EI providers should be aware of such resources in order to support parents in this very important routine.

When one looks at developmental checklists and assessments, there is quite a bit of discrepancy between expectations regarding toilet training. As Choby and George (2008) discuss, there have been changes over the years in expectations regarding when toilet training should be initiated. Societal changes and cultural trends have greatly affected this milestone. Though many sources discuss readiness signs, including removing clothes, walking, following directions, and verbalizing the need to use the bathroom, many children who have difficulties with those skills are successfully toilet trained. In order to be toilet trained a child must first demonstrate the ability to stay dry for several hours at a time. This is the first and foremost prerequisite to being toilet trained. Until a child is neurologically able to do this, he or she will not be successfully trained. Another important step is being willing to sit on the potty or toilet and then making the connection that the bladder and the bowels are emptied while there. At first, most children void when taken to the bathroom and later initiate that they need to use the bathroom. Many children are able to stay dry during the day but continue to use diapers at night for longer periods of time.

There are few hygiene skills expected of infants and young toddlers, but they are an important part of a child's daily routine. Young children get their hands wiped or washed, their teeth brushed, and their noses wiped often, and as with dressing, participation in these routines lead to increased independence and are also a vehicle for embedding language, motor, cognitive, and social skills.

This chapter contains milestones in the area of self-care/adaptive skills. Each of the skills and its importance is discussed. Ways to facilitate the skill's development in daily routines and activities are offered, and tips and hints to support development are presented. The language used is that which an EI provider would say to parents and caregivers in order to coach and support them.

SUCKING ON THE BOTTLE, BREAST, AND PACIFIER

Sucking from the bottle or breast involves using the lips, tongue, cheeks, and jaw to draw liquid into the mouth.

Importance: Successfully drinking formula or breast milk requires coordination of sucking, swallowing, and breathing. Being able to keep a pacifier in the mouth also requires coordination of the lips, tongue, and cheeks. Infants and young children often suck on a pacifier or other object to help them attain or maintain a calm, relaxed state.

How to Incorporate into Routines:

Mealtime/Snack Time: Provide a quiet, calm environment so the child can concentrate on sucking the bottle, breast, or pacifier. As skills improve, expose the child to more distractions so he or she learns to eat in a variety of environments.

Playtime: Provide a variety of safe objects on which the child can suck—washcloths, rattles, teethers, or a caregiver's clean finger.

Tips and Hints

Holding the child while rocking rhythmically, as in a rocking chair, may help establish a pattern that is helpful for a child whose suck is somewhat disorganized or for a child who needs some help being calm.

For children who are not able to take liquids by mouth, sucking on a pacifier during tube feedings is recommended so the child associates sucking with satisfying his or her hunger. If the child is able to have oral feedings in the future, the correlation will be already established. In addition, the oral stimulation of sucking and having objects in the mouth is beneficial for children who do not have a medical reason that precludes oral stimulation.

HOLDING THE BOTTLE

Holding the bottle first occurs in a semireclined position; holding the bottle while sitting upright is mastered later.

Importance: Holding the bottle is one of the first milestones toward independence.

How to Incorporate into Routines:

 Mealtime/Snack Time: Place the child's hands on the bottle and gradually decrease your support.

Tips and Hints

Some children have the physical ability to hold the bottle but resist doing so. It is often helpful to pause momentarily before placing the nipple into the mouth, as often the child will grab the bottle and pull the nipple into the mouth. Also, occasionally playfully interrupting the sucking and pulling the bottle out after the child has taken enough of the liquid to get rid of the intense hunger encourages some children to place their hands on the bottle to pull it back in. When this occurs, barely support the bottle and then let go to see if the child holds it independently.

If the child has difficulty holding the bottle while sitting up, form a wedge with a blanket or pillows so he or she will be successful. Gradually place more and more support under the head so the child will be more upright over time. This technique should be used under supervision to ensure safety and so help can be provided if needed.

MAKING THE TRANSITION FROM PUREES TO TABLE FOOD

Making the transition from purees to table food begins with soft mushy foods and progresses until the child is eating most of the textures and foods that the rest of the family is eating.

Importance: The transition from baby food to table food involves many new skills, including learning to accept new textures in the mouth and learning to chew, which involves coordinating the jaw, lips, tongue, and cheeks. A list of ideas of foods to try and more information about the progression of foods can be found in the "Progression of Drink and Food" section in Appendix A.

How to Incorporate into Routines:

Mealtime/Snack Time: When introducing new foods, first try a tiny amount. As the child accepts the new taste and/or texture, gradually increase the size of the bite, keeping in mind the size of the child's mouth and avoiding amounts that are too large. As the child begins to accept these thicker textures, try new textures by fork-mashing preferred foods. After the child accepts more textures, try tiny pieces of easily dissolvable foods, placing them at first on the chewing surface (where the molars are or will be) so the child does not need to move the food from the center of the mouth to the side. Once he or she has mastered this, present the pieces to the middle of the mouth.

Tips and Hints

To increase the texture of the foods from thin to thick, use baby cereal or cracker crumbs.

Many children do not tolerate mixed textures (lumps in purees) when first making the transition from purees. When given a mixed texture, they often swallow and are unaware the food was different, which results in the hidden lump triggering a gag and/or cough. Some children quickly learn to accept mixed textures, whereas others will do well with purees and those foods that need to be chewed but not the combination. Frequently, children make a transition to many solids before accepting mixed textures.

To help a child learn to accept new flavors and new textures, present a new food followed by a bite of a preferred food.

For a child who is very sensitive to changes, first set a goal of one or two bites of a new food at a given meal or snack and gradually increase the goal.

For children who tend to put too much in their mouths, place only one or two items in front of them until they are able to successfully manage larger portions.

Be aware of the signs of aspiration, including coughing, watery eyes, and changes in respiration or color. Should these signs be observed on more than one occasion or if the first occasion appears serious, the child's physician should be notified immediately.

Some children are more likely to try new foods when they are presented in a new situation such as in a restaurant, on a picnic, or from someone else's plate. Though the child needs to learn to eat as part of the typical routine, a change of scenery can be helpful for broadening experiences.

FINGER FEEDING AND TAKING BITES

Finger feeding involves picking up small bits of food and putting them into the mouth. Taking bites occurs when a child takes bites from food that is held for him or her and later when he or she brings larger pieces of food to the mouth, takes a bite of food, chews, swallows, and then takes another bite.

Importance: Finger feeding and taking bites of larger pieces of food are important milestones in independence with feeding. These skills involve coordination of grasp and release; control of the jaw, lips, and tongue; and judgments about how much to put in the mouth and when to take another bite.

How to Incorporate into Routines:

Mealtime/Snack Time: Place in front of the child one or two small bits of a type of food that the child has successfully eaten while being fed. He or she may instantly attempt to pick them up and put them in the mouth. If the child has difficult picking up the items, stabilize the forearm on the table or tray and, if needed, stabilize his or her wrist to help him or her use the fingers (see Photo 8.3). It will be easier for the child to release small bits into the mouth if you hand the child the food in the fingertips, as he or she will be more likely to use a pincer grasp. Larger pieces of food are easier to pick up than tiny bits, but it is important not to try larger pieces until the child is safely eating them when fed.

Tips and Hints

At first, very young children may need portion control—just giving them one or a few pieces at a time to ensure they don't stuff too much in their mouths.

Sometimes it is necessary to experiment with the size of the piece given to the child. If pieces are relatively small, the child may tend to put the whole piece in the mouth instead of taking bites. Larger pieces of food are easier to pick up than tiny bits, but it is important not to try larger pieces until the child is safely eating that size when fed. If a child generally needs a lot of sensory input before sensations are noticed (underreactive or has low muscle tone), he or she may be more likely to stuff or pocket food.

Handing the child the food from your fingertips will encourage the child to use a pincer grasp, which will facilitate an easier release into the mouth than a grasp that results in the food being stuck in the palm (see Photo 8.2).

When first having the child take bites of food held for him or her, place your thumb as a stop to mark where the child should take a bite. For example, when holding a cookie or a piece of banana, hold the food so there is about one quarter to one half inch of food beyond your index finger and thumb. If the child tries to take a large bite, he or she will "run into" your thumb and not be able to bite off a piece that is too large.

Verbal cues, hand-over-hand assistance, and/or portion control may be needed until the child safely takes the correct size bites or until he or she does not stuff too much in the mouth.

UTENSIL USE

Most toddlers use a spoon before a fork, but some children enjoy the challenge of stabbing food more than scooping and use a fork before the spoon.

Importance: Utensils are one of the first tools that young children use independently. The use of utensils requires eye–hand coordination and further improves eye–hand coordination through practice.

How to Incorporate into Routines:

Mealtime/Snack Time: With the child holding the spoon, loosely grasp his or her hand and help guide the spoon into a bowl to scoop, but then allow the child to bring the spoon to the mouth. As the child's skills progress, decrease the help until the child is independent. The process is similar with using a fork. Help the child stab the food (many children enjoy selecting the specific piece they want to pierce) and allow him or her to bring the piece to the mouth.

Self-Care/
Adaptive

Playtime: Place a bowl, pan, or pot filled with dry cereal on the floor on an old table-cloth, towel, or shower curtain and give the child some plastic cups and a spoon to practice filling and dumping. Once children are passed the stage when they put items into their mouths during play, you may use birdseed, dried corn, dried pasta, dried beans, or sand. If the child enjoys pretend play, he or she may enjoy using a fork to poke store-bought or homemade modeling clay or dough to "feed" a stuffed animal or doll.

Tips and Hints

Learning to use the spoon is easiest with sticky foods such as yogurt, pudding, and applesauce.

Choose a fork that fits the child's mouth and one that is not too sharp and not too dull so it is safe, but not too frustrating for the child when he or she is stabbing the food!

For children who have challenges with motor control, oral motor skills often show less coordination when they attempt to self-feed as compared to when they are fed. The child's drive for independence must be balanced with facilitating quality of movement and safety.

CUP DRINKING

Children should first learn to take sips from a cup held for them before drinking from a sippy cup, because the adult can control the amount of liquid to ensure safety and appropriate oral motor skills. Once they are able to take sips from a cup held by someone else, children may drink from a sippy cup. After mastering sippy cups and showing the ability to control impulses so the liquid does not turn into a puddle on the floor, the child is ready to begin to take sips from an open cup.

Importance: Drinking from cups necessitates and facilitates coordination of the jaw, lips, and cheeks as well as the tongue. Drinking also involves a high degree of coordination of the swallowing muscles, which, when working correctly, prevent one from aspirating or "swallowing down the wrong pipe."

How to Incorporate into Routines:

Bath Time: Introduce using an open cup in the tub (as long as the child is not one who enjoys drinking the bath water). Using lukewarm water in the cup means that spills will not be a problem for children who do not like cold water on their bodies!

Grooming and Hygiene: Provide a small open cup at toothbrushing for the child to take sips and/or to rinse the mouth.

Mealtime/Snack Time: When giving the child sips from an open cup, first give one sip at a time to ensure the child coordinates the swallow without coughing and choking. If consistently successful with one sip, cautiously progress to two consecutive sips. Once the child can take several consecutive sips without coughing, he or she is ready for a sippy cup. There are many varieties of cups, and some children can use a variety while others find a certain spout to be preferred. The child should use the lips to draw in the liquid rather than placing the tongue under the spout. If the child uses his or her tongue, try a cup that has a slit rather than a spout. Once the child is successful with sippy cups, it may be time to try an open cup if the child is mature enough to not spill on purpose. Using a very small cup works best, as it will help the child learn to take small amounts and spills will be minimized.

Photo 9.1.

Tips and Hints

If a child has difficulty sucking from a cup with a nonspill valve, it works very well to remove the valve, hold the cup for the child, and give several sips, one sip at a time, and then replace the valve. If the child continues to have difficulty drawing in the liquid, remove the valve and repeat the process again.

Some children use a suckle pattern whereby the tongue is under the spout. A prolonged use of a suckle can affect the position of the teeth, chewing, and sound production (Dos Santos & Noguiera, 2005; S. E. Morris, personal communication, August, 26, 2012).

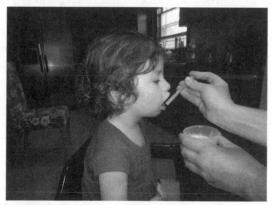

Photo 9.2.

Some sippy cups have soft, pliable spouts, and some children bite on them, which expels the liquid. It is best to attempt to find other types of spouts that facilitate a more typical drinking pattern.

For children who are very resistant to moving from the bottle to a sippy cup, try using a sippy cup in situations where the child does not typically take a bottle, such as when going for a walk and other places in the community.

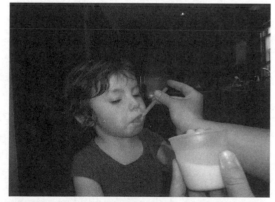

Photo 9.3.

DRINKING FROM A STRAW

Drinking from a straw involves coordinating the lips and the cheeks as well as coordinating sucking, swallowing, and breathing.

Importance: Straw drinking is another milestone marking independence in self-care skills. It helps to strengthen lip muscles and helps children gain control of muscles needed for speech and for managing saliva.

How to Incorporate into Routines:

Mealtime/Snack Time: There are several methods that may help the child gain success in learning to drink from a straw. For the first method,

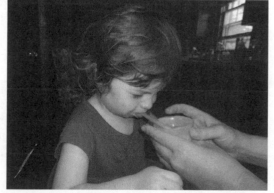

Photo 9.4.

gently hold a juice box and place the straw in the child's mouth, squeezing just enough for the liquid to move up the straw, being careful not to squeeze too much into the child's mouth. After practice, the child may learn to suck the straw. Similarly, for the second method, placing plastic tubing, which can be purchased from a hardware store's plumbing section, into a plastic squeeze bottle suitable for drinking also works for some children. The third method involves using a flexible straw or plumbing tubing about 5 inches long. Place the straw in a cup filled with the child's favorite beverage. The straw will fill with liquid to the level of the liquid in the cup. Put the tip of the index finger on the top of the straw to form a seal (Photo 9.1). Place the other end of the straw into the child's mouth, keeping the sealed end of the straw upright so gravity will cause the liquid to flow into the child's mouth once you take your finger off the opening and release the liquid (Photo 9.2). Wait until the child puts his or her lips together around the straw (keep the straw on the tips of the lips to avoid biting), allow the liquid to flow by removing your finger from the tip of the straw (Photo 9.3). Repeat this procedure many times until the child has good lip closure on the straw. If you hesitate a second, you may feel the child suck on the straw. When this happens, quickly place the end of the straw where your finger was into the cup, keeping the other end in the child's mouth (Photo 9.4). The child may then suck the liquid into the straw. If not, try the procedure again, making sure you wait for good lip closure before releasing the liquid. The child may need several days of repetition before learning to use a straw with this technique. As you teach the child to suck from the straw, make sure he or she does not get too much liquid at once, as sometimes young children aspirate, or get too much in their mouths at once, and the liquid may "go down the wrong pipe."

Tips and Hints

Once children master drinking from a straw, thickening their drinks and having them use a straw can help further strengthen mouth and cheek muscles.

Shorter straws are easiest and long, curvy straws are more difficult to suck from. Wide straws are generally easier than thin ones.

Some children need help stopping to take a breath after two sips to ensure they do not aspirate.

COOPERATING AND HELPING WITH DRESSING AND UNDRESSING

Children first cooperate with dressing by holding out their arms when presented with a sleeve and by holding out their feet when presented with pant legs, shoes, and socks. Then children actively push their limbs into the openings of shirts and pants. The same is true when a child is putting on clothes by him- or herself. Pants are much easier than shirts, though pulling up pants over the buttocks is quite a challenge for most young children!

Importance: When a child helps with dressing and undressing, the task is much easier for parents and is another step toward independence for the child.

How to Incorporate into Routines:

Diapering and Dressing: At first, help the child by putting his arm into the sleeve, but as time goes on, do less and less, and playfully ask "Where is your hand?" to encourage him or her to push the arm through the sleeve. Do the same with pants; at first help the child put the legs into the opening of the pants or shorts and over time do less and less. Pause part way through the routine to see if the child completes the step. When putting on the child's shoes and socks, pause before picking up the child's foot to see if he or she moves the foot toward the item.

Tips and Hints

Play Peekaboo as you take off and put on the child's shirt to help make dressing and undressing fun.

Singing made-up songs about dressing can also help a child cooperate. For example, singing, "This is the way we push our arms through, push our arms through, push our arms through; this is the way we push our arms through, so early in the morning" may help a child who would rather be exploring or playing!

Dressing and undressing the child sitting up rather than lying down may help the child be more active in the process.

For a child who uses one side of the body better than the other, first encourage him or her to push the limb on the side that has better motor control into the opening. After he or she is successful with this, encourage the child to push the other arm and leg through the opening.

TAKING OFF CLOTHES

Children usually undress themselves before they try to put on their clothes. Hats and bibs, followed by shoes and socks, are usually the easiest items to remove. Shorts, loose pants, and finally shirts are later-developing undressing skills. Variability in the sequence is affected by the child's motivation, physical coordination and strength, and the snugness of the clothing.

Importance: Trying to remove socks and loosened or untied shoes is often the first sign a child is interested in undressing. Some children learn to take off their clothes and love to practice this while others do not show much interest. Learning to undress involves awareness of the body, sequencing movements, and coordination.

How to Incorporate into Routines:

Bath Time: Utilize the opportunity to capture motivation for the child who loves to take a bath by playfully saying "Quick, take off your _____ so you can get in the tub" and provide the minimal amount of help to ensure success.

Diapering and Dressing: A technique called *backward chaining* is very useful when teaching a child to help with undressing. When doing backward chaining, first do all the steps for the child except the last one, which the child then does. When the child masters the last step, do everything except the last two steps, then the last three, and so on. For example, when using this method to help a child take off socks, take off the socks almost all the way, leaving them on the toes. The child then removes the socks from the toes. Do this a few times to ensure the child is successful, then take off the socks just over the heels, and have the child take off the socks from the foot. Once that is mastered, push the socks to the heel and help the child hook his or her thumb into the sock and have him or her pull it over the heel and off the foot and toes. The last step would be completely taking off the sock. This technique is very helpful when teaching a child to remove each item of clothing.

Mealtime/Snack Time: After the child is done eating, unfasten the bib and tell the child to hand it to you.

Playtime: Playfully put bracelets on the child's arms and legs to entice him or her to slide them off, a fun way to practice the movements needed for undressing. Similarly, playfully putting large socks on the child's arms and legs can be a fun way to get ready for undressing skills.

Tips and Hints

To decrease frustration, encourage undressing when clothing items are fairly loose fitting. It is helpful to have the child sit on your lap when helping to take off shoes and socks, as the child's hands can easily be guided.

For a child who has difficulties with balance, have the child sit against a wall when he or she is undressing.

PUTTING ON CLOTHES

Putting on clothes is much more difficult than taking off clothes for most children, and in the early years children typically assist but are not independent in dressing. If children try to put on clothes by themselves, they often have pants on backward and shoes on the wrong feet.

Importance: Helping with portions of dressing gives practice for upcoming independence in later years.

How to Incorporate into Routines:

Community Outings: When getting ready to go out in chilly weather, have the child put on his or her hat and jacket. Over time, decrease the help by providing fewer and fewer physical and verbal cues.

Diapering and Dressing: When dressing your child, have him or her help with many of the steps. For example, when putting on the child's pants, pause and tell him or her to "Put in your foot." After both feet are in, tell the child to stand up, you pull up the pants most of the way, and then have the child pull the pants up the rest of the way (backward chaining). Giving verbal directions throughout the process helps with language skills as well as dressing skills. Over time, as the child progresses, decrease both physical assistance and verbal cues to help him or her become more independent.

Playtime: Give the child bracelets to put on and take off arms and legs to practice the movements and to help develop body awareness. Playing dress-up with larger clothing items can be a fun way to practice dressing skills: provide Dad's hats, Mom's shoes, or an older sibling's shirt to encourage pretend play as well as the motor movements needed for dressing.

Tips and Hints

It is helpful to have the child sit on your lap when helping him or her put on shoes and socks, as the child's hands can easily be guided.

Providing help but pausing frequently is a good way to see if the child is beginning to learn new steps in the sequence of dressing.

For a child who has difficulty with balance, have the child sit with his or her back against a wall when putting on clothes.

WASHING HANDS AND FACE, WIPING NOSE, AND HELPING WITH BATHING

Washing hands often begins with playing in water at the sink or wiping the hands on a napkin or baby wipe at meal time after eating something sticky and progressing to attempting to truly wash hands. Many young children do not like having their faces wiped but will gladly help do it themselves, though at first they do not do so very thoroughly. The same is seen with wiping the nose. Many children initially resist this, then help by wiping and later blowing their noses. Children often enjoy helping to wash a few body parts in the tub at a young age.

Importance: Washing and wiping the face and hands and wiping the nose are early milestones in independence in hygiene.

How to Incorporate into Routines:

Bath Time: Ask the child to wash one or two easily reached body parts and gradually increase expectations.

Mealtime/Snack Time: Take the child to the sink or provide a washcloth or wipe before mealtime or snack time and afterward if the child's hands are messy. After a meal, give the child a small mirror and ask him or her to wipe his face, providing help if needed.

Playtime: Incorporate washing, wiping, and bathing into pretend play with a play partner or with dolls or plastic animals.

Tips and Hints

Some children love messy play while others do not. Having a paper towel or washcloth within reach helps the reluctant child interact with sticky substances and also encourages beginning hygiene skills.

Adapt such songs as "If You're Happy and You Know It" to include verses such as "wash your hands" and "wipe your nose" to facilitate pretend play and to give practice for the needed motor patterns.

Self-Care/
Adaptive

For children who fuss during face wiping, always cue them before wiping by using a gesture and a statement such as "time to wipe your face." Count to 10 during wiping, always stopping at 10 so the child knows when you will be finished.

BRUSHING TEETH

Oral hygiene begins with parents and caregivers rubbing the gums and new teeth and progressing to using a toothbrush. Very young children then begin to use the toothbrush themselves, but in order to properly clean the teeth, adults still need to take a turn.

Importance: Proper care of the teeth is necessary for dental and overall health and is an important hygiene skill that gets started in early childhood and is necessary for the life span.

How to Incorporate into Routines:

Grooming and Hygiene: Provide a soft toothbrush and brush the child's teeth. Have the child help, telling him or her to move the brush to the different areas of the mouth, providing touch and verbal cues.

Playtime: Incorporate toothbrushing into pretend play. Have the child take turns brushing a stuffed animal's or doll's teeth and brushing his or her own teeth.

Tips and Hints

It is often helpful to brush a few strokes and then pause so the child can swallow.

For those children who do not readily accept toothbrushing, it is helpful to sing a particular song (such as "This is the way we brush the teeth, brush the teeth, brush the teeth"), always stopping at the end of the song. For children who find brushing teeth very aversive, it is often helpful to count to 10, always stopping on 10 so the routine is predictable. As the child's tolerance increases, the counting can be slowed so the time of brushing is extended.

Caregivers should check with their dentist for recommendations as to when to begin using toothpaste rather than just water on the brush.

TOILET TRAINING

Toilet training is a process that depends on both physical and emotional readiness. Before a child is ready to be toilet trained, he or she needs to stay dry for several hours at a time. Though bowel control often happens before bladder control, many children urinate on the toilet or potty before they have a bowel movement in the toilet or potty. Many children will use the toilet when taken but do not initiate the need to use the toilet until they are older.

Importance: Toilet training is a milestone that is very important to most parents. Many parents feel pressure from others about toilet training. It is important to remember that a child must show the physical readiness signs to be successful. Toilet training is quite different in different cultures. The accepted time of toilet training has changed over the years, and many times children are not toilet trained until they are 3 years old.

How to Incorporate into Routines:

Playtime: Incorporating toileting in pretend play with a stuffed animal or doll is a way to introduce and talk about toilet training.

Tips and Hints

If other family members are comfortable using the bathroom in the presence of the young child, this can be a helpful way to introduce toilet training.

Children should feel secure when sitting on the toilet or potty, and for most this means using an insert on the toilet or a potty that fits them well.

To help a child become accustomed to sitting on the potty or toilet, one can count to 10 very quickly and then tell the child he or she is done and may get up. As time goes on, count more slowly to increase the time on the potty.

Having routines such as sitting briefly on the toilet or potty before getting into the tub or before brushing teeth can help establish patterns. Some children like to look at books or sing favorite songs while sitting.

Most children first urinate in the toilet or potty accidentally and then associate the necessary muscle control with the task.

NAPPING

Infants and young children sleep varying amounts during the day, depending on their age. Newborns typically sleep much of the day, and as time goes on babies nap several times a day and progress to taking only one nap a day as toddlers.

Importance: Napping is necessary for young children because there are not enough hours in the night for them to get the amount of sleep necessary.

How to Incorporate into Routines: To help children develop good sleep routines, there are several factors to consider. First, basic needs must be met in order for the child to be comfortable so he or she can relax. Children who are hungry, thirsty, or wet do not sleep well. The environment is important, and naps will be most successful if after active play there is a period of lower stimulation activities such as quiet rocking, reading, and so forth. Lighting should be dim, noises should be at a minimum, and ideally, when at home, the child should nap in the same room where he or she sleeps at night. It is important that young children learn to put themselves to sleep without the aid of a parent or caregiver so that they can learn to put themselves back to sleep during normally occurring awakenings.

Tips and Hints

There are many resources for parents and caregivers to assist with sleeping difficulties. There are differing styles of strategies, including methods where children learn to self-soothe, which may involve crying for short periods of time, as well as those that do not involve letting the child cry.

SLEEPING THROUGH THE NIGHT

Newborns and very young infants typically wake up to eat during the night, but as time goes on babies are expected to sleep through the night.

Importance: Learning to sleep through the night is a skill important to the child's health as well as that of the parents' and caregivers'.

How to Incorporate into Routines: Children should fall asleep within a short period of time after going to bed, and once they are past the age and weight of needing nighttime feedings they should sleep through the night unless sick or uncomfortable. Having a good sleep routine is important to set the stage for a good night's sleep. Active play should stop before the bedtime routine begins, and calm, relaxing activities should set the stage for going to bed. Children should have consistent routines that signal bedtime is coming, which may include having a small snack, brushing teeth, looking at books, and singing relaxing songs. It is important that the child be put into bed awake or he or she will develop the dependence that makes intervention in the night necessary.

Tips and Hints

As there are for napping, there are many resources for parents and caregivers to assist with sleeping difficulties. There are differing styles of strategies, including methods where children learn to self-soothe, which may involve crying for short periods of time, as well as those that do not involve letting the child cry.

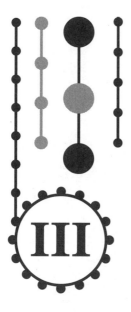

Daily Routines Across Domains

Infants and toddlers participate in many routines and activities throughout their typical weeks. In this section of the book, eight of these routines and activities are highlighted in the following subsections and tables: book time, taking a walk, at the playground, grocery shopping, riding in the car, diapering and dressing, taking a bath, and playing independently when parents and caregivers are busy. In contrast to Section II, which shows how a specific skill can be practiced in a variety of routines, this section exemplifies how many skills from all domains can be facilitated in a given routine regardless of the child's developmental level.

These tables show *approximate* age levels for the various skills and may help EI providers gain an understanding of the developmental sequences; however, they should not be used as age equivalents. For children whose development is progressing at approximately the same rate in each domain, skills to be targeted will fall at approximately the same age levels, whether the age level matches the child's own or not. For example, for the child who has an outcome related to using first words, the tables provide ideas for ways to facilitate this skill in the various routines. Because skill development in many children in EI is uneven, meaning their developmental profiles show relative strengths in some domains and weaknesses in others, these tables can be used to help target skills at various developmental levels in several areas simultaneously. For example, a child may have outcomes related to both learning to sit and making choices, skills that emerge at different times in typical development. The EI provider can use the tables to garner ideas to facilitate both of these skills during the various routines, such as when taking a walk or when grocery shopping.

BOOK TIME

Table III.1. Daily routines across domains: book time

Approx. dev. age level	Behavior regulation and social skills	Cognitive/receptive language skills	Expressive language skills	Gross motor skills	Fine motor skills	Self-care/adaptive skills
Birth to 4 months	**Being calm and regulated:** Read aloud using a slow, soothing voice. Rocking slowly may calm an upset infant or toddler. **Initiating and maintaining eye contact:** Hold the child closely or place in an infant seat and read short books, pausing now and then to see if the child looks at you.		**Cooing and vocalizing:** Allow the infant to hold a soft book that can be mouthed. Use a sing-song voice and talk about the book. Pause to wait for the child to make sounds back to you.	**Tummy time/ sidelying:** Lie or sit on the floor while holding the book for the child to see as you read.	**Visual fixation and attention/ visual tracking:** Hold a colorful book in front of the child. Slowly move it to encourage the child to follow it as it moves horizontally and vertically.	
4–8 months	**Gaining attention:** Read aloud and pause, waiting to see if the child uses his or her body or voice to get your attention.			**Sitting:** Provide as little support as needed to the child while you read to him or her. Have him or her sit in a seat, between your legs, in the corner of a sofa, in a box, or against a wall if needed.		
8–14 months	**Playing social games:** Play Peekaboo hiding behind the book.	**Cause and effect and using movements to continue an activity:** Imitate actions in the book with your body and pause to see if the child takes your hand to do it again. For example, if the book is about a spider, "crawl" your fingers across the page playfully saying "crawl, crawl, crawl." Pause to see if the child takes your hand to do it again.		**Pulling to stand:** Sit on a chair or sofa and hold out the book so the child can see. Entice him or her to pull to stand to see the book. Begin reading as the child pulls to stand and continue to read as the child stands.	**Poking and pointing:** Take the child's hand and help him or her to isolate the index finger, pointing to various items in the book.	

130

Imitation of actions with objects and with the body: Imitate actions in the book or make up some of your own and tell the child, "You do." If he or she doesn't imitate you, help him or her. For example, if there is a picture of a baby in the book, tickle the baby and tell the child to "Tickle baby." If he or she doesn't initiate the action, help him or her "tickle" the picture.

Object permanence: Use a tissue, bib, or cloth to drape over the page, saying, "Uh oh! Where did the _____ go?"

Demonstrating understanding of words: Have the child find pictures of the objects you read about or talk about.

Functional use of objects: Model how to use objects that are pictured in the book. If possible, provide the actual object. For example, if the book has a picture of a brush, get your brush and model brushing your hair after you read or talk about the brush.

Following directions: Tell the child, "Go get a book," giving cues as needed to help him or her be successful. Give the child directions related to pictures in the book, such as "Kiss the baby" or "Pat the doggy," providing a model if needed. When finished reading, tell the child to put the book away.

Making choices: Hold up two books and ask the child which one he or she wants to read.

Using first words: Repeat some single words when talking about the pictures or when reading to encourage the child to imitate. Read books with a line of predictable, short language that repeats throughout the book.

Standing unsupported: Have the child stand with his or her back against a stable surface such as a wall or heavy chair. Read the book, holding it so the child can easily see the pictures. At times, move the book slightly farther away to see if the child leans or takes a step to look at or hold the book.

Walking: Read a few pages with the child standing to listen and look at the book. Move a few steps away to see if the child walks to where you moved.

Using both hands: Have the child hold the book with one hand and turn pages with the other.

14–18 months

(continued)

Table III.1. (continued)

Approx. dev. age level	Behavior regulation and social skills	Cognitive/receptive language skills	Expressive language skills	Gross motor skills	Fine motor skills	Self-care/adaptive skills
18–24 months			**Answering questions:** Ask questions about commonly associated sounds or actions when reading, such as, "What does a cow say?" If he or she does not respond, model answer. **Using different types of words/using phrases and sentences:** Repeat two- and three-word combinations to emphasize them. Use a variety of types of words including nouns, verbs, and adjectives. Model directions and questions for the child to repeat, for example, "Tell doggy, no-no!" and "Let's ask him, 'Are you okay?'"			
24–30 months		**Matching and sorting:** Have the child put away the book when finished, placing it in a box or bin with other books. **Concept development:** Have the child find named pictures. When finished reading, give directions containing prepositions such as "Put the book on the table" or "Put the book under the table or in the bookshelf." At the end of the book, say, "The end!"		**Jumping:** If reading books in which the characters are jumping or in which there are animals that can jump, model the jumping and provide any needed hand support to help the child jump.		
30–36 months	**Turn-taking and sharing:** Take turns with the child when choosing books, turning the pages, naming pictures, imitating actions, and talking about the pictures. **Testing limits/becoming independent/accepting limits:** Tell the child ahead of time that you will read a certain number of books. When finished, let your child know, "All done. No more books."	**Matching and sorting/concept development:** Have the child find pictures of a certain color, shape, or function on a page. For example, have him or her find big or little items, things to eat, or all the circles.	**Using different types of words/using phrases and sentences:** Hand the book to the child and tell him or her to read the story to you.			

SPECIAL CONSIDERATIONS

In their article "First Stories, Emergent Literacy in Infants and Toddlers," Zeece and Churchill (2001) describe the developmental progression and benefits of becoming literate. They describe first books as needing to be "touchable, bendable, and even lickable" (p. 102). Many infants and young toddlers do not have a long attention span for being read to, but they often will sit as parents and caregivers talk about the pictures using simple words and phrases. As their attention spans increase, they begin to sit and listen to the words being read to them. Using preferred subjects and familiar themes helps infants and toddlers to sit and listen. Books made from photo albums using photographs of family members, friends, pets, favorite foods, favorite toys, and special items such as blankets or stuffed animals are often great first books to help children pay attention to books and practice language skills.

For children who have difficulty turning pages due to motor coordination difficulties, adaptations can be made by using large paper clips and foam pieces glued to the pages. Internet resources are abundant for adapting books for infants and toddlers.

For children who have visual impairments, commercially available tactile or "feely" books are helpful. These can also be made by using scraps of fabric, cardboard, plastic lids, and so forth cut into pictures. Helpful guidance can be found at the web site of Tots-n-Tech: http://tnt.asu.edu.

For children who have language-processing difficulties, adapting the text of the book to simplify the reading can help them focus on the language. Using just one or two words throughout the book can help the child attend to the pictures by, for example, pointing and saying "dog!" for each picture of a dog. Reading slowly and emphasizing key words further supports comprehension. Pause between pages to give the child time to process the information.

For children with hearing impairment, reading face to face may help them by adding facial cues to the expression of the text and the content of the story. Direct the child to attend to the pictures to support the text by pointing to the pictures in the book. Pause so the child looks up at your face as well.

For children who are difficult to engage, cards with text and pictures may help them to attend. Hand the card to the child after he or she looks at it. The child can then hold the cards, collect them in a pile, or put them into a box.

Provide books with an element to manipulate, such as textured pages or flaps, to make books more alluring. Some children may have little interest in books; leaving books out in the environment may help them explore books.

Ryan was a 20-month-old with cerebral palsy. He sat with support and liked to play on his back but hated to be on his belly. Ryan was able to reach for toys in supported sitting and at times was able to grasp and briefly hold objects. Ryan used his eyes to tell his parents what he wanted, and he was able to vocalize to get attention. He inconsistently used a few vowel sounds but was unable to say any consonants. Ryan was able to look at named objects and pictures from a group of four, and he was beginning to use a picture board to communicate choices of food, movies, and toys. He loved to be read to and enjoyed picking what book he wanted. His EI provider recommended that Ryan's parents use his favorite book to increase Ryan's tolerance of being on his belly. At first they read two pages, and then they held him in their lap for the rest of the story, but over the span of a week Ryan was able to stay on his belly for the entire book. Ryan's EI provider also showed his parents how to have Ryan move his hand to named pictures, giving him support at the elbow, and having him move his hand toward large pictures they named. At first Ryan was able to reach pictures only on the bottom left side of the book, but after several weeks he was able to reach ones that were at the top of the book as well as those on the right side. As Ryan's ability to direct his hand improved, his parents were able to have Ryan touch smaller pictures that were closer together. Ryan also liked to look at books while in his stander. His EI provider showed his parents how to make a book for Ryan using a photo album with foam pieces between the pages so he could turn the pages by himself. To help

Ryan with his expressive language, the provider suggested they together make a book of animals to use when singing "Old MacDonald." The repetition of *E-I-E-I-O* gave Ryan practice of consistently producing vowel sounds during an enjoyable activity.

Brooke was a 34-month-old child who had no interest in books. Her father was concerned that she did not like to be read to, and therefore he thought she was missing lots of opportunities to build her vocabulary. The EI provider and the father talked about what Brooke did like and decided to make their own book using digital pictures. They took pictures of Brooke's five favorite toys, printed them, and laminated them at an office supply store. Then, using a hole punch, they put the pages together with metal rings to form a book. Brooke's father gave her the book when she was in the car and at night he read it to her quickly during their nighttime routine, calling it "Brooke's favorite toys." Brooke did indeed enjoy the book. The provider and the father planned to take pictures throughout an activity that Brooke performed to make another homemade book. They took pictures of her during play with her dolls, and her father narrated the book with simple sentences such as "Baby night-night" and "Brooke is holding her baby." After Brooke attended to these homemade books, her father got a book with her favorite TV character in it and read the book by pointing and saying the character's name. Brooke was able to tolerate the book reading and seemed even to enjoy it. After Brooke enjoyed this book, her father began to slowly expand its scope by putting a bit more narration into the pages. The EI provider suggested taking Brooke to the library for storytime for toddlers and seeing if peers would serve as a model for Brooke to sit and listen to a book. Because the local library augmented reading with songs and crafts, Brooke attended well to the activities. When she was allowed to pick out her own books at the library, she seemed to feel proud and happy with her choices and looked at books she chose. Brooke's father was feeling much better about her response to books and felt that he no longer needed the EI provider's help to support Brooke's enjoyment of books.

TAKING A WALK

Table III.2. Daily routines across domains: taking a walk

Approx. dev. age level	Behavior regulation and social skills	Cognitive/receptive language skills	Expressive language skills	Gross motor skills	Fine motor skills	Self-care/adaptive skills
Birth to 4 months	**Being calm and regulated:** If the child is upset or irritable, consider sensory overload and try to decrease the visual and/or auditory stimulation if possible. Stop and soothe the child. **Initiating and maintaining eye contact:** When the child is in the stroller, occasionally stop and talk and smile.		**Cooing and vocalizing:** Look into the child's eyes and make comments such as "Oooh, we are on a walk-walk-walk!" using a sing-song voice with high affect.		**Visual fixation and attention:** During the walk, show the child colorful items such as wildflowers and leaves.	
4–8 months	**Gaining attention:** Stop the stroller and see if the child tries to get your attention using his or her body movements or voice to see why you stopped, to engage you, or to tell you to move on.	**Encouraging listening and attention:** Use exclamations and intonation to alert the child when commenting about what you see and hear, such as the dogs barking, the cars honking, or the wind blowing. **Turning to name:** When handing the child items or when pointing out items of interest that you see while walking, use the child's name.	**Making vowel and early consonant sounds:** Talk to the child about what you are doing and seeing, emphasizing early developing sounds such as vowels and /p/, /m/, /b/, and /d/. Pause and wait. If the child vocalizes back, imitate his or her sounds or make another comment using these sounds.	**Sitting:** Position the child as upright as possible, using pillows, towel rolls, or foam if needed.	**Grasping:** Provide toys for the child to grasp and mouth while walking. Attach a short ribbon to toys and to the stroller to help keep them from falling or being dropped.	
8–14 months	**Playing social games:** Play Peekaboo, for example from behind the stroller, a telephone pole, or a leaf. Wave to familiar people or even animals.	**Cause and effect and using movements to continue an activity:** Playfully start a game by starting and stopping while pushing the stroller saying "Go-go-go...STOP!" Wait for the child to use his or her voice or body to indicate he or she wants to move again.	**Using gestures:** When picking the child up from the stroller ask "Up?" and wait for the child to raise his or her arms. If needed put out your hands and/or touch the child's hands. Wave to things or people you pass or greet.			**Cooperating and helping with dressing and undressing:** During colder weather when sweaters and jackets are needed, provide decreasing help so the child pushes his or her arms through the sleeves.

(continued)

135

Table III.2. *(continued)*

Approx. dev. age level	Behavior regulation and social skills	Cognitive/receptive language skills	Expressive language skills	Gross motor skills	Fine motor skills	Self-care/adaptive skills
		Demonstrating understanding of words: Use key words you think the child knows, such as "Truck!""Beep-beep," and "Doggy." Watch for him or her to turn to look. If he or she doesn't, draw attention to the person or object so the child looks.				
14–18 months		**Following directions:** While walking along, tell the child to give you named items such as a stick, a piece of grass, or a stone. If the child is in a stroller, tell him or her to look at or point to a dog, a car, or other familiar objects/people.	**Making choices:** Find opportunities to offer choices, such as which toy to hold or which shoes to wear. Hold up the available choices so the child can indicate by reaching, pointing, or naming. Affirm the choice by saying the name of the chosen item. **Using first words:** Emphasize names of common objects and familiar people you see, such as car, dog, and Daddy. Speak slowly and repeat the word to encourage imitation.	**Walking:** Hold the child's hand or have him or her push a toy or the stroller, providing resistance if necessary so the wheels do not go too fast. Progress to walking with less support such as with one hand instead of two or by holding on to the item being pushed with less force.	**Using both hands/container play:** Give the child a bucket or bag and hand him or her objects to put in.	
18–24 months		**Imitation of actions with objects and with the body:** Throughout the walk, pick up two of the same items, one for you and one for the child. Model an action with the object, such as throwing a stick and blowing on a dandelion and tell the child, "You do." Play imitation games such as waving to people, putting arms up, stomping, and blowing kisses while walking along.	**Answering questions:** Ask questions about what the child sees or what the child or others are doing. Pause, and if the child does not answer, model the needed word. **Using different types of words/using phrases and sentences:** After the child answers a question or spontaneously comments, at times expand the child's utterance by one word. For example, if he or she says, "doggy, respond by saying, "big doggy" or "doggy barking."	**Running:** Chase the child playfully on grassy surfaces or throw a ball for him or her to chase. **Ball play:** Have the child throw a ball to you, into a box, or at a tree to practice throwing with aim.		

136

24–30 months

Testing limits/ becoming independent/ accepting limits: The child may want to get out of the stroller or, if out of the stroller, may run ahead and refuse to hold an adult's hand. Give choices such as "Do you want me to carry you or do you want to hold my hand?" Or, use statements such as "Walk with me or I will carry you." For children who become upset going inside after a walk, focus on preferred items inside by saying things like "Let's go in and get a drink" or giving choices such as "Do you want to play with your trains or a puzzle when we go in?"

Turn-taking and sharing: Collect items such as leaves and stones and give some to the child. Tell the child to get you some.

Matching and sorting: Hold up an object such as a leaf or rock and have the child find one like yours.

Have the child put two different objects such as leaves and rocks into two boxes, bags, or buckets.

Following directions/ concept development: Ask for one leaf, one stone, or one jump while walking along. Have the child complete a two-step direction such as "Touch the mailbox then wave bye-bye to the squirrel."

Riding toys: Have the child sit on a riding toy and push it if the child is unable to propel it. Move the child's feet, one at a time, emphasizing "one foot, other foot."

Taking off clothes: If the child's jacket has a zipper, have the child help pull the zipper down when it is time to take it off. Pull off the first sleeve and part of the second sleeve and have the child pull the sleeve the rest of the way off. Over time, try to help a little less so gradually the child is doing more independently.

30–36 months

Pretend play: Have the child pretend to fly like a bird, bark like a dog, or deliver mail to the mailboxes.

Concept development: Present two different sizes of sticks or blades of grass and ask for the big one. If the child chooses the wrong one, say, "This is the ____ one," naming the one that you asked for.

Matching and sorting: Have the child match and sort objects by color or size, such as big stones in one bag and small ones in another or green leaves in one bucket and yellow leaves in another.

Riding toys: Help the child keep feet on the pedals of a trike and emphasize one foot then the other.

Putting on clothes: When dressing the child in a jacket with a zipper, start the zipper and have the child pull it up the rest of the way. Help put the child's jacket on and each time try to help a little less.

SPECIAL CONSIDERATIONS

For children who need help to sit, modifications to their stroller can be made using towel rolls, phone books, foam, and other materials to assist upright posture. Attaching toys to the stroller using links or ribbon that is short to avoid the possibility of strangulation helps keep toys such as teethers accessible for children who have difficulty maintaining a grasp.

For a child who has a visual impairment, the parents and caregivers should comment on what is being seen.

For a child with a hearing impairment, the parents and caregivers should provide a myriad of gestures and/or signs to augment what the child is experiencing during the walk. They should talk face to face so the child will be able to gain as much information as possible about facial gestures, movements of lips, and nonverbal cues such as smiling or frowning.

For the child who is generally hypersensitive to stimuli such as noisy environments, the parents and caregivers should look for signs of overstimulation and distress (crying or fussing) and attempt to comfort the child, move to an environment that is less distressing such as shadier or less noisy places, and gradually progress to exposing the child to more challenging surroundings.

For a child who has difficulty sitting in the stroller for short walks, parents and caregivers should be encouraged to start with the amount of time the child sits successfully without showing signs of distress (crying or fussing) and gradually increase the time and distance over several excursions.

Finally, for children who have difficulty being confined in a stroller, those who have difficulty holding hands in areas where it is not safe, and/or those who have tendencies to run away, parents and caregivers should be encouraged to balance times when the child can walk or run in enclosed, safe areas with time in the stroller or holding an adult's hand.

Joey was a 2-year-old who was working on using words to communicate his wants and needs and was beginning to match and sort in play. His understanding of language was progressing more quickly than his expressive language. He had mild weakness in his left side. His behavior was fairly typical for his age, and like other 2-year-olds he was somewhat impulsive and had a difficult time with transitions. He walked and ran and was beginning to jump, though his left-side weakness made it difficult for him to keep his feet together. He tended to use his right hand more than his left. He, his mother, and his EI provider went for a walk around the neighborhood during the session. His mother and the EI provider took along two small paper bags. As they walked, the EI provider modeled skills such as jumping over the crack in the sidewalk, and Joey tried to imitate but was unsuccessful. The provider asked the mother to hold Joey's hands to help him jump a few times. The provider then walked ahead and asked Joey to run to her, practicing impulse control and following directions. As they went down the street they saw a lot of stones and leaves in an empty lot. The provider gathered two leaves and two stones and showed Joey how to put them into bags to sort them and asked Joey and his mother to help her get more. The EI provider gave Joey one bag and gave the other to his mother so Joey had to use two hands to gather; one holding and the other manipulating. As he bent down to pick up the stones, he practiced his ability to move from standing to squatting with control. The provider coached his mother on how to provide him with visual and verbal cues to help him sort and then coached her when to decrease her cues. The EI provider asked Joey to give her one stone, which he did successfully. She then held out two stones and asked for a big one. He handed her the little one, and she then used the opportunity to teach him *big* by using multiple examples of big and little. As they returned home, the provider and the mother helped Joey make the transition into the house by offering a snack. The EI provider suggested that Joey's mother break a cookie into two pieces, one big and one little, and asked Joey which one he wants. He chose the big one, which the provider labeled as the *"big* cookie." When Joey asked for another, his mother broke the cookie in two unequal pieces and asked if he wanted the big or the little one, showing him each as she labeled their size. As expected, Joey responded "big one" and reached for the cookie.

Maria was a 15-month-old who had significant motor delays and a cortical visual impairment. She made vowel and a few consonant sounds. Maria communicated by crying and was beginning to use eye gaze to indicate what she wanted in structured situations, such as when given a choice of two foods or toys. She had a new adapted stroller and tolerated being in it for about 20 minutes at a time before she cried. Maria's grandfather, Juan, watched her during the day while her mother worked. Juan and the EI provider took a walk to help Maria learn to get used to her stroller. The EI provider noticed that Maria cried whenever they went over bumps in the sidewalk and when a noisy car went by. The provider explained to Juan that Maria may have been confused about the new feelings she was experiencing, and they experimented by telling Maria before there would be a bump. When they heard a car approaching, they prepared her by saying "Here comes a car.... Get ready, Maria." They also made a game over going over the bump and said "one, two, three, bump" so that Maria could become more comfortable with the movement. Maria soon accommodated to the noises and bumps on the walk and was smiling happily. The EI provider then began to facilitate Maria's communication skills. She was learning to use her voice and her body to request that she wanted more. The provider asked Juan to stop pushing her to see what she would do. The EI provider asked, "Maria, do you want to go?" Maria vocalized and rocked her body forward, and Juan resumed their walk. When they got home, he removed her sweater and the provider asked him to stop before he pulled off the second sleeve. Maria asked, "Give me your hand." Maria did not move her hand, so the EI provider asked Juan to tap on her hand and ask her the question again. He did, and Maria moved her hand toward him. He pulled part of the sleeve off and paused as the provider had shown him before, and Maria pulled her arm from the sleeve.

AT THE PLAYGROUND

Table III.3. Daily routines across domains: at the playground

Approx. dev. age level	Behavior regulation and social skills	Cognitive/receptive language skills	Expressive language skills	Gross motor skills	Fine motor skills	Self-care/adaptive skills
Birth to 4 months	**Being calm and regulated:** Sit on a swing and hold the child, swinging slowly and rhythmically, talking to the child in a soothing voice. **Initiating and maintaining eye contact:** Talk to the child with your face near his or hers while in the stroller, on your lap, on the slide, or on the swing **Gaining attention:** As you walk or play on equipment, look for signs such as a change in facial expressions, a vocalization, or a body movement communicating that your child wants your attention.	**Encouraging listening and attention:** Push the child's stroller or carry the child to where other children are playing so he or she can easily see and hear them. Direct speech to the child as you narrate what you see, using a sing-song voice, such as "Ooooh, they are swinging. Swing-swing."	**Cooing and vocalizing:** When the child acts excited by what he or she sees and coos or vocalizes, talk back to the child using a sing-song voice.	**Tummy time:** Place the child on a blanket so he or she can watch children playing.		
4–8 months	**Playing social games:** As your child swings, playfully cover your eyes and uncover them to play Peekaboo and look for smiles.	**Turning to name:** Call the child's name when he or she is in the swing, the stroller, or on other play equipment and comment on what he or she is doing and what is happening nearby.	**Making vowel and early consonant sounds:** Use simple words like "whee" and "go-go-go" and repeat with a sing-song voice. Repeat back to the child sounds the child makes. When picking up the child to look at swings or other children, repeat early developing vowels and consonants like "up-up-up!" or "Momma. Momma has you!"	**Sitting:** Place the child in an infant swing and use small blankets or towels for side supports if needed.	**Grasping:** Provide rattles and teethers for the child to hold while in the stroller or when being held.	

(continued)

8–14 months

Playing social games: As your child swings, play Peekaboo and watch for the child to imitate you.

Peer interaction: Talk about what other children are doing as the child looks in their direction. If a peer comes over to the child, speak for your child to facilitate interaction.

Cause and effect and using movements to continue an activity: Push the child on the swing and stop. Watch for body movements to indicate the child wants more.

Object permanence: Hide behind a tree next to where the child is sitting after saying, "Where's Mommy?"

Using gestures: Hold your hands out when asking the child if he or she wants to get out of the stroller and wait for the child to reach.

Using first words: Label what the child is doing or looking at with single words. Support the comments with repetition and gesture, such as "Birdie!" paired with a point.

Walking: Hold the child's hands and walk around the park. Hold only one hand when the child is comfortable walking with less support.

14–18 months

Peer interaction: As the child approaches peers or as they approach him or her, help the child wave or say hi.

Demonstrating understanding of words: Ask the child "Where's ___" focusing on names of familiar people and objects nearby. If the child does not indicate by looking or pointing, call his or her attention to the named person or item, saying, "There's ___"

Imitation of actions with objects and with the body: Stop the swing and model a gesture that represents "go." Tell the child "Show me go!" Help the child by guiding his or her hands if he or she does not imitate.

Functional use of objects: Provide shovels for digging and show the child how to use them.

Following directions: Tell the child to throw the ball to Mommy, to Daddy, or to the dog.

Using different types of words: Label vocabulary associated with the playground, such as *swing, slide, sand, tree, grass, walk, run,* and *play.*

Walking: Help the child walk on uneven surfaces such as in the grass, and up and down inclines, providing as little support as necessary to maintain balance.

Table III.3. *(continued)*

Approx. dev. age level	Behavior regulation and social skills	Cognitive/receptive language skills	Expressive language skills	Gross motor skills	Fine motor skills	Self-care/ adaptive skills
18–24 months	**Peer interaction:** In the sandbox, help the child hand shovels and buckets to other children who may come to play. **Testing limits/becoming independent/ accepting limits:** If the child runs ahead or resists redirection, give clear expectations in simple language such as "Walk with Mommy." **Turn-taking and sharing:** After a turn on the swing or slide, allow another child to take a turn. If another child wants what your child has or vice versa, try to provide another similar object so they each have a fun toy or turn on a piece of equipment. As other children go down the slide, model "His turn. Now it's your turn."	**Matching and sorting:** Give the child two buckets and help him or her put stones in one and leaves in another. **Following directions:** Tell the child to get the ball and kick it to Daddy or get a leaf and put it on the table.	**Using different types of words/ using phrases and sentences:** Describe what the child sees and touches, for example "wet sand," "green grass," and "big slide." Talk about verbs associated with the park, such as *walk, run, climb,* and *swing.* Model asking, calling, and commenting for the child to imitate.	**Walking:** Put a ball on a hill or on an uneven surface and tell the child to go get it. **Ball play:** Model kicking a ball forward and tell the child to do the same. Tell the child to throw the ball to you.	**Using both hands:** Have the child pick up stones or leaves to put in a bucket that he or she is holding in the other hand.	
24–30 months	**Testing limits/becoming independent/ accepting limits:** Give the child choices that are acceptable options, such as "Walk with me or ride in your stroller."	**Concept development:** Talk about big and little, sizes of the equipment, colors and number of items, such as one slide and two swings. **Matching and sorting:** Give the child two buckets and have him or her put red leaves in one and green leaves in another.	**Answering questions:** Occasionally ask questions about the playground and what is happening that are yes/no, *who, what, what doing,* and *where* questions. Give visual cues if needed.	**Running:** Playfully chase the child to encourage a running pattern. **Riding toys:** On a smooth surface such as an unoccupied basketball court or a safe area of a parking lot, encourage the child to propel a riding toy to get a desired object or treat.	**Prewriting:** With a stick model drawing circular, horizontal, and vertical strokes in the sand or in the dirt and encourage the child to imitate.	

Following directions: Tell the child to get the ball and put it on his or her head.

Navigating stairs: Walk up the climbers and the slides ahead of the child so he or she will follow you.

Jumping: Help the child jump down from a step on the slide, the bench of a picnic table, or on a leaf providing as little help as possible until he or she is independent.

Ball play: Throw a ball to the child to catch. Start close to the child and throw gently. Gradually increase the distance as the child succeeds.

Tearing and cutting: Give the child leaves to tear.

30–36 months

Following directions: Give two-step unrelated directions such as "Give Mommy the shovel and go to the swings."

Being understood: When the child says words about the playground that are not clear, such as win/swing, ah/up, wide/slide, say them back to the child slowly and clearly model the correct sounds.

Navigating stairs: Encourage the child to go up the slide ladder or steps with a step-over-step pattern.

Climbing: Help the child go up climbers, providing as little support as necessary.

Jumping: Model jumping over a small stick or a dandelion in the grass and encourage the child to do the same.

SPECIAL CONSIDERATIONS

For a child who is not able to walk around the playground and who is not yet using words or pointing to indicate where he or she wants to play, look for eye gaze and take the child to where he or she is looking. Provide support so that the child can participate by holding the child on your lap on the swing or on the slide. If the child needs minimal support to sit well, use small towels or blankets to help keep the child from leaning to the side or too far forward or backward.

For a child with a hearing impairment, talk in view of the child's eyes so he or she can watch your face. Support the message you are saying with gestures. Divide the message into shorter segments rather than using a long narration. Pair words with sounds to emphasize and teach about sounds: for example, squeak, chirp, plane, and kids.

For a child who has a visual impairment, talk to the child about what options there are from which he or she may choose. Provide needed physical and verbal cues such as guidance to the slide and verbal cues such as "Hold on to the railing... Go up the step ... and now we go down the slide."

For a child who is uncomfortable with movement, begin with activities that the child can tolerate. For example, for the child who does not like slides, have the child sit at the bottom of the slide and progress to moving the child higher and higher up while providing support to come down. Similarly, for the child who does not like to swing, first allow the child to become comfortable in the swing without it moving, perhaps sitting on an adult's lap. Then progress by providing increasing amounts of movement, watching the child closely for signs of distress.

Mario was a 26-month-old boy who had Down syndrome. He was beginning to walk without support but fell frequently. He communicated by pointing to what he wanted, and he used a few single words to request and to comment. Mario imitated single actions well. He cried whenever his dad, Giorgio, rough-housed with him, as he did not like having movement imposed upon him. At the park, the EI provider recommended that Giorgio offer his hand for support until Mario became comfortable with the new environment and suggested that later, once Mario felt comfortable, they encourage him to walk independently. The provider and Giorgio walked around to show Mario what was available and to see if he showed an interest in a piece of equipment. Mario pointed to the slide, and after he walked there he began banging on it. The EI provider suggested Giorgio also playfully bang on the slide, and when he did, Mario laughed heartily. The EI provide suggested Giorgio sit on the end of the slide and bang on it. Again Mario laughed. The EI provider put Mario on his dad's lap and they banged together. The provider then suggested to Giorgio that he wiggle upward a few inches and playfully bang on the slide again. Once Mario was having fun banging, the EI provider coached Giorgio to securely hold Mario and gently slide down and bang again as soon as they arrived at the bottom of the slide. Mario enjoyed this, and after several more times Giorgio was able to help him climb the steps and playfully bang at the top before the pair slid down with big grins on their faces. The EI provider suggested to Giorgio that the next time they go to the park he take cues from Mario as to whether or not Mario will need time to get accustomed to the slide by again playing the banging imitation game or if he would be ready to go down the slide. They talked about a plan for future trips to the playground and decided that, once Mario felt more comfortable on the slide, they would help him adjust to the swing. The EI provider also mentioned that once Mario felt comfortable he would likely be more interested in the other children, and Giorgio could then work on peer interaction and more complex gross motor skills.

Benny was a 12-month-old boy with a moderate sensorineural loss in both ears. He wore bilateral hearing aids. The EI provider and Benny's babysitter, Mary, planned a trip to the park with Benny's brother using the family's wagon for the day's session. Mary brought the wagon out in preparation. The EI provider coached Mary to allow Benny to signal his desire to get into the wagon by moving toward it and trying to climb in. Mary then modeled "up?" and held out her hands until Benny reached for her hands. She made certain to position herself face to face and said "up!" to Benny, repeating it one more time, "up!" When Benny responded with "ah" she imitated his sound and said "Up! That's right! Up!" While walking to the park she walked backward intermittently while pulling, so that Benny could see her face, and she would describe what Benny was looking at on the way, stopping to pick up and label things such as "stick," "leaf," and "pine-cone." When a plane flew overhead, she stopped the wagon, looked at Benny and called his name to get his attention. She pointed to the sky and said "plane," modeled "aaaaaaaaaa" to signify the sound of the motor and asked the brother to point to the plane as well so Benny would see his brother attending to the plane also. Upon arrival at the park, the brother got out of the wagon and went to the swing. The provider coached Mary to wait until Benny signaled what he wanted. Benny reached and leaned toward his brother, and the caregiver brought Benny over to the brother. With Benny on her hip, she pushed the brother on the swing, labeling "push," looking at Benny, and labeling "push" again. The swing happened to be squeaky, and the provider coached Mary to point to her ear, label "squeak," and point to Benny's ear, saying "Squeak. The swing is squeaky." The provider coached Mary to talk about other sounds around them. For example, Mary saw a group of laughing children and pointed, saying, "Kids! Laughing." She then pointed at the brother to label different things he was doing, such as "off," "all done swinging," "climbing," and "sliding." On the way home, the EI provider coached Mary to label "bump!" when the wagon went over the bump and to call attention to cars going by and to other environmental sounds.

GROCERY SHOPPING

Table III.4. Daily routines across domains: grocery shopping

Approx. dev. age level	Behavior regulation and social skills	Cognitive/receptive language skills	Expressive language skills	Gross motor skills	Fine motor skills	Self-care/adaptive skills
Birth to 4 months	**Initiating and maintaining eye contact:** After getting items off the shelf, glance to see if your child is looking at you and comment about what you or the child is doing.	**Encouraging listening and attention:** When getting items off the shelves, talk to the child about the item or an associated idea in a sing-song voice: "Daddy needs more cereal" or "Yummy snack. Your brother likes his snacks!"	**Cooing and vocalizing:** While shopping, vocalize in response to the child's sounds. Initiate vocalizations as well. Pause, see if the child alerts to voice.		**Visual fixation and attention:** Show various items to the child that are being purchased, presenting them from different directions.	
4–8 months	**Gaining attention:** When the child vocalizes, turn to the child and comment, for example, "What? What are you saying?" or "Is that so?"	**Encouraging listening and attention:** Talk to the child in a sing-song voice. **Turning to name:** Call the child's name in an excited tone of voice and show him or her an item of interest before putting it in the cart.	**Making vowel and early consonant sounds:** Exaggerate vowel and early consonant sounds related to the items you put in the cart, such as "'Mmm, yuuummy milk."	**Sitting:** Position the child as upright as possible using a diaper bag or blanket, if needed.	**Using both hands:** While he or she is sitting in the cart or stroller, have the child hold large items with two hands and/or an item in each hand that is safe from mouthing or breaking.	
8–14 months	**Playing social games:** Hold a cereal box over your face, remove it and say, "Peekaboo." While pushing the cart, quietly sing to the child. Get closer when you sing important words and smile. Watch for a smile from the child too.	**Cause and effect and using movements to continue an activity:** Occasionally stop the cart and playfully say "Stop" to play the game of waiting for the child to indicate by a movement or sound or word for the cart to move again. **Imitation of actions with objects and with the body:** When showing a food item, pretend to take a bite or chew. Playfully tap the cart handle. Wave bye-bye to foods you pass. After each action, pause and say, "You do it!" **Demonstrating understanding of words:** Hold up two familiar food items and tell the child to point to the one you name. Play "Where's the _____" with foods in the child's view.	**Using gestures:** Name something in the child's view and encourage pointing with "Do you see _____?" or "Where is the _____?" Wave to people you know. If the child is allowed to open a snack, move your hands to signal "Open." Encourage the child to imitate. If a child does not want a choice, encourage a gentle push away gesture. Shake your head yes or no and encourage the child to shake his or her head yes or no too.			

146

Age			
14–18 months	**Demonstrating understanding of words:** Hold up two familiar food items; tell the child to point to the one you name.	**Making choices:** When appropriate, hold up two items for the child to choose one, such as different types of apples or different boxes of crackers. **Using first words:** Model the names of items the child is familiar with, for example, apple, milk, cheese, and chicken nuggets. Name the foods as you put them into the cart. Look at the child expectantly after saying a name. If the child can imitate, encourage imitation of a sound or the word, depending upon the child's ability.	**Walking:** Have the child hold someone's hand or the side of the cart for short periods of time.	**Finger feeding and taking bites:** Provide a snack for the child to finger feed while sitting in the cart.
18–24 months		**Answering questions:** Ask simple questions such as "What is that?" "Who is that?" (when familiar cartoon characters are on boxes), and yes/no questions (e.g., "Do you like cookies?"). **Using different types of words/using phrases and sentences:** When placing food in the cart, use nouns (e.g., cereal, beans). Use words of location such as in while putting items in the cart, under if using the lower part of the cart, on when placing items on the checkout counter, and verbs for actions, such as push, eat, pay, carry, and lift. Use adjectives such as heavy, big, little, cold, and so forth. To encourage words for different functions, model asking questions, commenting, requesting, and answering.	**Using both hands:** Have the child hold a bag in the produce area and hand him or her fruits and vegetables to place in the bag.	

(continued)

147

Table III.4. (continued)

Approx. dev. age level	Behavior regulation and social skills	Cognitive/receptive language skills	Expressive language skills	Gross motor skills	Fine motor skills	Self-care/adaptive skills
24–30 months	**Testing limits/becoming independent/accepting limits:** Use choices such as "Walk with Mommy or ride in the cart," following through if the child runs ahead.	**Matching and sorting:** When identical items are being purchased, hold up one and tell your child to find another from the shelf. **Concept development:** Tell the child to put "one" piece of produce in the bag. Ask the child if he or she wants "more" of a snack. Point out "big" packages, such as 10-pound bags of dog food and "little" packages such as individual servings. When you put the child in the cart, label "up"; when you take him or her out, label "down." Use the word one, such as "We need one can of corn" and all such as "We packed all our groceries into bags."	**Answering questions:** Ask later developing questions such as "where," such as "Where does milk go?" or "When do we eat pancakes?" **Using different types of words:** Show the child one item and then two items to teach plurals. For example, say, "Here is one apple and here are two apples." When talking about who the intended recipient is for a particular food, use possessives, such as "Daddy's juice" or "PJ's crackers." Model endings on verbs such as "I am pushing," "I am paying," and "He is packing."	**Jumping:** Have the child jump down the aisle if he or she is able to stay next to you safely.	**Hand preference and hand dominance:** Hand the child items at mid-line to place in a bag or in the cart.	
30–36 months	**Turn-taking and sharing:** Take turns putting items in the cart saying "my turn" and "your turn."	**Matching and sorting:** Before shopping, make a list using several pictures from the Internet or by using cutout package labels or pictures. Have the child find the items that match the list when in front of the appropriate shelves. **Concept development:** Tell the child to name items such as the green apples, the big pears, or the little cucumber, holding up choices if necessary.	**Using different types of words/using phrases and sentences:** Combine words to form simple sentences to model sentences for the child to understand and imitate, such as "I like popcorn," "We need macaroni," and "Our cart is full!"			

SPECIAL CONSIDERATIONS

Grocery shopping is often a difficult routine for children and caregivers; however, using a child's strengths and motivating interactions geared toward the child's developmental level can help make shopping less stressful, fun, and productive for the child and the caregiver. For children who have difficulties with self-regulation and sensory processing, stores may be overstimulating with bright lights, unexpected sounds, and unpredictability. Trips may need to be carefully planned to increase a child's tolerance of the sensory stimulation gradually.

For children who are active, sitting still or staying with a caregiver is often quite challenging. Providers should help caregivers see the shopping routine from the infant's or toddler's perspective to help the caregiver understand why the child may not be pleasant in the store; caregivers should look at factors such as hunger, tiredness, and duration of the time of the shopping trip. Short successful trips to the store with gradual increases in duration often help with success. EI providers' knowledge of behavioral principles can vastly improve the success of shopping trips by helping caregivers in the timing and delivery of the popular method of using a snack to "get through the store." Many times the snack is given to the child as soon as he or she starts crying, fussing, or otherwise acting up. This timing is very likely to increase the unwanted behaviors as the child quickly learns that certain behaviors result in being handed a bag or box of a favorite food. EI providers can guide caregivers on how to increase wanted behaviors by giving the snack or treat when the child is calm, staying next to the caregiver, and showing other desirable behaviors.

For children who have delayed gross motor skills and who may use adapted strollers or wheelchairs, grocery shopping with one adult can be challenging, because pushing the child and handling a cart simultaneously may be difficult. It may be helpful to use the tray and the push handles to hold clear bags (to avoid perception of shoplifting).

Combining gestures with speech, speaking at a slower rate to allow for processing time, and allowing pauses between sentences may help a child with language-processing difficulties understand. To help comprehension, support the message with visual cues, such as holding up the cereal box as you name it. When choices are appropriate, encourage the child to reach for things he or she likes, which is practice in using gestural communication. Listen for the child's vocalizations that may be attempts to gain attention and help the child realize that sound has a communicative function.

Be sure that children with hearing impairments can see your face when you talk to them. Label sounds to give the child an opportunity to make sense of what he or she hears—for example, squeaky wheels, children laughing, an airplane overhead as you load the car, a car beeping, or a fire engine going by. While the child is in the shopping cart, stand nearby in different positions—for example, on the right side, the left side, and slightly behind the child to help with auditory localization skills.

Tiffany was a 13-month-old who had global developmental delays, a cortical visual impairment, and a seizure disorder. She had significant periods of irritability in new situations. Her grandmother, her legal guardian, must take her shopping while the grandmother's teenage children were at school, and she was embarrassed by the onlookers' stares as Tiffany wailed through the store. The EI provider accompanied Tiffany and her grandmother to the store to observe a typical shopping trip. Tiffany sat in the car seat in the shopping cart at an angle that was more upright than in the car. In this position, Tiffany's head tended to tilt to the side. The EI provider suggested rolling up a small blanket to help keep Tiffany's head in mid-line so she could better see and be more comfortable. While Tiffany's grandmother was focused on her shopping list, the EI provider was able to observe that Tiffany was calm when the cart was stopped for several minutes or when the cart was moving for several minutes, but with each stop and start, Tiffany cried. The EI provider suggested that Grandma use a phrase such as "Here we go" or "Let's go get some _____" when she was ready to move the cart and to cue Tiffany of an upcoming movement. She also suggested giving

Tiffany her favorite blanket to hold and mouth while shopping. The EI provider suggested that for several weeks Grandma break up the weekly shopping trip into two or three trips so Tiffany could learn to be calm for gradually increasing amounts of time, building up to the typical 45-minute excursion. Once Tiffany was able to shop without crying, the EI provider showed Grandma ways to facilitate Tiffany's visual attention to grandmother, her reach and grasp, and her understanding and use of language.

 Elliot was a 20-month-old child who was very self-directed and did not use words. Elliot had spina bifida and did not walk. He pulled to stand and crawled rapidly. He did not like to have his freedom of movement restricted—for example, when his mother carried him or he had to be in a stroller. Elliot screamed and cried when grocery shopping. His mother reported, "It's embarrassing, and some days I just want to sit down and cry." Elliot's mom and EI provider decided to go shopping together to see if the EI provider could think of any strategies that would help Elliot's mother. The EI provider coached Elliot's mother to provide opportunities for movement before taking Elliot shopping, such as having him play one of his favorite games, crawling rapidly, and playing Peekaboo behind the ottoman. The provider and mother arranged for the trip to occur at 10:00 a.m., which gave Elliot time to expend some energy before the trip, which was to occur long before naptime so he was not tired and irritable. Elliot's mother was encouraged to have a list so that shopping would be efficient and take less time. The EI provider showed Elliot's mother how to playfully facilitate choice-making by holding up two identical items for Elliot and putting the one back that he did not select. To help keep Elliot engaged and moving, he was given safe items to drop into the cart. When Elliot began to fuss, the EI provider suggested Elliot be allowed to walk holding the cart for support. Prior to putting Elliot back into the cart, his mother gave him a package of food he liked to hold so that the transition was eased. When Elliot was lifted back into the cart, the EI provider coached Elliot's mom to model "up, up, up!" which Elliot imitated. Items were labeled with single words throughout the trip, e.g., "apples," "potatoes," and "juice," to help Elliot understand more words. To work on following directions, the EI provider coached Elliot's mother to use simple directions such as "Take it" and "Put it in," which not only helped Elliot comply with directions but also helped him be actively involved in the shopping trip. Over time, Elliot's mother was able to build on Elliot's sounds to encourage him to attempt words, and more skills were adding into shopping trips. Elliot fussed much less during trips when the strategies were used.

RIDING IN THE CAR

Table III.5. Daily routines across domains: riding in the car

Approx. dev. age level	Behavior regulation and social skills	Cognitive/receptive language skills	Expressive language skills	Gross motor skills	Fine motor skills	Self-care/ adaptive skills
Birth to 4 months	**Initiating and maintaining eye contact:** After placing the child in the car seat, take a moment to see if the child is looking at you. If not, gain the child's attention by talking to and/or stroking him or her. Tell him or her where he or she is going.		**Cooing and vocalizing:** When putting the child in the car seat, talk to the child in a sing-song voice.		**Visual fixation and attention:** After placing the child in the car seat, talk to him or her, and as you move away, watch to see if the child follows you with his or her eyes.	
4–8 months	**Gaining attention:** Listen for the child's sounds and respond to the child by commenting when you hear them.	**Encouraging listening and attention:** While fastening the child in the car seat, sing or talk in a sing-song voice about what you are doing.	**Making vowel and early consonant sounds:** Label and repeat words with early developing sounds such "Car, car, car! Off we go!" or "Bye-bye, Nana. Bye-bye."		**Using both hands:** Provide toys to hold such as stuffed animals, rattles, and teethers.	
8–14 months			**Using gestures:** During the ride, model gestures such as waving hi, bye, and throwing kisses. Model pointing to familiar items as you label them, both in and out of the car. Playfully show the child gestures such as moving fists up and down to represent driving and one fist pounding the other to represent "beep–beep."			
14–18 months	**Following directions:** Tell the child to put his or her arms through the straps.		**Making choices:** Offer the child a choice of toys to hold while in the car seat. Wait for the child to reach or name.	**Walking:** Have the child walk to and from the car.		

(continued)

Table III.5. (continued)

Approx. dev. age level	Behavior regulation and social skills	Cognitive/receptive language skills	Expressive language skills	Gross motor skills	Fine motor skills	Self-care/adaptive skills
18–24 months	**Testing limits/ becoming independent/ accepting limits:** If the child throws items or purposely bothers others, try to determine the purpose of the behavior.		**Using first words:** Use single-word models associated with car rides, such as *go, car, ride,* and *store.*			
24–30 months		**Following directions:** Tell the child, "Climb in and get your buckle."	**Using different types of words/using phrases and sentences:** When the child uses one word, add one more word to provide two-word models. When the child says "up," model "go up." When the child says, "car," model "car ride."	**Jumping:** Have the child jump to and from the car. **Climbing:** Have the child climb into the car and get into the car seat.		
30–36 months	**Turn-taking and sharing:** Take turns choosing songs to sing.	**Concept development:** Have the child tell you things he or she sees out of the window that are big, little, or named colors or that have a specific function.	**Using different types of words/using phrases and sentences:** When the child uses word combinations that are not linked by appropriate grammar, provide a model for the missing or incorrect structures. If the child says, "We goed store," model "We went to the store," or if the child says, "Baby crying," model "Baby is crying."	**Climbing:** Have the child climb out of the car seat and out of the car with decreasing support after the fasteners have been removed by an adult.		

SPECIAL CONSIDERATIONS

Some children have motor impairments that necessitate specialized car seats, which EI providers can help procure through durable medical equipment companies. The National Highway Safety Administration has a website that helps to locate child car seat inspection stations (http://www.nhtsa.gov/cps/cpsfitting/index.cfm) to ensure parents and caregivers have properly fitting and positioned car seats

For children who have visual impairments, parents and caregivers should talk about what they see and hear as they travel.

Eli was a 29–month-old who had Down syndrome. He walked with one hand held and stood alone briefly. He used a few single words. Eli's dad, Mike, decided to take Eli and his twin sister, Ella, out for ice cream and incorporated many of the strategies recently learned from Eli's EI providers. Mike held both of Eli's hands on the steps and one on the way to the car while Ella walked beside them. As Eli crawled into his car seat, Mike told him to give him his hand and waited for him to do so before helping him guide his arm through the harness. After checking to see if Ella was safely buckled in her seat, they headed to get ice cream. Ella asked Dad to sing the "Wheels on the Bus" and Dad gave Eli the choice of singing "beep" or "swish." After the singing, Mike took turns asking the twins questions about what they saw, tailoring the questions to each child's ability. He asked Ella to find something green, and as they passed a dog being walked, Mike asked Eli, "What does a doggy say?" Upon arriving at the ice cream stand, Mike showed Eli the pictures on the wall, and Eli pointed to an ice cream sandwich to indicate his choice. Ella later remarked that her ice cream tasted "really yummy," which Dad repeated for Eli to imitate. Mike then told the twins to wipe their faces and asked Ella to stand in front of Eli so he could imitate her. They walked to the car, and on the drive home they again talked about the "yummy" ice cream. Mike asked Ella to give Eli the book of song pictures the EI provider made for them and Eli pointed to the picture of the star, which Ella relayed to Dad. They sang "Twinkle, Twinkle, Little Star" until they reached the house. Eli was very tired, so Mike carried him into the house, deciding to practice walking another time.

Leigha was a 27-month-old child whose aunt, Jo, watched her during the day while her parents worked. Leigha used approximately 12 words and her most frequent word was *car*. She enjoyed looking at and touching her family's car when it was parked in the driveway, but she did not like being in her car seat or riding in the car. When Jo attempted to put her in her car seat, Leigha arched her back and cried. In addition, when they arrived at their destination, Leigha wanted to stay in the car to play and screamed when Jo took her out. Jo asked the EI provider if she could help Leigha be calmer both in the car and when they reach their destination. The EI provider suggested allowing Leigha to hold special toys in the car seat. This idea did not help, as Leigha continued to scream, but the suggestion gave Jo the idea to give Leigha a sippy cup. Using this strategy was successful during the ride, but not when they arrived at their destination. The EI provider suggested several strategies to help Leigha willingly get out of the car. Before unfastening her, the EI provider modeled helping Leigha focus on where she was going rather than what she was leaving by saying, "Let's go look for the balloons." In addition, the provider and Jo attempted playful transitions, such as jumping into the store, being pushed "fast" in a cart from the parking lot, and providing highly motivating toys to hold. Through this process, Leigha learned to be calm and regulated and accept direction, which made car rides and shopping much more pleasant for both her and her aunt.

DIAPERING AND DRESSING

Table III.6. Daily routines across domains: diapering and dressing

Approx. dev. age level	Behavior regulation and social skills	Cognitive/receptive language skills	Expressive language skills	Gross motor skills	Fine motor skills	Self-care/adaptive skills
Birth to 4 months	**Initiating and maintaining eye contact:** Sing to the child and look for eye contact before, during, or after diapering and dressing.		**Cooing and vocalizing:** While face to face, vocalize with the child.	**Playing on the back:** Encourage head to mid-line by positioning your face in front of the child.	**Visual fixation and attention/visual tracking:** During diaper changes and dressing, move your face into the child's visual field and sing, talk, and/or make mouth movements to get the child's attention. Slowly move to encourage the child to follow with the eyes.	**Undressing:** Help the child pull off socks by taking them off most of the way.
4–8 months	**Playing social games:** Play This Little Piggy and Peekaboo before, during, or after diapering and dressing.		**Making vowel and early consonant sounds:** Playfully repeat consonants and vowels that the child says, using a sing-song voice.	**Playing on the back:** Encourage hands to knees and hands to feet by bringing the legs up during diapering. **Sitting:** Put on the child's shirts, socks, and shoes in supported sitting, such as in your lap or propped against the side of the sofa.	**Batting and reaching/grasping:** Hold clothing items, the diaper, or toys for the child within reach. **Transferring from hand to hand:** Have the child hold a small article of clothing, diaper, or toy in one hand. When you are ready to help put that hand into the sleeve, help the child transfer the item to the other hand.	
8–14 months	**Being calm and regulated:** Give the child a safe and interesting object to explore, one that is available only at this time.	**Object permanence:** Hide interesting items under the clothing, diaper, or blanket for the child to find. **Demonstrating understanding of words:** Establish predictable games such as "I'm going to get your toes." and over time see if the child anticipates your action of tickling his or her toes. When the child does so, add a new word such as "belly" and look for the child discriminating toes from belly.	**Using gestures:** When finished changing the child, hold out your hands and ask "Up?" Wait for the child to extend his or her arms toward you.	**Moving in and out of sitting:** Help the child move from back to sitting by rolling to the side and pushing up and sitting after dressing and diapering. **Pulling to stand:** Help the child move from sitting to hands and knees to sitting to pull up pants.	**Releasing:** Have the child hand you items such as a diaper, a shirt, or a shoe. **Using both hands:** Give the child two items, one for each hand, to hold, such as two shoes, two socks, or two diapers. **Banging objects and clapping:** When the child is holding two objects, help him or her bang them together, then pause to see if the child bangs. **Poking and pointing:** Show the child pictures on the diaper or the wipes container and help him or her point. Model poking your finger into button holes and help the child do the same.	**Taking off clothes:** When removing the child's shirt, keep it on top of the child's head for the child to pull off. Remove one arm from the sleeve and remove most of the other arm from the sleeve for the child to pull off the rest of the way. **Putting on clothes:** Hold the sleeve out for the child to put in his or her arm. Tap the arm to give cues if needed.

Age			
14–18 months	**Functional use of objects:** Hand the child an item, such as a sock, asking, "Where does that go?" If necessary move the sock toward the foot. **Demonstrating understanding of words:** Say to the child, "Do you see your diaper?" and see if he or she looks for it.	**Using first words:** Label each clothing item as you take it off or put it. Pause for the child to imitate.	
18–24 months	**Testing limits/becoming independent/accepting limits:** Give warnings to help with transitions. **Following directions:** Tell the child to bring you a diaper or get his or her shoes. **Problem solving:** Playfully put the child's sock on his or her hand. Wait to see if he or she indicates it goes on the foot by moving the foot, pointing, and so forth.	**Using different types of words/ using phrases and sentences:** Model two-word sentences for the child to imitate, such as "dirty diaper," "all clean," or "all done."	**Taking apart and putting together:** If the child has hook-and-loop fasteners, show him or her how to take them apart and put together and help him or her do the same. **Taking off clothes:** Pause during undressing to see if the child does the next step. Give verbal or physical assistance as needed.
24–30 months	**Using or showing "mine" and defending possessions:** Playfully pretend to put the child's shirt on your head and look for child to say or show "mine." **Matching and sorting:** Remove one sock and one shoe and put them next to the child. Have him or her take off the others and put them with the matching item. **Following directions:** Tell the child to get his shoes and give them to Daddy.	**Answering questions:** Ask the child questions (that he or she can answer), such as "What is Mommy doing?" or "Is that your tummy?"	
30–36 months	**Turn-taking and sharing:** Take turns putting on and taking off items of clothing, saying "Your turn to put on this sock and my turn for that sock." **Problem solving:** Ask the child what he or she needs to get dressed depending on the situation. For example, "It's time for bed. What do you need to put on?"		**Putting on clothes:** Pause during the dressing sequence to see if the child does the next step. Give verbal or physical assistance as needed.

SPECIAL CONSIDERATIONS

Many toddlers do not like to stop their activities for diapering and dressing. Being playful, having the child help as much as possible, and distracting him or her with novel items used only during these routines often work well. Give warnings such as "Let's run one more time and then it's time to get dressed" helps to prepare reluctant children. Focus on what the child will do afterward by saying "Let's quick get dressed so we can go outside." Try changing toddlers with them in standing position instead of on their backs when practical. Give choices such as "Should we change your diaper in the bedroom or in the living room?" to give the child a sense of control.

For children who have visual impairments or who are sensitive to textures or touch, talking to them about what you are doing can help them prepare for what comes next.

For children with hearing impairments, signal that it is time for a diaper change by tapping the child to gain his or her attention. Showing the diaper and using gestures will help the child participate.

For children who have increased muscle tone, relaxing activities before diapering and dressing can make moving limbs easier. For those who have lower muscle tone, providing support can help the child maximize his or her independence. For example, to encourage a child who is unstable to push an arm into a sleeve, providing support at the trunk may help him or her isolate arm movements more easily. For children who have a significant difference in motor control on one side as compared to the other, first undressing the arm or leg with greater control will allow the child to assist more and will also aid the caregiver in undressing the child more easily. Conversely, when dressing the child, starting with the limb with decreased control will allow the child to assist more and will also aid the caregiver to dress the child more easily.

Joey was a 23-month-old who had cerebral palsy. He could roll to his side from his back and from his belly. He had increased muscle tone, greater on his right side than his left. He had two IFSP outcomes; one was that he would sit unsupported and crawl so he could move from one area of the house to another, and the other was that he would communicate what he wanted in ways other than crying. Though the outcomes did not specifically address diapering and dressing, the EI provider showed his parents how to use diapering and dressing as a time to stretch his muscles by having him reach for his toes, to practice supported sitting when putting on his shoes and socks, and to help him roll during dressing when they need to pull up his pants. Because his right side was very tight, the EI provider showed the family how to put his right arm in the sleeve first when dressing him and how to take the left arm out first when undressing him. Joey tended to get fussy when diapering and dressing took more than a few minutes, so the provider and the family brainstormed about what might make Joey a little more patient, and they decided playing Peekaboo and singing would give the family a few extra minutes when needed. Diapering and dressing also provided opportunities to work on Joey's communication skills. The EI provider showed the family how to prolong the vowel sounds in songs so Joey could vocalize in imitation. She also showed them how to work on vocabulary by telling him to find his diaper when they held up a diaper and another item and waited to see if Joey looked at the diaper. If he did not, they moved it to attract his attention, and when he looked they excitedly said "Yes, there's your diaper." They then repeated this until Joey looked at the diaper without the prompt of the movement. The EI provider also showed the family how to give Joey a choice during dressing. Though he did not care about colors of clothing, he loved trains, and when given the choice of his train shirt and a shirt without a train, Joey used his eyes to tell his parents the one he wanted. The EI provider also discussed hand use with the family to provide them with important developmental information and because of its relevance to moving and communicating. The provider showed the family how to encourage Joey to reach for his clothes and his diaper, help close the wipes box, and drop his clothes in the hamper to practice the next steps in fine motor development.

David was a 30-month-old child diagnosed with autism spectrum disorder. David did not consistently look at others' eyes, reach for what he wanted, or attend to others' language. David entertained himself by wandering and rocking. His father often tried to play with him, but unless they were rough-housing, David had no interest and walked away. When David needed a diaper change during a session, his father held him while David arched his back, cried, twisted away, and pushed his father. During the struggle, diaper contents spread to the couch, David's legs, and his father's clothes. David's father reported that this scenario was typical and very frustrating, as was dressing, diapering, brushing teeth, and mealtime. The EI provider and the father decided that it would be helpful during sessions to address not only David's play and communication skills but also his challenging behavior during routines. The father was eager to learn strategies for keeping David calm, especially during diapering and dressing. The EI provider and David's father first explored position to see if David's behavior was different when he was standing for diaper changes than when he was lying on his back. They found he was more cooperative when he was standing, though David's father found this was not practical after a bowel movement. The EI provider then coached David's father to lay David on his back and act as if this were part of their routine of playfully blowing raspberries on David's belly. This helped him lie still until he realized he was about to get his diaper changed, at which point he started to fuss again. After much problem solving and trial and error, the EI provider and David's father discovered that singing to David and allowing him to hold small favorite toys decreased his difficult behaviors, although it did not eliminate them. To help David be calm during dressing, he was allowed to walk around and his father would momentarily stop him to put on one article of clothing. David's father felt that though some of the strategies helped at times, many routines remained quite challenging. The EI provider and David's father planned to continue to work on David's ability to be calm and cooperative during diapering and dressing and then explore using strategies within other routines such as mealtime and brushing teeth.

TAKING A BATH

Table III.7. Daily routines across domains: taking a bath

Approx. dev. age level	Behavior regulation and social skills	Cognitive/receptive language skills	Expressive language skills	Gross motor skills	Fine motor skills	Self-care/ adaptive skills
Birth to 4 months	**Being calm and regulated:** Be cognizant of the environment, and if the child is irritable, try to determine if the cause of the distress is due to the temperature of the water or the room, the amount of tactile pressure of the washing, hunger, or tiredness and attempt to make changes for the duration of the bath or for future ones. If the child is distressed, talk quietly to calm the child. If the child is sleepy and lethargic and it is not almost bedtime, talk playfully to alert the child. **Initiating and maintaining eye contact:** While washing the child, look into his or her eyes and talk to him or her. While washing the child, watch for the child to look at your face, and as soon as he or she does so, respond with smiles and exclamations of praise and warmth.	**Encouraging listening and attention:** When placing the child in the tub, talk to him or her gently with a smile on your face. Watch for the child's eyes on your face.	**Cooing and vocalizing:** When the child coos or vocalizes, imitate his or her sounds.		**Visual fixation and attention/visual tracking:** Hold bath toys near the child's eyes. Talk to the child so he or she will focus on your face. Once the child focuses, move the object or your head slowly so the child has the opportunity to follow.	
4–8 months	**Playing social games:** Play Peekaboo with the washcloth. Watch for smiles. As the child gains hand skills, help him or her pull off the cloth from his or her face until, over time, he or she no longer needs the assistance. When bathing, play "I'm gonna get your _____ (toes, fingers, belly)" with the washcloth, your hands, or kisses.	**Encouraging listening and attention:** Narrate the bath experience with sentences such as "That feels so good when Mommy washes your belly." Sing made-up songs while washing, such as "Wash, wash, wash your belly."	**Making vowel and early consonant sounds:** When naming, reduplicate early developing consonants and vowels in words playfully, such as "wash, wash, wash – wa-wa-wa-wa-wa – wash, wash, wash" or "ba-ba-ba – bath, bath, bath."	**Sitting:** Provide a bath ring or have the child sit in a small plastic laundry tub if he or she needs only a little support. As soon as the child is a safe sitter, have him or her sit for bathing.	**Batting and reaching/grasping:** Present tub toys near the child's hands to encourage him or her to touch them and hold them. **Releasing:** Put small plastic bottles in the child's hands and playfully ask for them, helping the child to release if necessary. **Transferring:** Give the child a toy or bottle to hold in one hand. When it is time to wash that hand, help him or her transfer the item to the other hand. **Using both hands:** Provide small tub toys or bottles for the child to hold in both hands at the same time.	

158

| 8–14 months | **Gaining attention:** When the child vocalizes in response to splashing, the water, bubbles, or other bath time events, respond with verbal and visual attention. | **Turning to name:** Perform an action the child will turn toward and enjoy, such as pouring water over his or her toes. Call the child's name, and as soon as he or she turns, perform the action again.

Demonstrating understanding of words: Use short sentences such as "Time to wash your foot" and pause to see if the child looks toward the foot or moves it. If not, tap the child's foot and label it to help the child make the association. Wash a few strokes and repeat to give more opportunities for practice.

Cause and effect and using movements to continue an activity: When washing the child's leg or arm, playfully say, "wash, wash, wash." Watch for the child to move his or her limb to indicate the wish to continue.

Playfully pat the water to make tiny splashes. Watch for the child to pat the water too or make a patting motion.

Object permanence: Playfully hide a bath toy, cup, or the child's toes and ask, "Where's your ____?"

Hide a favorite bath toy under the washcloth and ask, "Oh-oh! Where did (ducky, fishy) go?" Wait for the child to pull off the washcloth. | **Using gestures:** Hold out the washcloth or a bath toy the child wants. Wait for reach and then give the object to the child.

Making choices: Hold out two objects for playing in the tub. Allow the child to choose one. Wait for reach toward the object.

Using first words: Label objects and actions with single words, such as *duck, boat, soap,* and *wash.* Use high affect and smile. | **Pulling to stand:** Provide minimal support and fade over time when the child needs to stand for washing the buttocks and for getting in or out of the tub.

Walking: Have the child walk to and from the bathroom providing the least amount of support needed. | **Pointing and poking:** Blow bubbles and catch one on the wand. Have the child poke it to pop it. |

(continued)

Table III.7. *(continued)*

Approx. dev. age level	Behavior regulation and social skills	Cognitive/receptive language skills	Expressive language skills	Gross motor skills	Fine motor skills	Self-care/adaptive skills
14–18 months		**Using gestures/ making choices:** Hold out two objects for playing in the tub. Allow the child to choose one. Wait for reaching or pointing toward the object. **Imitation of actions with objects and with the body:** Wash the child's leg or other easy-to-reach area and then hand him or her the cloth and say, "You do," looking for any attempt to rub the cloth. Pretend to wash your hair. Say, "You do." Rub your hands together, saying, "Wash, wash, wash!" Say, "You do."	**Using different types of words:** Use a variety of vocabulary associated with the tub: names of toys and things in the bathroom, such as *tub, towel, soap,* and *rug;* adjectives such as *big, little, dirty,* and *clean;* verbs such as *wash* or *splash;* and words of location such as *in, out,* and *on.* **Answering questions:** Point to a body part, toy, or bathroom object and ask, "What is that?"		**Using both hands/container play:** Give the child a container to hold with one hand and have him or her collect washcloths from the tub to put them in it. Provide plastic containers to fill with water and dump.	
18–24 months	**Testing limits/becoming independent/accepting limits:** If the child splashes too much, use phrases such as "Water stays in tub." If he or she continues to splash too much, try to redirect to an activity such as pouring from cup to cup. If the child continues to splash, give a choice such as "Stop splashing or get out of the tub."	**Imitation of actions with objects and with the body:** Use tub toys or cups and perform a simple action such as making the duck swim or the cup dump water. Hand the child the item and say, "You do."	**Using phrases and sentences:** Use word combinations, such as "No wash" or "More wash." Comment on what people are doing, such as "Mommy is washing your hair," "You are washing your belly." Talk about possession, e.g., "your nose," "Daddy's nose."			**Taking off clothes:** Have the child take off articles of clothing, providing as little assistance as needed, before he or she gets into the tub.

Functional use of objects: Hand the child the washcloth, towel, cup, and brush at the appropriate time. If the child does not use the object appropriately, model the action needed and hand it to him or her again. If needed, use physical guidance to gain success.

Pretend play: Show the child how to wash a waterproof doll or action figure. Unless the child will drink the water, show him or her how to give the doll/figure a pretend drink from a cup.

Following directions: Introduce directions into the routine that the child will be able to follow for most bath times such as "Throw your diaper in the trash" before he or she gets in the tub or "Give me the soap" while in the tub. Use visual cues and fade them as the child succeeds.

Answering questions: Ask the child "What are you doing?" Listen for use of *ing* on the end of the verb. Ask Yes/No questions, such as "Are you all done?"

(continued)

Table III.7. (continued)

Approx. dev. age level	Behavior regulation and social skills	Cognitive/receptive language skills	Expressive language skills	Gross motor skills	Fine motor skills	Self-care/ adaptive skills
24–30 months	**Testing limits/becoming independent/accepting limits:** Establish routines for bath time, such as having the child throw away his or her diaper before getting in the tub, and set limits, such as if the child splashes too much he or she must get out of the tub without playing with toys. **Turn-taking and sharing:** Take turns pouring water into containers, washing, or filling the cup used to rinse the child's hair.	**Problem solving:** During specific parts of the routine, ask the child, "What do you need?" For example, when preparing to get him or her out of the tub, remark how the child is all wet and ask what he or she needs to dry off. Provide various sizes of plastic containers to nest inside each other. **Concept development:** Give directions, such as "Put the washcloth on your head" or "Put the duck in the cup," helping the child if needed. Talk about colors of the items in the tub. Tell the child to give you one hand, then two hands to wash. **Following directions:** Give the child novel directions, such as "Put the duck on your leg." Work on two-step related directions by saying body parts to wash, "Wash your toes and then your leg."	**Using phrases and sentences:** Model phrases and short sentences that contain grammatical structures such as a/the ("a duck," "the water"), is/are ("It is wet," "They are clean"), present progressive verb tense ("washing," "drying"), past tense verbs ("we wiped," "we washed"), and typical sentence structure such as noun plus verb ("Ducky swims").		**Prewriting:** Provide foam soap or liquid soap and place a small amount on the side of the tub. Show the child how to make circular scribbles, vertical lines, and horizontal lines.	**Cup drinking:** Give the child an open cup to drink from while in the tub where spills will not be a problem. **Toilet training:** Have the child sit on the potty or toilet before getting into the tub to establish the routine.
30–36 months	**Testing limits/becoming independent/accepting limits:** Encourage the child to do as much dressing, undressing, washing, and drying as the child is able.	**Following directions:** Work on two-step unrelated directions by saying silly things such as "Wiggle your toes then wash your belly."				

SPECIAL CONSIDERATIONS

For the child who cries when put in the tub, try having the child play, while fully clothed, with a favorite waterproof toy in the empty tub. Progress to having the child play with the toy while the child is undressed. Over time, add a little water, and as the child gets more comfortable, add more water. Observe the child's behavior and regulatory state with changes in depth.

For the child who gets very excited at bath time, plan the bath long before it is time to go to bed. For the child who gets very relaxed at bath time, give a bath shortly before time to go to sleep.

For the child who has difficulty sitting, try having the child sit in a bath seat. If one is not available, try having the child sit in a small, plastic laundry basket.

Always give a warning to the child who is sensitive to touch: for example, "I'm going to wash your face now." If the child dislikes the water running over his or her eyes during hair rinsing, try putting a picture or large sticker on the ceiling so the child will look up to tilt the head back. Also try holding a washcloth over the child's eyes.

For the child who resists bath time or has difficulty making a transition to bath time, provide the child with as much choice as possible by having him or her pick out the towel, decide on bath toys, and say, "Off" when the water should be turned off or "On" to start the water flow. Sing songs during bath time, telling the child "After this song is done, bath time is over." Focus on a fun activity that comes next, saying, for example, "Let's go pick out a book or have a drink."

For the child who is fearful of bath time, try filling a baby tub or small baby pool with just a bit of water, next to the tub. Later, move the pool or tub into the tub. Gradually add water in the tub around the pool or baby tub, fading the pool or baby tub over time.

For the child with hearing impairment, having a rug, towels hung on racks, and a shower curtain will reduce the sounds in the room so the child can better attend to voice versus environmental sounds. Positioning yourself face to face as often as possible will help the child attend to speech. Label and describe the sounds in the bathroom—water running, splashing, talking—and the absence of sound, such as when the water is turned off, so the child can understand what he or she is hearing.

For the child with a visual impairment, allow as much touching, holding, and feeling as possible to give the child the opportunity to use other senses in the tub.

For the child with cleft lip or palate, water on the face may go into the mouth or nose and cause the child to resist face washing. Use a damp wash cloth and wash the face gently rather than exposing the face to greater amounts of water.

Jimmy was a very active 30-month-old child who had difficulty with self-regulation and communication. He used single words to communicate. His play was very rough, and his parents described him as always on the go. His mother reported that he had terrible tantrums every night at bath time when it was time to get out of the tub. It took his parents 2 hours to get him to bed after his bath. The EI provider asked if she could watch bath time during the next session, and Jimmy's mother agreed. At the start of the session, Jimmy's mother asked him if he wanted to take a bath, and he raced toward the bathroom. He started to jump around the room, and his mother raised her voice to tell him to calm down. The louder she yelled, the more he jumped. The EI provider suggested his mother quietly begin to sing one of Jimmy's favorite songs. He immediately stopped jumping and started to join in the song. The provider suggested his mother quietly sing, "This is the way we take off your clothes, take off your clothes, take off your clothes. This is the way we take off your clothes, so early in the morning" and change each verse to a different article of clothing. As she did this, the provider showed her how to guide Jimmy's hands to take off the item she began to sing about. Once Jimmy was in the tub, the EI provider showed his mom how to replace his active behaviors that annoyed her with more appropriate ones. For example, when Jimmy started to dump water on the floor, they gave him a bowl into which he could pour the water. The provider showed the mother how to take turns with the pouring and to pause until Jimmy would say "me." When it was time to get out, the EI provider asked Mom how she typically got Jimmy out of the tub. She remarked that she told him it was time to get ready for bed. The provider suggested that Jimmy's mom think of a calm activity that Jimmy enjoyed. His mother said he loved it when she read the book *Brown Bear, Brown Bear, What Do You See?* (Martin & Carl, 2010). The provider told her to tell Jimmy, "Let's go read *Brown Bear.*" Jimmy quickly stood up and started to get out of the tub. Because the transition was the priority, the EI provider decided not to put any other demands on Jimmy at that time. Once Jimmy's behavior got better, she planned to show his mother how she could use bath time to work on Jimmy's problem-solving and communication skills.

Mohammad was a 26-month-old child diagnosed with autism spectrum disorder. Mohammad was not yet talking and communicated primarily by crying. When he wanted something, he would get it by himself. His mother described bath time as a "nightmare." Mohammad cried the entire time, flailed his limbs in an attempt to get out of the tub, and refused to sit down. His mother believed that Mohammad was afraid of the bathroom; he cried whenever he was in the bathroom for any purpose. The provider asked permission to help with bath time over a period of several weeks. The mother suggested bathing in a different room, and she set up a child's tub in the playroom, a room where Mohammad was always happy. The provider honored her suggestion, and Mohammad did indeed sit quietly in the child-sized tub without crying. Over the next few weeks, the tub was moved closer and closer to the bathroom at about 2-foot intervals, and Mohammad maintained being calm in the tub. At bath time only, Mohammed was given waterproof toys he loved to hold to help him feel secure and to distract him from whatever he felt was unpleasant about the bath routine. The small tub was finally moved into the bathroom and then into the bathtub without any difficulty. Mohammad remained calm. Over time, the bathtub and the small tub were filled with water to the same level. It was a long process before Mohammad would sit in the bathtub, and he still needed to hold his toys to remain calm. The provider suggested the next step be working on the other routines, such as dressing and eating meals, which were also difficult for the family.

PLAYING INDEPENDENTLY WHEN CAREGIVERS ARE BUSY

Table III.8. Daily routines across domains: playing independently when parents and caregivers are busy

Approx. dev. age level	Behavior regulation and social skills	Cognitive/receptive language skills	Expressive language skills	Gross motor skills	Fine motor skills	Self-care/adaptive skills
Birth to 4 months			**Cooing and vocalizing:** Provide the child with a child-safe mirror for the crib to encourage cooing and vocalizing to the reflection.	**Tummy time/sidelying:** Give the child time in a variety of positions.	**Visual fixation and attention/visual tracking/batting and reaching:** Hang brightly colored or reflective items such as toys and spoons above or in front of the child.	
4–8 months			**Making vowel and early consonant sounds:** Provide the child with a child-safe mirror for the crib to encourage making early sounds to the reflection.	**Rolling/commando crawling/moving in and out of sitting/crawling on hands and knees:** Place some favorite toys and objects out of reach to encourage moving to get them. For children who are not moving from one place or one position to another, move them so they can interact with different toys/objects to keep them interested in playing and exploring. **Sitting:** If needed, use an infant seat or safely prop the child in a laundry basket or box.	**Grasping/releasing/transferring from hand to hand/banging objects/using both hands:** Place a variety of sizes and shapes of toys, teethers, socks, and other safe items within reach. **Using both hands:** Provide stuffed animals and other toys or safe objects that require both hands.	
8–14 months		**Cause and effect and using movements to continue an activity:** Provide safe kitchen utensils, such as spoons and cups, pots, and pans for banging. Place several cause-and-effect toys that the child can activate near where the child is sitting or lying. **Preliteracy:** Provide the child with simple familiar books that he or she is content to look at on his or her own.			**Container play:** Provide plastic bowls, bins, and sturdy boxes to put socks, balls, cups, spoons, and other household items to take out and put in.	

(continued)

Table III.8. *(continued)*

Approx. dev. age level	Behavior regulation and social skills	Cognitive/receptive language skills	Expressive language skills	Gross motor skills	Fine motor skills	Self-care/adaptive skills
14–18 months					**Container play:** Give the child boxes with slots and tops from large plastic containers to put into the slots.	
18–24 months		**Using gestures with songs:** Have music playing with songs the child knows such as "The Wheels on the Bus" or "Twinkle, Twinkle, Little Star."	**Making choices:** Give the child a choice of two toys or activities to do independently.		**Using both hands:** Give the child a small-mouthed bottle and a bowl of small crackers or cereal and have the child put the snack food into the bottle.	
24–30 months	**Testing limits/ becoming independent/ accepting limits:** Set up the environment so the child will be as safe as possible.	**Matching and sorting:** Give the child a group of items such as spoons and clothespins to sort into two bowls. **Pretend play:** Provide the child with a direction to make lunch or serve tea in the play kitchen. Encourage the child to feed stuffed animals or dolls that you set up for the meal or tea time.			**Prewriting:** With the child safely sitting in a highchair or booster seat, have him or her color with crayons.	
30–36 months		**Matching and sorting/ concept development:** Give the child items to sort by color or size, such as socks or spoons.			**Using both hands/ tearing:** Give the child paper to tear into pieces and place into a basket, bowl, or paper bag to later use for a gluing activity.	

SPECIAL CONSIDERATIONS

Caregivers should be within sight and earshot of an infant and toddler to ensure safety; however, it is often necessary for the caregiver to leave a child for a few minutes to attend to household and personal routines. For young children to learn to be independent, they need short periods of time to learn to entertain themselves. EI providers should help caregivers understand that they must balance the child's need for interaction, the child's needs to learn independence, and the caregivers' needs to care for themselves and their other responsibilities. The interactive skills that the EI provider and the caregivers facilitate during sessions help the child gain skills so he or she has a greater variety of options to choose from to entertain himself or herself. It is sometimes necessary for children to entertain themselves in ways that are not ideal so the caregiver can accomplish what needs to be done. For example, some families resort to television or movies because they know their children are safe and happy so the laundry or cooking gets done.

Quaneisha was a 14-month-old child who had global developmental delays. Her aunt, Diyana, watched her while her mother attended classes several days a week. Diyana told the EI provider she had difficulty getting her housework done because Quaneisha cried whenever she left the room. Quaneisha was not sitting independently but could sit for about 10 minutes in a corner seat the physical therapist lent the family before her head began to flop forward or to the left side as she tired. Quaneisha could grasp lightweight toys and bring them to her mouth. She used her left hand a lot more than her right. Diyana put toys to Quaneisha's right side to encourage her to use her right hand more when in the corner chair. To help with separation issues, the EI provider recommended that Quaneisha's aunt play Peekaboo, hide her toys under a cloth and make them reappear, and playfully hide and reappear calling Quaneisha's name as she reappeared, hiding for an increasing number of seconds. The provider recommended that when Diyana was not there to help and when working on independence to put Quaneisha's toys where she could most easily use them, on her left side. The provider also recommended alternating Quaneisha's position from sitting to sidelying to lying on her back when Diyana needed to leave the room. Being on her belly was very difficult for Quaneisha, and the EI provider suggested using this position for Quaneisha's favorite activities such as playing a kissing game when Diyana kisses Quaneisha's forehead as she makes an "ah" sound. The EI provider and Diyana made some special toys to use to help Quaneisha entertain herself when her aunt was busy. They put rice in two small empty plastic spice container so Quaneisha could hold them, shake them, and bang them, and they put colored water and glitter in an empty water bottle for Quaneisha to explore by rolling, shaking, and mouthing. They also looked through Quaneisha's toys and separated them into those that were good for playing with help and those good for playing when alone. This helped Diyana set up the environment so she could more easily play independently when her aunt was not with her.

Joshua was an 8-month-old child who had a cleft lip and palate and other developmental delays from a rare genetic syndrome. Joshua was tube fed, tucked his finger into his unrepaired cleft often, had low muscle tone, and did not sit or consistently reach or grasp toys. Joshua's mother, Kelli, asked the EI provider for ideas to help her balance the needs of Joshua and his two siblings as well as her own needs—she was taking classes to become a nurse. Over the next two months, the EI provider and Kelli discussed ways to balance the issues. With Kelli's permission, the provider looked at Joshua's crib, where he received his tube feedings. They discussed safe toys for in the crib that would promote batting and reaching. They put a simple cloth book, a mobile, two soft animals, and a vibrating teething toy in the crib. Kelli gathered other soft, safe toys into a basket to rotate so that Joshua would be able to experience a variety of toys over time. The provider suggested putting some blankets and toys on the floor near the kitchen. This allowed Joshua to lie on the floor and practice reaching, grasping, and rolling to his side. In addition, he could see his mother and she could periodically move him, as he did not tolerate one position very long. Kelli also enlisted his siblings to play with Joshua for short periods of time, making him laugh, handing him toys, or patting his head or belly, which kept his hands busy so his hands were not in his mouth or his cleft. During the sessions, the provider and Kelli worked together to encourage Joshua to put safe toys in his mouth to explore and to facilitate awareness of his lips and tongue. While sitting and reading with the other children, the EI provider showed Kelli how to support Joshua's body with her own body so that Joshua could watch the activity and be content doing so. This helped strengthen his trunk muscles. Over time, Joshua was able to explore more readily using his hands and his mother was able to study as he played independently.

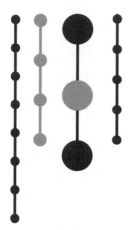

References

Ahola, D., & Kovacik, A. (2007). *Observing and understanding child development: A child study manual*. New York, NY: Thomson Delmar Learning.

Alabama Department of Rehabilitation Services. (2012). *Alabama's early intervention system*. Retrieved from http://www.rehab.state.al.us/individuals-and-families/early-intervention

Alaska Department of Health and Social Services, Office of Children's Services. (2011). *FAQ about the infant learning program*. Retrieved from http://dhss.alaska.gov/ocs/Pages/infantlearning/program/program_faq.aspx#4

American Academy of Pediatrics. (1992, June 1). *Positioning and SIDS*. Retrieved from http://pediatrics.aappublications.org/content/89/6/1120.abstract

American-Speech-Language Hearing Association. (2005). *Cultural competence*. Retrieved from http://www.asha.org/policy/ET2005-00174.htm

Arizona Department of Economic Security. (2012). *Eligibility*. Retrieved from https://www.azdes.gov/main.aspx?menu=98&id=2506

Ayres, A.J. (1985). *Developmental dyspraxia & adult-onset apraxia: A lecture prepared for Sensory Integration International*. Torrance, CA: Sensory Integration International.

Baillargeon, R., Spelke, E.S., & Wasserman, S. (1985). Object permanence in five-month infants. *Cognition, 20*(3), 191–208.

Barton, E.E., & Wolery, M. (2008). Teaching pretend play to children with disabilities: A review of the literature. *Topics in Early Childhood Special Education, 28*(2), 109–125.

Bellugi, U., & Brown, R. (Eds.). (1964). The acquisition of language. *Monographs of the Society for Research in Child Development, 29*(1), 1–192.

Bergen, D. (2002). The role of pretend play in children's cognitive development. *Early Childhood Research and Practice, 4*(1), n.p.

Bernheimer, L.B., & Weisner, T.S. (2007). "Let me just tell you what I do all day…:" The family story at the center of intervention research and practice. *Infants & Young Children, 20*(3), 192–201.

Bloom, L., & Lahey, M. (1978). *Language development and language disorders*. Somerset, NJ: John Wiley & Sons.

Blue-Banning, M., Summers, J.A., Frankland, H.C., Nelson, L.L., & Beegle, G. (2004). Dimensions of family and professional partnerships: Constructive guidelines for collaboration. *Exceptional Children, 70*(2), 167–84.

Brown, R. (1973). *A first language*. Cambridge, MA: Harvard University Press.

Brownell, C.A., Ramani, G.B., & Zerwas, S. (2006). Becoming a social partner with peers: Cooperation and social understanding in one- and two-year-olds. *Child Development, 77*(4), 803–821.

Bruder, M. (2010). Early childhood intervention: A promise to children and families for their future. *Exceptional Children, 76*(3), 339–355.

Bruner, J.S. (1973). Organization of early skilled action. *Child Development, 44*, 1–11.

Buzhardt, J., Greenwood, C., Walker, D., Carta, J., Terry, B., & Garrett, M. (2010). A web-based tool to support data-based early intervention decision making. *Topics in Early Childhood Special Education, 29*(4), 201–213.

Camaioni, L., & Laicardi, C. (1985). Early social games and the acquisition of language. *The British Journal of Developmental Psychology, 3*(31), 31–39.

Campbell, P.H. (2004). Participation-based services: Promoting children's participation in natural settings. *Young Exceptional Children, 8*(1), 20–29.

Campbell, P.H., & Sawyer, L.B. (2007). Supporting learning opportunities in natural settings through participation-based services. *Journal of Early Intervention, 29*, 287–305.

Campbell, P.H., & Sawyer, L.B. (2009). Changing early intervention providers' home visiting skills though participation in professional development. *Topics in Early Childhood Special Education, 28*(4), 219–234.

Campbell, P.H., Sawyer, L.B., & Muhlenhaupt, M. (2009). The meaning of natural environments for parents and professionals. *Infants and Young Children, 22*, 264–278.

Capirci, O., Iverson, J., Pizzuto, E., & Volterra, V. (1996). Communicative gestures and the transition to two-word speech. *Journal of Child Language, 23,* 645–673.

Capone, N.C., & McGregor, K.K. (2004). Gesture development: A review for clinical and research practices. *Journal of Speech, Language, and Hearing Research, 47,* 173–186.

Carpenter, M., Nagell, K., & Tomasello, M. (1998). Social cognition, joint attention, and communicative competence from 9 to 15 months of age. *Monographs of the Society for Research in Child Development, 63*(4), 1–174.

Casasola, M. (2005). Can language do the driving? The effect of linguistic input on infants' categorization of support spatial relations. *Developmental Psychology, 41,* 183–192.

Case-Smith, J., Fisher, A., & Bauer, D. (1989). An analysis of the relationship between proximal and distal motor control. *American Journal of Occupational Therapy, 43,* 657–662.

Choby, B.A., & George, S. (2008). Toilet training. *American Family Physician, 78*(9), 1059–1064.

Christelow, E. (1998). *Five little monkeys jumping on the bed.* New York, NY: Clarion Books.

Columbo, J. (2001). The development of visual attention in infancy. *Annual Review of Psychology, 52,* 337–367.

Cooper, J.O., Heron, T.E., & Heward, W.L. (2007). *Applied behavior analysis.* Upper Saddle River, NJ: Pearson.

Courage, M.L., & Howe, M.L. (2002). From infant to child: The dynamics of cognitive change in the second year of life. *Psychological Bulletin, 128,* 250–277.

Cowden, J.E., & Torrey, C.C. (2007). *Motor development and movement activities for preschoolers and infants with delays: A multisensory approach for professionals and families.* Springfield, IL: Charles C. Thomas.

Crais, E., Watson, L., & Baranek, G. (2009). Use of gesture development in profiling children's prelinguistic communication skills. *American Journal of Speech-Language Pathology, 18,* 95–108.

Cripe, J.W., & Venn, M.L. (1997). Family-guided routines for early intervention services. *Young Exceptional Children, 1*(1), 18–26.

Daehler, M.W. (2008). Milestones: Cognitive. In J.B. Benson & M.M. Haith (Eds.), *Language, memory, and cognition in infancy and early childhood* (pp. 337–346). Oxford, UK: Elsevier.

Dale, L.P., O'Hara, E., Keen, J., & Porges, S. (2011). Infant regulatory disorders: Temperamental, physiological, and behavioral features. *Journal of Developmental & Behavioral Pediatrics, 32*(3), 216–224.

DeGangi, G. (2000). *Pediatric disorders of regulation in affect and behavior: A therapist's guide to assessment and treatment.* San Diego, CA: Academic Press.

Dodici, B.J., Draper, D.C., & Peterson, C.A. (2003). Early parent-child interactions and early literacy development. *Topics in Early Childhood Special Education, 23,* 124–136.

Dos Santos, M.T.B.R., & Noguiera, M.L.G. (2005). Infantile reflexes and their effects on dental caries and oral hygiene in cerebral palsy individuals. *Journal of Oral Rehabilitation, 32,* 880–885.

Dunfield, K.A. (2010). *Redefining prosocial behaviour: The production of helping, sharing, and comforting acts in human infants and toddlers.* (Unpublished doctoral dissertation, Queen's University, Kingston, Ontario, Canada.)

Dunfield, K.A., Kulmeier, V.A., O'Connell, L., & Kelley, E. (2011). Examining the diversity of prosocial behavior: Helping, sharing, and comforting in infancy. *Infancy, 16,* 227–247.

Dunst, C.J. (2001). Participation of young children with disabilities in community leaning activities. In M.J. Guralnick (Ed.), *Early childhood inclusion: Focus on change* (pp. 307–334). Baltimore, MD: Paul H. Brookes Publishing Co.

Dunst, C., Bruder, M.B., Trivette, C.M., Raab, M., & McLean, M. (2001). Natural learning opportunities for infants, toddlers, and preschoolers, *Young Exceptional Children, 4*(3), 18–25.

Dunst, C.J., Hamby, D.W., & Brookfield, J. (2007). Modeling the effects of early childhood intervention variables on parent and family well-being. *Journal of Applied Quantitative Methods, 2*(3), 268–288.

Dunst, C.J., Hamby, D., Trivette, C.M., Raab, M., & Bruder, M.B. (2000). Everyday family and community life and children's naturally occurring learning opportunities. *Journal of Early Intervention, 23*(3), 151–161.

Dunst, C.J., Trivette, C.M., & Deal, A.G. (1994). Enabling and empowering families, In C.J. Dunst, C.M. Trivette, & A.G. Deal (Eds.), *Supporting and Strengthening Families: Vol. 1. Methods, strategies, and practices* (pp. 2–11). Cambridge, MA: Brookline Books.

Early Childhood Outcomes Center. (n.d.). *Federal requirements.* Retrieved from http://projects.fpg.unc.edu/eco/pages/fed_req.cfm

Early Intervention Programs for Infants and Toddlers with Disabilities, 34 C.F.R. § 303.344(c) (2011).

Early Intervention Services. (2003). 55 Pa. Code § 4226.

Education of the Handicapped Act Amendments of 1986, PL 99-457, 20 U.S.C. §§ 1400.

Edutopia. (2007). *What is successful technology integration?* Retrieved from http://www.edutopia.org/technology-integration-guide-description

Erhardt, R. (1994). *Erhardt developmental prehension assessment.* Maplewood, MN: Erhardt Developmental Products.

Fagan, M.K., & Montgomery, T.R. (2009). Managing referrals for children with receptive language delay. *Clinical Pediatrics, 48*(1), 72–80.

Fagard, J., & Marks, A. (2000). Unimanual and bimanual tasks and the assessment of handedness in toddlers. *Developmental Science, 3*(2), 137–147.

Featherstone, H. (1980). *A difference in the family: Life with a disabled child.* New York, NY: Basic Books.

Ferber, R. (2006). *Solve your child's sleep problems.* New York, NY: Fireside.

Florida Department of Education Technical Assistance and Training Center. (2009, May). *Families and their children with disabilities—Grieving or dealing with acceptance?* Retrieved from http://www.tats.ucf.edu/docs/eupdates/FamilyInvolvement-8.pdf

Forman, D.R. (2007). Autonomy, compliance, and internalization. In C.A. Brownell & C.B. Kopp (Eds.), *Socioemotional development in the toddler years: transitions and transformations* (pp. 285–319). New York, NY: Guildford Press.

Gallagher, P.A., Fialka, J., Rhodes, C., & Arceneaux, C. (2002). Working with families: Rethinking denial. *Young Exceptional Children, 5*(2) 11–17.

Gentner, D., & Goldin-Meadow, S. (Eds.). (2003). *Language in mind: Advances in the study of language and thought.* Cambridge, MA: MIT Press.

Gopnik, A., & Meltzoff, A.N. (1997). *Words, thoughts, and theories.* Cambridge, MA: MIT Press.

Groce, N.E., & Zola, I.K. (1993). Multiculturalism, chronic illness, and disability. *Pediatrics, 91*, 1048–1055.

Gulick, R., & Kitchen, T. (2007). *Effective instruction for children with autism: An applied behavior analytic approach.* Erie, PA: Dr. Gertrude A. Barber National Institute.

Gumperz, J.J., & Levinson, S.C. (Eds.). (1996). *Rethinking linguistic relativity.* Cambridge, UK: Cambridge University Press.

Halverson, H.M. (1931). An experimental study of prehension in infants by means of systematic cinema records. *Genetic Psychology Monographs, 10*, 107–286.

Hanft, B.E., Pilkington, K.O. (2000). Therapy in natural environments: The means or end goal for early intervention? *Infants and Young Children, 12*(4), 1–13.

Hanft, B.E., Rush, D.D., & Shelden, M.L. (2004). *Coaching families and colleagues in early childhood.* Baltimore, MD: Paul H Brookes Publishing Co.

Hebbeler, K., Spiker, D., Bailey, D., Scarbarough, A., Malilik, S., Simeonnsson, R., & Singer, M. (2007). *Early intervention for infants & toddlers with disabilities and their families: Participants, services, and outcomes. Final report of the National Early Intervention Longitudinal Study (NEILS).* Retrieved from http://www.sri.com/work/publications/national-early-intervention-longitudinal-study-neils-final-report

Howard, V.F., Williams, B.F., Port, P.D., & Lepper, C. (1997). *Very young children with special needs: A formative approach for the 21st century.* Upper Saddle River, NJ: Merrill.

Howes, C. (1980). Peer play scale as an index of complexity of peer interaction. *Developmental Psychology, 16*(4), 371–372.

Iverson, J.M., & Goldin-Meadow, S. (2005). Gesture paves the way for language development. *Psychological Science, 16*, 368–371.

Jan, J.E., Owens, J.A., Weiss, M.D., Johnson, K.P., Wasdell, M.B., Freeman, R.D., et al. (2008). Sleep hygiene for children with neurodevelopmental disabilities. *Pediatrics, 6*, 1343–1350.

Kresak, K., Gallagher, P., & Rhodes, C. (2009). Siblings of infants and toddlers with disabilities in early intervention. *Topics in Early Childhood Special Education, 29*(3), 143–154.

Kushnir, T., Wellman, H., & Gelman, S. (2008). The role of preschoolers' social understanding in evaluating the informativeness of causal interventions. *Cognition, 107*(3), 1084–1092.

Lantz, C., Melén, K., & Forrsberg, H. (1996). Early infant grasping involves radial fingers. *Developmental Medicine and Child Neurology, 38*, 668–674.

Lawhon, T., & Cobb, J.B. (2002). Routines that build emergent literacy skills in infants, toddlers, and preshcoolers. *Early Childhood Education Journal, 30*(2), 113–118.

Ledford, J., & Wolery, M. (2011). Teaching imitation to young children with disabilities: A review of the literature. *Topics in Early Childhood Special Education, 30*(4), 245–255.

Lencioni, P. (2002). *The five dysfunctions of a team: A leadership fable.* San Francisco, CA: Jossey-Bass.

Levinson, S.C. (1997). Contextualizing "contextualization cues." In S.L. Eerdmans, C.L. Prevignano, & P.J. Thibault (Eds.), *Language and interaction* (pp. 31–40). Lausanne, Switzerland: Beta Press.

Libby, M.E., Weiss, J.S., Bancroft, S., & Ahearn, W.H. (2008). A comparison of most-to-least and least-to-most prompting on the acquisition of solitary play skills. *Behavior Analysis in Practice, 1*, 37–43.

Liddle, T.L., & Yorke, L. (2004). *Why motor skills matter.* New York, NY: McGraw Hill.

Lindeman, D., & Woods, J. (1999). *Implementing information about adult learners in family-guided activity based intervention: A checklist.* Retrieved from http://www.facets.lsi.ku.edu/pdf/AdultLearner.pdf

Lupyan, G., Rakison, D.H., & McClelland, J.L. (2007). Language is not just for talking: Labels facilitate learning of novel categories. *Psychological Science, 18*(12), 1077–1083.

Lynch, J.I., Brookshire, B.L., & Fox, D.R. (1980). *A parent-child cleft palate curriculum: Developing speech and language.* Tigard, OR: CC Publications.

Marshalla, P. (2001). *Becoming verbal with childhood apraxia: New insights on Piaget for today's therapy.* Kirkland, WA: Marshalla Speech and Language.

Martin, B., & Carl, E. (2010). *Brown bear, brown bear, what do you see?* New York, NY: Henry Holt.

Maryland State Department of Education. (2011). *Birth to 3: A family guide to early intervention services in Maryland.* Retrieved from http://www.marylandpublicschools.org/NR/rdonlyres/E94CADE8-6143-4300-A2B8-7FDF00E709EC/29915/BlueBirth3Guide18x11.pdf

McConnell, S.R. (2000). Assessment in early intervention and early childhood special education: Building on the past to project into our future. *Topics in Early Childhood Special Education, 19*, 43–48.

McConnell, S.R., McEvoy, M.A. & Priest, J.S. (2002). Growing measures for monitoring progress in early childhood education: A research and development process for individual growth and development indicators. *Assessment for Effective Intervention, 27*, 3–14.

McWilliam, R.A. (2003). The primary-service provider model for home- and community-based services. *Piscologia, 17*, 115–135.

McWilliam, R.A. (2010). *Routines-based early intervention: Supporting young children and their families.* Baltimore, MD: Paul H. Brookes Publishing Co.

McWilliam, R.A., & Scott, S. (2001). A support approach to early intervention: A three-part framework. *Infants and Young Children, 13*(4), 55–66.

Miller, N.B. with Burmester, S., Niedermeyer, S., Callahan, B.G., & Diertele, J. (1994). *Nobody's perfect: Living and growing with children who have special needs.* Baltimore, MD: Paul H. Brookes Publishing Co.

Munakata, Y., McClelland, J.L., Johnson, M.H., & Siegler, R.S. (1997). Rethinking infant knowledge: Toward an adaptive process account of successes and failures in object permanence tasks. *Psychological Review, 104,* 686–713.

NAEYC (National Association for the Education of Young Children) & Fred Rogers Center. (2012, January). *Technology and interactive media as tools in early childhood programs serving children from birth through age 8.* Retrieved from http://www.naeyc.org/files/naeyc/file/positions/PS_technology_WEB2.pdf

National Institute for Literacy. (2008). *Developing early literacy: Report of the National Early Literacy Panel.* Retrieved from http://lincs.ed.gov/publications/pdf/NELPReport09.pdf

Natural Environments. (2012). 34 CFR § 303.26.

New Jersey Early Intervention System. (2012a). *Policies and procedures.* Retrieved from http://www.state.nj.us/health/fhs/documents/njeis-02.pdf

New Jersey Early Intervention System. (2012b). *System of payments and family cost participation handbook.* Retrieved from http://www.nj.gov/health/fhs/eis/documents/system_payment_family_cost_policies_procedures.pdf

North Carolina Department of Human Services. (2012, August 29). *North Carolina Infant-Toddler Program: Frequently asked questions.* Retrieved from http://www.beearly.nc.gov/index.php/faq

Pantley, E. (2002). *The no-cry sleep solution: Gentle ways to help your baby sleep through the night.* New York, NY: McGraw Hill.

Pantley, E. (2005). *The no-cry sleep solution for toddlers and preschoolers: Gentle ways to stop bedtime battles and improve your child's sleep.* New York, NY: McGraw Hill.

Parks, S. (1992–2011). *HELP Strands.* Palo Alto, CA: VORT Corporation.

Paul, R. (2007). *Language disorders from infancy through adolescence: Assessment & intervention* (3rd ed.). St. Louis, MO: Mosby Elsevier.

Pennsylvania Department of Public Welfare. (2012). *Early intervention services: Information for parents and families.* Retrieved from http://www.dpw.state.pa.us/forchildren/childcareearlylearning/earlyinterventionservices/index.htm

Peterson, N. (1987). *Early intervention for handicapped and at-risk children: An introduction to early childhood special education.* Denver, CO: Love.

Pretti-Frontczak, K., & Bricker, D. (2004). *An activity-based approach to early intervention* (3rd ed.). Baltimore, MD: Paul H. Brookes Publishing Co.

Proctor, A. (1989). Stages of normal noncry vocal development in infancy: A protocol for assessment. *Topics in Language Development, 10,* 26–42.

Rescorla, L., & Achenbach, T. (2002). Use of the language development survey (LDS) in a national probability sample of children 18 to 35 months old. *Journal of Speech, Language, and Hearing Research, 45,* 733–743.

Richards, J.E., Reynolds, G.D., & Courage, M.L. (2010). The neural bases of infant attention. *Current Directions in Psychological Science, 19*(1), 41–46.

Ross, H., Vickar, M., & Perlman, M. (2010). *Early social cognitive skills at play in toddlers' peer interactions.* Hoboken, NJ: Wiley-Blackwell.

Rowland, C., & Schweigert, P. (2004). *First things first: early communication for the pre-symbolic child with severe disabilities.* Portland, OR: Design to Learn.

Salls, J.S., Silverman, L.N., & Gatty, C.M. (2002). The relationship of infant sleep and play positioning to motor milestone achievement. *American Journal of Occupational Therapy, 56,* 577–580.

Sander, E.K. (1972). When are speech sounds learned? *Journal of Speech and Hearing Disorders, 7,* 55–63.

Sawyer, L.B., & Campbell, P.H. (2009). Beliefs about participation-based practices in early intervention. *Journal of Early Intervention, 31*(4), 326–343.

Smith, A.B. (2004). How do infants and toddlers learn the rules? Family discipline and young children. *International Journal of Early Childhood, 36*(2), 27–41.

Snedeker, J., & Gleitman, L. (2004). Why it is hard to label our concepts. In D.G. Hall & S.R. Waxman (Eds.), *Weaving a lexicon.* Cambridge, MA: MIT Press.

Sobel, D., & Kirkham, N. (2007). Bayes nets and babies: Infants' developing statistical reasoning abilities and their representation of causal knowledge. *Developmental Science, 10*(3), 298–306.

Stone, W., Ousley, O., & Littleford, C. (1997). Motor imitation in young children with autism: What's the object? *Journal of Abnormal Child Psychology, 25,* 475–485.

Thal, D., & Bates, E. (1988). Language and gesture in late talkers. *Journal of Speech and Hearing Research, 31,* 115–123.

Tots-n-Tech. (2013). *Adapting books.* Retrieved from http://tnt.asu.edu/helpdesk/pdf/adapting-books

Turnbull, A.P., & Turnbull, H.R., III. (2001). *Families, professionals, and exceptionality: Collaborating for empowerment.* Upper Saddle River, NJ: Merrill.

Ulrich, M.E., & Bauer, A.M. (2003). Levels of awareness: A closer look at communication between parents and professionals. *Teaching Exceptional Children, 35*(6), 20–24.

U.S. Census Bureau. (2009). *American community survey, C16005, nativity by language spoken at home by ability to speak English for the population 5 years and over.* Retrieved from http://www.census.gov/compendia/statab/2012/tables/12s0055.pdf

U.S. Census Bureau. (2010). *New Census Bureau report analyzes nation's linguistic diversity: Population speaking a language other than English at home increases by 140 percent in past three decades.* Retrieved from http://www.census.gov/newsroom/releases/archives/american_community_survey_acs/cb10-cn58.html

Van Tatenhove, G.M. (2007). *Normal language development, generative language & AAC*. Retrieved from http://www.vantatenhove.com/files/NLDAAC.pdf

Van Tubbergen, M., Warschausky, S., Birnholz, J., & Baker, S. (2008). Choice beyond preference: Conceptualization and assessment of choice-making skills in children with significant impairments. *Rehabilitation Psychology, 53*(1), 93–100.

Valvano, J. (2004). Activity-focused motor interventions for children with neurological conditions. *Physical and Occupational Therapy in Pediatrics, 24*(12), 79–107.

Velleman, S. (2003). *Childhood apraxia of speech: Resource guide*. Clifton Park, NY: Thomson/Delmar Learning.

Vermont Department for Children and Families. (2012). *IDEA part C—Early intervention services for infants and toddlers*. Retrieved from http://dcf.vermont.gov/cdd/cis/IDEA_Part_C_early_intervention

Waldburger, J., and Spivak, J. (2008). *The sleepeasy solution: The exhausted parents guide to getting your child to sleep*. Deerfield Beach, FL: Health Communications.

Walker, D., Carta, J.J., Greenwood, C.R., & Buzhardt, J. (2008). The use of individual growth and developmental indicators for progress monitoring and intervention decision making in early education. *Exceptionality, 16*(1), 33–47.

Weir, K., McMahon, S., Barry, L., Masters, I.B., & Chang, A.B. (2009). Clinical signs and symptoms of oropharyngeal aspiration and dysphagia in children. *European Respiratory Journal, 33*, 604–611.

Weiss, CE (1982). *Weiss Intelligibility Test*. Tigard, OR: CC Publications.

West, K., & Kenen, J. (2010). *The sleep lady's good night sleep tight: Gentle proven solutions to help sleep well and wake up happy*. New York, NY: Vanguard.

Wilcox, M,J., & Woods, J. (2011). Participation as a basis for developing early intervention outcomes. *Language, Speech, & Hearing Services in Schools, 42*(3), 365–378.

Williamson, G.G., & Anzalone, M.E. (2001). *Sensory integration and self-regulation in infants and toddlers: Helping very young children interact with their environment*. Washington, DC: Zero to Three.

Woodruff, G., & McGonigel, M. (1988). Early intervention team approaches: The transdisciplinary model. In J. Jordan, J. Gallagher, P. Hutinger, & M. Karnes (Eds.), *Early childhood special education: Birth to three* (pp. 163–181). Reston, VA: Council for Exceptional Children.

Woods, J., Kashinath, S., & Goldstein, H. (2004). Effects of embedding caregiver-implemented teaching strategies in daily routines on children's communication outcomes. *Journal of Early Intervention, 26*(3), 193–195.

Woods, J., & Lindeman, D. (2008). Gathering and giving information with families. *Infants & Young Children, 21*(4), 272–284.

Workgroup on Principles and Practices in Natural Environments. (2008). *Agreed upon mission and key principles for providing early intervention services in natural environments*. Retrieved from http://www.nectac.org/ pdfs/topics/families/Final missionandprinciples3_11_08.pdf

World Health Organization. (2002). *Towards a common language for functioning, disability and health: ICF, the international classification of functioning, disability and health*. Retrieved from http://www.who.int/classifications/icf/training/icfbeginnersguide.pdf

Zachry, A.H., & Kitzmann, K.M. (2011). Caregiver awareness of prone play recommendations. *American Journal of Occupational Therapy, 65*, 101–105.

Zeece, P.D., & Churchill, S.L. (2001). First stories, emergent literacy in infants and toddlers. *Early Childhood Education Journal, 29*(2), 101–104.

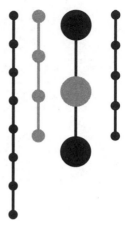

Appendix A

Resources

SUBSTITUTIONS:
Using common household items instead of bringing toys

If you do not have	For	Try
Toy bars	Batting and reaching	Hanging toys on a wrapping paper tube
Small stepstool	Climbing and jumping	Phone books
Exercise ball	Movement to facilitate sounds and requesting more; strengthening muscles; relaxation	Holding the child across your lap or sitting the child on your knees
Blocks	Eye–hand coordination	Small cans such as tuna cans, small boxes, or plastic containers
Nesting cups	Problem solving	Small boxes or plastic containers; measuring cups
Pegboards	Eye–hand coordination	Clothespins in egg cartons or straws in parmesan cheese container with lid
Shape sorter	Visual discrimination	Shoe box with slits of different sizes and shapes to fit small plastic bottles, small pieces of cardboard, etc.
Bowling set	Rolling with aim; turn-taking	Plastic water, soda, or juice bottles
Basketball set	Throwing with aim	Socks (stuffed with paper or tied in pairs) and a laundry basket or large box
Sandbox	Sensory play	Dry cereal (for those who put things in their mouths) or dry pasta, beans, etc. (for those who no longer put things in their mouths)
Picture cards or books	Communication book	Labels from food, cereal boxes, pictures from magazines, photos, pictures from the Internet
Table for the floor	Playing surface when sitting	Cardboard box cut to be a small table
Tub seat	Positioning a child who needs a little support in the tub	Plastic laundry basket
Ring stack	Eye–hand coordination	Bracelets on paper towel tube or empty CD spool
Water table	Sensory play	Large pan or plastic boxes
Bubbles	Blowing	Packing foam, small piece of tissue or paper rolled into a ball, cotton ball, feather

TIPS FOR TODDLERS:
Encouraging the behavior you want

1. Give choices throughout the day when the child truly has a choice. For example, give choices of foods, clothing, or where to have a diaper change. Give visual choices to help with comprehension of the choices. Make sure the possible choices are agreeable to you.

2. When the child does not have a choice, give clear, simple directions. For example, when it is time to eat, time to go in, or time for a diaper change, do not ask the child if he or she wants to do these things. Avoid asking "okay?" at the end of a direction that needs to be followed. When the child does not have a choice, avoid saying or asking, "It's time to go in, okay?"; "Will you go to your high chair?"; or "Do you want to go to bed?" Instead say, "It's time to go in"; "Go to your high chair"; or "Time to go to bed."

3. When the child does not have a choice in that the direction must be followed, giving the option "Do it or I will help you" gives both you and the child control.

4. Acknowledge the child's communication attempts. Often adults think that if they ignore a request the child will stop asking. This rarely happens, but being ignored often frustrates the child because he or she does not know if the adult understood the request.

5. If the child is asking for something that is not allowed, rather than ignoring, say, "You can't have _____, but you may have _____ or _____." Giving a choice of two items is typically accepted more than when given only one. Often, a child who is upset will say no to any item offered after he or she has been denied something, but giving a choice of two gives the child control.

6. When a preferred activity is ending, rather than emphasizing that the fun activity is over, emphasize what the child will be doing next. For example, when it is time to go inside, rather than repeating that it is time to go inside over and over to the screaming toddler, try to focus on something fun the child can do inside. Giving two choices is helpful in this situation. For example, when it is time to go in, tell the child "Time to go in. Let's go play with _____" or "Time to go in. Shall we play with ____ or _____?"

7. To help with transitions such as in the situation above, having an item such as a preferred toy, a drink, or a snack at the door may be helpful. Saying goodbye to items a child can no longer have is also helpful for transitions. For example, if a child is looking at a toy at the store and the family is not going to be purchasing it, saying goodbye to it is often helpful.

8. Try to give only directions that you can help the child carry out if he or she does not do as told. If you are frequently giving directions and not having the child follow through, when you really want the child to follow through, he or she has no way to know when you mean it and when you do not.

9. Remember that toddlers test limits to learn rules and understand consequences. The consequence should fit the situation. Be as consistent as possible so the child understands the rules and can predict the consequence.

10. If you use time-outs, remember the purpose of a time-out is for the child to not receive any attention. The time-out must occur so the child does not need attention to stay in the time-out.

11. For turn-taking and daily routines that the child does not like, try counting to 10. At 10, the other person gets a turn for the count of 10, and the counting repeats. Similarly, if a child does not like getting teeth brushed, count to 10 while brushing, and then stop. As the child tolerates the routine, the counting can be slowed. The child knows that the difficult routine will always stop at 10.

12. If diaper changes are difficult, try having a goodie bag with small items that are fun and that are used only at diaper time. Rotate the items to keep them novel. If a child is playing with something small and it is time for a diaper change, allow the child to take the item with him or her.

13. Give warnings for transitions. Use cues such as "It is almost time for _____" so the child can prepare as much as possible.

14. Do not make threats you cannot carry out. If you tell the child, "If you don't come now, I am going to leave without you," at first he or she will come, but as time goes on children learn that you did not speak the truth. Trust is very important, and children have no way to know when adults are telling the truth and when they are not if they are exposed to deception.

15. Use "first this, then that" statements once the child understands this concept, but be sure you do not get in a position of not being able to follow through. Making statements such as "You can leave the table if you take one more bite" or "You can get down when you say 'all done'" may put you in a position of not being able to follow through if the child refuses.

16. When children have separation anxiety, many adults sneak out of, for example, a child care setting, thinking the child will fare better if there is no separation to trigger tears. Though the child may cry when the adult says goodbye, this interaction instills trust. If a parent disappears without warning, the child never knows when the parent is going to disappear, which can foster more anxiety.

17. Try to put yourself in the shoes of the toddlers. Remember that they do not understand why situations are unsafe or unhealthy.

18. Try to make less preferred activities as fun as possible. Using clean-up songs or being silly can help make a less preferred activity more fun.

19. Tell the child what to do rather than what not to do. This helps the child know what to do and also avoids language that may be too complex. For example, instead of saying, "Don't throw," give the child a direction such as "Give it to me" or "Put it down gently."

20. Do not expect toddlers to share or to understand others' feelings well. Empathy begins in the early years but takes a long time to develop fully.

21. Use the presence of others to encourage behavior you want. Praise a sibling, parent, or peer for good cleaning up; good tasting the new food; or nice using the spoon.

22. Carefully look at the function of the behavior and teach a replacement behavior whenever possible. If a child is hitting because another child is in his or her space, he or she needs to learn to communicate "move." If a child is hitting because another child took a toy, he or she needs to communicate "mine." If the child is hitting to get attention, he or she needs to learn an appropriate way to gain attention. Telling a child "gentle hands" will not solve any of these problems, and the behavior will likely persist.

23. As much as possible, pay a lot of attention to the desired behaviors and as little attention as possible to the undesired behaviors. Catch children being good and give a lot of attention then. When a child must be redirected or needs a consequence, say and do as little as possible when carrying out the consequence.

24. Use praise frequently and be specific about the desired behavior. For example, saying, "I like the way you are using your spoon" and "Nice walking next to me" teaches a lot more than "good boy" or "good girl."

25. Avoid power struggles as much as possible and choose your battles.

26. Take into account how your child is feeling, physically and emotionally. Reduce demands when your child is not at his or her best.

27. Prioritize when there are many behavior challenges.

28. Be aware that sometimes things get worse before they get better. If a child cries when Mom or Dad does not lie down on the bed until he or she falls asleep, and the parents decide they no longer want to do this, the child will likely cry harder or even resort to behaviors such as hitting or throwing to try to get the parents to change their minds. Often the crying gets worse for several days, and then the child will figure out it is not working and the crying will decrease and finally stop.

Progression of drink and food

Thickened liquids allow the child more time to process and organize a swallow and are helpful when introducing cup drinking. Juices such as apricot, mango, or peach nectar tend to be thicker than many other beverages for infants and toddlers; infant cereal, pudding, yogurt, or applesauce may be mixed with thinner liquids to produce the desired thickness. Commercially available products can also be used to thicken liquids after consultation from a physician or therapist specializing in swallowing.

The following is a list of foods progressing from easier to more challenging textures and consistencies.

1. Infant cereal
2. Pureed fruits and vegetables of one texture
3. Applesauce
4. Yogurt without fruit or other pieces
5. Pudding
6. Mashed banana
7. Mashed potatoes
8. Mashed cooked egg yolk
9. Mashed cooked squash
10. Mashed canned or cooked fruit
11. Scrambled eggs or omelet cut in small squares
12. Canned meat or liverwurst, thinned with broth if needed
13. Cottage cheese
14. Mashed cooked vegetables (other than corn, lima beans, and peas)
15. Soup mixed with baby cereal or cracker crumbs to make texture consistent
16. Commercially available easily dissolvable finger foods
17. Dry cereal, graham crackers, butter cookies
18. Sandwich spreads
19. Canned spaghetti rings
20. Thinly sliced cheese, deli meats, or toddler meat sticks
21. Ground meat
22. Cooked vegetables other than corn, peas, and lima beans
23. Hot dogs cut into thin slices then quartered
24. Diced chicken
25. Ground beef
26. Cooked corn, lima beans, peas
27. Raw and dried fruits and vegetables

Mixed textures (e.g., those found in commercial baby food for older babies and young toddlers), soups, stews, or chunky applesauce are very difficult for many children. These children tend to swallow the food without chewing the more solid pieces, and this may cause gagging or coughing. Many of these children are able to chew and swallow small pieces of foods without difficulty when the small pieces are given separately rather than mixed with a puree.

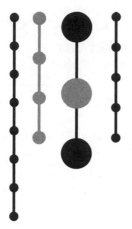

Appendix B

Progress Monitoring Examples

PEER INTERACTION:
Sample chart for monitoring progress

Plays near other children with little to no awareness of them	Plays near other children and watches them	Communicates verbally or nonverbally with a peer	Plays games such as chase or Peekaboo with a peer
6/22	7/3	8/28	10/2
6/25	7/8	8/30	10//
6/30	7/10	8/31	10/9

TESTING LIMITS/BECOMING INDEPENDENT/ACCEPTING LIMITS:
Sample Antecedent, Behavior, Consequence (ABC) chart for monitoring progress (throwing)

Date	Time	What was happening before? (antecedent)	What behavior did you see? (behavior)	What did you do? (consequence)	What happened next/ what stopped the behavior(s)?
7/15	8:00 a.m.	Playing with sister who took toy from him	Threw cup	Told him no throwing	He walked away
7/15	11:00 a.m.	Wanted yogurt and I told him no	Threw pacifier	Time-out for 2 minutes	Wanted to be held
7/15	12:00 p.m.	Eating lunch and was ready to get down	Threw food on floor	Got him down	He went to play

      Appendix B

CAUSE AND EFFECT AND USING MOVEMENTS TO CONTINUE AN ACTIVITY:
Sample chart for monitoring progress

Date	How child demonstrated understanding, by responses such as reaching, shaking, or bouncing, that body movements cause actions	Date	How child demonstrated understanding, by crying, vocalizing, or making sounds, that cause others to behave in certain ways	Date	How child moved to indicate continuance of activity
3/13	Repeatedly batted at rattle to hear the sound	4/13	Cried and vocalized "Mama" when woke up from nap	5/6	Took Grandma's hands to clap them after Grandma stopped clapping
3/17	Bounced after pause in bouncing to indicate "more"	4/14	Repeated "Mama" after hearing "Mama" and looked expectantly to hear "Mama" again	5/8	Clapped when Grandma stopped clapping
3/19	Banged bottle repeatedly on tray to hear the noise	4/16	Said "baba" and looked at bottle	5/9	When Grandma put him/her down after playing "up" and "down" he/she raised hands to be picked up
3/20	Looked at light after flipping light switch on the wall				
3/21	Dropped food and looked at dog to see if he was going to come eat it				

MATCHING AND SORTING:
Sample chart for monitoring progress

	Matched		Sorted	
	Date	Items	Date	Items
Objects	2/1	Got matching shoes out of closet	2/1	Put blocks and balls in correct bins at clean up
Pictures to objects	2/18	Saw ball on TV and ran to get own ball		
	2/20	Saw duck in book and went to toy box to get own		
Pictures	3/8	Matched picture cards during therapy	4/2	Sorted pictures of Elmo and Big Bird
Colors	3/4	Matched blue and red socks	3/19	Put white spoons in one pile and red in another
			3/20	Sorted green, yellow, and red fish crackers
Shapes	4/10	Completed shape puzzle	5/1	Sorted pretzels by shapes
Sizes	6/2	Put two sizes of matching socks with their mates	6/15	Put little spoons and big spoons in appropriate slot in silverware holder

USING FIRST WORDS:
Sample chart for monitoring progress

Date	Routine used	Words	Word combinations
5/5	Laundry	Momma, my, hat	My shirt
5/12	Playtime	Go, up, whee	
5/19	Bath time	No, duck, bubble	Momma out

ANSWERING QUESTIONS:
Sample chart for monitoring progress

Date	Routine/ participation	What/what doing	Yes/no	Who	Where
6/2	Mealtime	Answered "What are you eating?"			
6/9	Playtime		Said "yes" to "Do you want to go outside?"	Answered "Daddy"	
6/16	Book time	Answered 4 *what* questions and 2 "What are you doing?" questions			

STANDING UNSUPPORTED:
Sample chart for monitoring progress

Stands alone momentarily at couch or chair	Stands with back against a surface	Stands alone momentarily in middle of floor	Stands alone for several minutes
12/2	12/26	1/10	2/26
12/4	12/27	1/15	2/27
12/5	12/28	1/16	2/28

BALL PLAY:
Sample chart for monitoring progress

Throws or rolls ball to entertain self		Throws ball with aim		Rolls ball with aim	Kicks ball	Catches ball
5/1	6/23	To Dad	5/10	To Mom	6/24	8/6
5/4	6/25	Into box	5/23	To brother	7/1	8/9
5/4	6/28	Knocked over empty water bottles	7/2	Knocked over empty juice bottles	7/5	8/11

BATTING AND REACHING:
Sample chart for monitoring progress

Bats at toys when on back		Reaches for toys in supported sitting		Reaches for toys when on belly		Reaches for toys when on hands and knees		Reaches for toys in standing	
Left	Right	Left	Right	Left	Right	Left	Right	Left	Right
7/1	10/2	9/12	12/8					12/9 (in stander)	
7/2	10/5	9/13	12/10						
7/3	10/6	9/15	12/11						
	10/7		12/12						

GRASPING PATTERNS:
Sample chart for monitoring progress

Grasps using palm and fingers		Grasps using thumb and fingers—no space between object and palm		Grasps using thumb and fingertips—space between object and palm		Grasps small objects such as cereal using thumb and pad of index finger or side of index finger		Grasps using a fine pincer grasp: tip to tip	
Left	Right	Left	Right	Left	Right	Left	Right	Left	Right
9/6	11/2	11/19	1/8	2/12	6/1	12/15		3/25	
9/7	11/7	11/20	1/25	2/13	6/7	12/16		3/26	
9/8	11/15	11/21	2/1	2/16	6/8	12/17		3/27	
	11/16			2/2	6/9				

MAKING THE TRANSITION FROM PUREES TO TABLE FOOD:
Sample chart for monitoring progress

Eats one or two smooth purees such as Stage 1 foods	Eats mashed or soft textures	Eats small pieces of easily dissolvable foods	Eats small pieces of soft table food of various food groups	Eats most foods that the family eats
2/3	4/1	8/17	10/6	2/6
2/4	4/2	8/18	10/7	2/9
2/5	4/3	8/19	10/8	2/10

TAKING OFF CLOTHES:
Sample chart for monitoring progress

Removes socks	Removes untied/ loose shoes	Pulls shirt off head after help with arms	Removes shorts	Removes pants	Takes off shirt
5/7	5/9	5/12	7/9	8/16	9/26
5/8	5/10	5/16	7/10	8/17	9/27
5/10	5/12	5/17	7/12	8/18	9/28

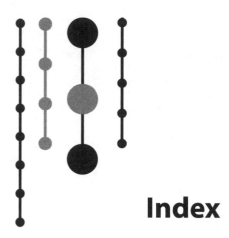

Index

Tables are indicated by *t*.